THE COLLECTED WORKS OF

ERIC VOEGELIN

VOLUME 21

HISTORY OF POLITICAL IDEAS

VOLUME III

THE LATER MIDDLE AGES

PROJECTED VOLUMES IN THE COLLECTED WORKS

HISTORY OF POLITICAL IDEAS
Series Editor, Ellis Sandoz

The Editorial Board offers grateful acknowledgment to the Earhart Foundation, the Windway Foundation, Liberty Fund, Inc., Robert J. Cihak, M.D., and John C. Jacobs, Jr., for support provided at various stages in the preparation of this book for publication.

The University of Missouri Press offers its grateful acknowledgment for generous contributions from the R. C. Kemper Charitable Trust and Foundation and from the Earhart Foundation in support of the publication of this volume.

THE COLLECTED WORKS OF

ERIC VOEGELIN

VOLUME 21

❦

HISTORY OF POLITICAL IDEAS

VOLUME III

THE LATER MIDDLE AGES

EDITED WITH AN INTRODUCTION BY
DAVID WALSH

UNIVERSITY OF MISSOURI PRESS

COLUMBIA AND LONDON

Library of Congress Cataloging-in-Publication Data
(Revised for volume III)

Voegelin, Eric, 1901–
    [Selections, 1997]
    History of political ideas / edited with an introduction by David
Walsh

    p.   cm.   — (The collected works of Eric Voegelin ; v. 21)
Includes index.
    Contents: v. III. The Later Middle Ages.
    ISBN 0–8262-1126-7 (vol. I : alk. paper)
    ISBN 0–8262-1142-9 (vol. II : alk. paper)
    ISBN 0–8262-1154-2 (vol. III : alk. paper)
    ISBN 0–8262-1174-7 (set)
    1. Philosophy.   2. History—Philosophy.   3. Political science—
Philosophy.   I. Walsh, David.   II. Title.   III. Series: Voegelin, Eric,
1901–   Works. 1989 ; v. 21.
B3354.V88   1989 v. 20
320'.09—dc21   97–13266
                                                          CIP

    ∞ ™ This paper meets the requirements of the
American National Standard for Permanence of Paper
for Printed Library Materials, Z39.48, 1984.

Designer: Albert Crochet
Typesetter: BOOKCOMP
Printer and binder: Thomson-Shore, Inc.
Typeface: Trump Mediaeval

Contents

THE LATER MIDDLE AGES

Editor's Introduction

Eric Voegelin's study of the high Middle Ages is surely one of the gems of his vast historical enterprise. It is a volume destined to belie the judgment of its author concerning the merits of the publication of his *History of Political Ideas*. Far from being the ineradicably flawed construction Voegelin came to regard his *History* as being, the work now emerges as one of the great scholarly achievements of the century. Undertaken with the intention of replacing the standard treatment of George Sabine's *History of Political Theory*, a work that has been revised but not superseded since 1937, Voegelin's survey is now poised to fulfill its original purpose. Since that time political theorists have lost both their nerve and their inclination to attempt vast single-author historical narratives, so that the belated appearance of Voegelin's monumental account is a landmark within the discipline. Even those who are not familiar with his later writings will recognize this as the work of one of the giants of the field.

Perhaps nothing is so indicative of Voegelin's stature as that supreme detachment with which he set aside the labor of more than a decade on the grounds that it was rooted in a theoretical misconception. After almost completing his vast survey of the history of political ideas, he came to the realization that the work was tantamount to an ideological deformation of reality. "There were no ideas," he explained, "unless there were symbols of immediate *experiences*."[1] Voegelin had discovered that his adoption of the conventional approach had led him to recount the history of

---

1. Eric Voegelin, *Autobiographical Reflections*, ed. Ellis Sandoz (Baton Rouge: Louisiana State University Press, 1989), 63.

I

political ideas as if it were a self-contained entity fully intelligible in its own terms. His work exemplified the approach, which has since become a standard within the discipline, of relating ideas about politics to their setting within political history.[2] But Voegelin saw that that was not enough. Neither political history nor political ideas exist on their own. They have meaning only in reference to a wider civilizational context in which fundamental conceptions of order, of man's place in the order of reality as a whole, are given expression. But what do such ordering conceptions rest on? Ultimately they arise from the living dynamism of human existence as it moves under the impetus of forces of moral and spiritual order that reach immediately into experience. It is in terms of such moving sources of order that the ideas of moral or political order have resonance. Once the underlying experiences shift, then the ideas cease to exercise any authoritative force in human life.

Few contemporary political theorists have yet reached this insight, and it is this failure that imparts a sense of incompleteness to their historical studies.[3] We are left with the impression of the derivative or secondary because their analyses do not reach as far as the motivating sources of the ideas they analyze. The flatness of their narratives is a direct consequence of their inability to explain what it was that made the idea of subjective rights or the slogan of liberty so attractive at a particular time. They can explain the conditions and the changes that occurred in the historical setting, but they cannot penetrate to the changes that occurred within the human beings who lived through them. Surely the most important task is to comprehend the dynamics of such inner shifts, and it can be done only by reaching the level of the immediate experiences of order that form the ultimate horizon of human existence. Voegelin recognized the indispensability of such an approach and therefore set out to write a very different kind of study, an account of the history of the experiences and symbols of order as they emerged within the human condition over space and time. In writing *Order*

2. The historical approach to political theory is represented most prominently by Quentin Skinner. For a discussion of the theoretical debate surrounding it see James Tully, ed., *Meaning in Context: Quentin Skinner and His Critics* (Princeton: Princeton University Press, 1988).

3. One of the interesting exceptions is Charles Taylor. His *Sources of the Self* (Cambridge: Harvard University Press, 1989) is a remarkable investigation of the sources of moral resonance that are not contained within the intellectual elaborations.

and History he left our contemporary historians of political ideas far behind.

But the abruptness of that transition in Voegelin's own career constituted a dual miscalculation on the author's part with important consequences for the way the remainder of his work has been viewed. The first misimpression is that his *History of Political Ideas* was not worth publishing, a view to which Voegelin himself lent credence by his own refusal to publish or to have it published as a whole during his lifetime. One can certainly understand the solicitude of an author to ensure that only his very best work appears before the public. But this may well be a case where the author's own assessment is tinged with an unnecessary degree of proprietary concern to the detriment of the reception of his work. Voegelin's decision strikes us in hindsight as both a substantive and a strategic misjudgment. It is not simply a case of the editors having lower standards, although that also may be true. For the history-of-ideas approach to political theory remains a viable mode of analysis, still evidently thriving today more than ever, so long as due acknowledgment is made of the limitations of context in the enterprise. There is no reason Voegelin's own vast contribution to this genre cannot appear before the public with this overarching caveat emblazoned above it.

Strictly in terms of the history of political ideas it provides a gigantic service, for it surveys the development of political theory from the Greco-Roman period up to the nineteenth century. While it does not attain the analytic penetration of the sources of order that Voegelin achieved in *Order and History*, it provides a compendium of political reflections unmatched by his later work and unequaled by any author this century. The wealth of detailed accounts of individual thinkers and specific complexes of ideas, organized with a historical sweep, is little short of breathtaking. It is elaborated with an erudition that is confirmed by the best historical research and often outshines that literature in the sheer novelty of the materials covered. The theoretical superiority of Voegelin's later work does not relieve the necessity for a detailed knowledge of the history of political thought, which is recounted nowhere as thoroughly as in the pages of his *History of Political Ideas*.

A neglected corollary to this observation is that the earlier study provides one of the best points of entry into the theoretical depth of the later Voegelin. Despite the author's abrupt statement of discontinuity, of a break in his enterprise, it is a mistake to expect that this earlier effort comes from a very different mind. Most readers are likely to be struck by the continuity of effort and of orientation, as they were when the only previously published segment of the *History* appeared as *From Enlightenment to Revolution.* Voegelin does use the language of ideas in this work, but clearly his interest is already moving toward the discovery of the "sentiments" that lie behind them. The organizing framework is composed of the "evocative ideas" that constitute the comprehensive ordering convictions of the epochs with which he is dealing. And in the case of individual thinkers his analyses unfailingly target the motivating centers of their thought; it is Voegelin's capacity to lay bare the *anima animi* from which the works have been written that constitutes the secret of his exegetical brilliance. Thus, far from being a discontinuous predecessor, *History of Political Ideas* is in fundamental continuity with Voegelin's later work and is an indispensable background for the analyses offered all too elliptically in that context. From the viewpoint both of the inherent value of the analyses themselves and of their role in amplifying the often difficult theoretical reflections of his later work, Voegelin's *History of Political Ideas* can no longer be withheld from publication.

The most poignant consideration within this context is the strategic consequence of his decision to postpone the work's publication. It has meant that Voegelin's largest, most accessible, and most impressive historical survey was denied to the public during his lifetime. Instead, the cryptic and elliptical conclusions of this vast study appeared as occasional lectures,[4] while the theoretically more challenging volumes of *Order and History* trailed off into the stratosphere of reflections where few readers were prepared to follow. Now at last the public will have a chance to explore this vastly more approachable infrastructure. The great wealth of historical study on which the later theoretical adumbrations are based now becomes apparent. Surely this will in time have the effect of presenting a very different perception of Voegelin than is now current. Not only will it cement his reputation as one of the

---

4. Two of the most obvious examples are the lectures that became *The New Science of Politics: An Introduction* (1952; Chicago: University of Chicago Press, 1987) and *Science, Politics, and Gnosticism: Two Essays,* trans. William J. Fitzpatrick, introduction by Ellis Sandoz (1968; rpt. Washington, D.C.: Regnery, 1997).

greatest political theorists of the twentieth century, but it may even have the happy consequence of reversing the curious status that he now enjoys within the discipline. With the appearance of *History of Political Ideas*, Voegelin may move from being one of the least read of major figures to becoming one of the most widely read.

Certainly the present volume on the later Middle Ages presents a masterful account of one of the most crucial periods in the history of political thought. Voegelin's analysis is unequaled in theoretical penetration of the epoch despite the profusion of studies that have appeared since he wrote. Naturally, there have been advances in the understanding of the empirical materials, especially by way of the recovery of critical texts and a more extensive appreciation of economic, social, and political factors. But there has not appeared a survey of the meaning and significance of the period as a whole that even approaches the insights Voegelin draws out of his study. When we ask what the medieval world was about, the specialists become tongue-tied and end by muttering platitudes about the wholeness of the medieval mind that obscure more than they reveal. The contribution of Voegelin's work in this volume is not only that he has found an organizing framework within which to understand the medieval order, but also that he has explained its crucial significance for the modern world that emerged from its disintegration.

The key to Voegelin's success in untangling this intricate relationship has been his penetration of the inner self-constitution of the medieval world. Drawing especially on the work of Alois Dempf, he identifies the *sacrum imperium* as the organizing principle of medieval civilization. On its face there is nothing exceptional about such a familiar overarching conception. But in the hands of Voegelin it yields a new depth and expansiveness that reveal its character as the defining self-understanding of the medieval universe. It functions, as he explains in the preceding volume, *The Middle Ages to Aquinas*, as the great evocative symbolization in terms of which the medieval world measured itself. This enables Voegelin to brilliantly organize the epoch along two great arcs of meaning. One is the integrating movement toward the realization of the *sacrum imperium* ideal; the other is the disintegrating movement as the *sacrum imperium* ceases to function as the authoritative ideal. In neither case does the *sacrum imperium* exist as a reality. It is a pure aspiration, and the degree of its efficacy determines the unfolding of medieval civilization.

When compared to the organizing perspective offered by even the best twentieth-century historians, Voegelin's approach stands out with a theoretical rightness that is unique. Primarily this is because it is the most faithful to the historical materials themselves. It does not inject extraneous or later concerns into the medieval world. Instead it seeks to understand the epoch as it was understood by the people who lived in it. The *sacrum imperium* was their construction of a defining ideal that they slowly came to abandon. Compared to this perspicuity, the approach that looks to the medieval world as the forerunner of modernity, whether in terms of the growth of constitutionalism, the emergence of secularism, or the rise of the spirit of self-determination, appears peculiarly anachronistic. Even a scholar of the stature of Walter Ullman found himself compelled to cobble together a makeshift framework by which medieval history narrates the transition from descending, authoritarian styles of government to ascending, democratically grounded forms of politics.[5] The only problem is that this was not how, or not principally how, medieval men and women themselves understood what they were doing. For them the struggle was centrally defined as the effort to realize a single order of temporal and spiritual authority, and to adjust to the movements and forces that rendered that aspiration finally impossible.

Before that collapse occurred, however, the struggle was to maintain a balance between two jurisdictions or offices, the sacerdotal and the royal, within one embracing public order that defined the medieval cosmion. It was never to be a "forerunner" for anything else. What constituted the whole character of the medieval world was the conviction that these two centers of authority can be held together within one order. They were convinced that there is only one order that has its source in God; as a consequence, all inferior orders must be capable of being harmonized within a comprehensive whole. In this sense the term *sacrum imperium* does not refer to a merely political conception. There is not even a necessary indication that it requires a strong central direction whether from its ecclesiastical or its imperial authorities. At its deepest level it simply expresses the consciousness of living within one common overarching order and the impossibility of severing the parts from

---

5. Walter Ullman, *A History of Political Thought: The Middle Ages* (Harmondsworth: Penguin, 1970).

6

it. The papal and imperial authorities occupy their position, not because of their achievement in organizing the whole, but primarily because there is a whole that must be given expression through the recognition of their cooperative authority. It is this wholeness of ethos, rather than of power, that accounts for the peculiar tolerance of resistance and diversity within the medieval commonwealth. It is also what accounts for the crucial contrast and continuity with the modern world that has emerged from it.

Modernity is defined by difference and separation. But it is a disassociation that exists within the memory of its medieval wholeness, and not just in such passing evocations as Western or Judeo-Christian civilization. It is haunted by a consciousness of unity between its elemental poles of church and state, public and private, individual and social, because such distinctions cannot even be maintained except by reference to a preexisting unity. Their separation presupposes a common order by which they can be distinguished and related. Even the modern world cannot utterly dispense with what was most featured in the medieval, a shared understanding of the overarching spiritual order within which human beings exist and under which human society can be organized. It is because Voegelin's analysis reaches to the ultimate horizon of the medieval self-understanding that he is also able to find the most adequate means of exploring its relationship to the modern world as well. It is not that the continuities of an emerging liberal constitutional order so often noted are not valid, but that their meaning can be properly identified only in relation to an overarching conception of the order of reality.

That recognition is the major strength of Voegelin's analysis in this volume. It enables him to see that the source of the medieval unity is primarily philosophical and that its disintegration is correspondingly philosophical. The political fragmentation reflects that inner symbolic fracture. Nowhere is this dynamic made as brilliantly clear as in his analysis of William of Ockham, whom he designates the first modern philosopher. Ockham is the first to "philosophize on problems that do not originate in a radical philosophical experience but are offered by the environment for an intellectual solution." The fact that William's formidable acumen is put to the service of protecting the integrity of the truths disclosed through faith does not in any way diminish the collapse of the sense of their continuity with the truths revealed by reason.

His nominalistic philosophical mode, with its reduction of all substantive questions to methodological and power relational issues,
announces the end of the medieval confidence in the unity of
all things. Voegelin rightly measures the revolution taking place
in Ockham's writings when he identifies it as "a civilizational
schism." This is a penetration that escapes most commentators
who are distracted by the spirituality of the Ockhamite orientation.
In some sense his fideism is more "medieval" than that of Saint
Thomas, but it is a faith that is no longer confident of its capacity
to find its integration with reason.

This is the inner division that finds its outer expression in the
gradual divergence between the church and the temporal sphere.
The institutional strains within the *sacrum imperium* cannot be
treated as an autonomous process, for their unraveling is com-
prehensible only in relation to the deeper dislocations within the
spiritual and intellectual life of medieval civilization. Voegelin's
analysis is fully attuned to that connection and therefore provides
the most adequate account both of the high Middle Ages and of their
relationship to the modern world. It is rooted in his understanding
of the aspiration to find the comprehensive unity of all things,
human and divine, temporal and spiritual, which is included under
the abbreviation *sacrum imperium*. From the disintegration of this
always implied but rarely articulated unity of faith and reason, the
components of the modern world emerge as the result of a long
process of differentiation. What is neglected in most analyses of
the modern world, as a consequence, is the prior unity from which
its parts have asserted their autonomy. The superiority of Voegelin's
perspective is that he enables us to recognize that the assumption of
the self-contained character of the spheres of reason and revelation,
politics and religion, is a modern conceit. Their character can be
assumed to lie just as much in the prior unity that constitutes them
as parts of a whole.

The real excitement of Voegelin's treatment in this volume is
that he compels us to think about such fundamental relationships,
and not just in terms of the more restricted continuities between
medieval and modern constitutional thought. He shows us where
the deeper philosophical struggles whose insolubility defines the
modern world have their origin. We recognize our world in his
account of the loss undergone by faith and reason in their bifur-
cation. Reason is severed from the substantive goal that directed it

and disconnected from the source of its confidence in the order that assures its efficacy. In its place we recognize the emerging instrumental reason that no longer knows either itself or its purpose in existence. The structure of nature can no longer be apprehended by reason since neither universals nor causality have any validity; knowledge of the external world is reduced to "a problem of organizing empirical materials by means of the conceptual instruments of the human mind." Moreover, faith does not fare any better. Now it exists without reference to rational control, and increasingly the church is deprived of the invigoration provided by the engagement in robust intellectual discussion. Shrunk to the essentials of dogmatic authority and the private mystical and devotional life, it is on the way toward losing all publicly authoritative significance in human life. "The tearing of this gap between the worldly sphere and the true Christian life unfolds its full consequences only in the Great Reformation. The order of the world is established as an autonomous human sphere outside the Christian order in the strict sense, and the Christian order is brought nearer to a monastic, ascetic conduct of life. The medieval temporal-spiritual double order is broken up into the two orders of a non-Christian politico-economic order and a Christian ascetic discipline. As a result, the order of the world will follow from now on its own principles without regard to the Christian order of life, or an attempt must be made to keep it within bounds through regulation from the monastic position."[6] Both of these variations were attempted, by Luther and Calvin respectively, and the modern world has oscillated between rationalism and fundamentalism ever since.

Voegelin brilliantly explores the emergence of this tension in the reflections of Dante, who confronts the modern recognition of the inability of the political realm to absorb the spirit of Christianity. The scene is dominated by political realists, of the type that eventually culminates in Machiavelli, and religious reformers, of the type that follows a long line from Saint Francis on. What is absent is a political thinker who can unite them in a new institutional evocation. Voegelin is able to make sense of the romantic quality of Dante's thought, which harks back to the empire at precisely the height of the interregnum that has exposed its obsolescence. He is able to interpret Dante's vision, not as an escapist or utopian response to

6. See below, 119.

the newly emerging reality, but as a very deliberate evocation of a new civilizational order. It is not any particular social or political order that Dante has in mind, but a publicly effective recognition of the eschatological openness that is the source of a common human order. It is the eschatological component of the medieval whole that is now in search of a new public expression. Now it is the poet and not the church, Voegelin points out, who steps forward to evoke the consciousness of the transcendent finality of human life on the basis of the personal authority of his vision.

With Dante the eschatological dimension of the *sacrum imperium* is in search of a new institutional evocation, but it has not yet found it, and perhaps, Voegelin suggests, it cannot be found. Instead eschatology is more likely to continue as a spiritual movement in search of a political expression. It is Voegelin's sensitivity to this level of ultimate spiritual meaning that enables him to unlock the peculiar political development that occurs within the subimperial zone of Germany, Bohemia, and the Italian *regnum.* This is generally the area of medieval politics and theory most neglected because it seems to fall outside the emerging pattern of the nation-state. Attention has recently been focused on the Italian city-states because they at least exemplify the new ideas of liberty and republican self-government.[7] But even when they are examined, it is generally without reference to the imperial context within which their existence was possible. Voegelin is virtually alone in bestowing attention on the peculiar problems of German particularism that prevented German consolidation into a state and of the idiosyncratic character of politics that inevitably resulted within this imperial zone. Such interest is not simply a reflection of Voegelin's own experience as a central European. It is primarily a consequence of his understanding of the dimension of spiritual universality that remains an abiding feature of political initiatives within this setting.[8]

---

7. A good example is Quentin Skinner, *The Foundations of Modern Political Thought,* vol. 1, *The Renaissance* (Cambridge: Cambridge University Press, 1978).

8. One of the most fascinating episodes is surely the intoxicatedly optimistic vision advanced by Pierre Dubois in his *De recuperatione terre sancte* (1306). The French lawyer elaborated the conception of a league of nations, complete with arrangements for collective security, as part of a scheme for realizing an age of universal peace. The modern and utopian dimensions of this work are not dismissed by Voegelin as purely fanciful, for he recognizes their source in the lingering medieval aspiration for an order to replace the *sacrum imperium.* See below, 61–65.

Cola di Rienzo is the figure who brings this puzzling relationship into focus. After leading a successful revolt in Rome (1347), Rienzo issued a series of letters to the Italian cities, the imperial electors, and the emperor, along with the pope. He proclaimed the advent of a *reformatio et renovatio,* which would be both spiritual and political, a new imperial Christianity that seemed to look back to the past rather than forward to the future. Certainly the rhetoric was apparently unrelated to his immediate political intentions of uniting Italy and restoring republican government. Again Voegelin is alone among commentators in getting to the core of this anachronistic behavior. It is, he explains, the residue of a universalistic consciousness that exists in unbroken continuity within the imperial political zone. Unlike the Western nations, "in the imperial zone the transfer of the *corpus mysticum* idea to the national bodies did not function quite smoothly." Instead there was a tendency to extend its application to the whole of Europe, a universalistic sediment from the imperial past that was present in more muted form in the nation-states as well. It was a preoccupation with the necessity for spiritual renovation reflected in such diverse figures as Savonarola and Machiavelli, which was virtually unknown in the nation-states. "In England," Voegelin explains, "the nation grew under the pressure of a strong kingship. In the imperial zone the nations gained political unity through the growth of a national spirit and, when the spirit had sufficiently matured, through military action that overcame the particularistic political entrenchments."[9]

The other side of this dissociation of the eschatological impulse, now in search of its institutional embodiment, is that the newly autonomous political entities of whatever type existed without reference to a universal order beyond themselves. Even the church, as Voegelin points out, was compelled in a world defined in terms of rival power organizations to accommodate itself to the new necessities. Breaking with the Hildebrandine assertion of the papacy's universal political authority, the popes set out to secure their own territorial bases first at Avignon and then in the papal states. The ground was well prepared theoretically through the work of the extreme papalists of the thirteenth and fourteenth centuries in a series of writings whose novelty in transforming the church into a

9. See below, 238, 244.

state Voegelin is particularly acute in recognizing. Giles of Rome (Aegidius Romanus and Egidio Colonna), for example, is roundly excoriated as a thoroughly modern intellectual whose sycophantic service toward both Philip the Fair and his nemesis Boniface VIII proves his unadulterated obsession with power. The result was that the Western world lost an institutional expression of its universal interests, and the papacy sought to utilize the political agreements as the primary instruments for meeting the challenges mounting against it. In the Conciliar movement this resulted in a papal victory in alliance with the national monarchs, but it prevented, Voegelin suggests, the development of a response to the calls for a reformation that eventually overwhelmed it.

For the new secular entities themselves the situation was not much better. Marsilius of Padua is the theorist who articulates the rise of this supreme secular state because he is the first to differentiate the source of its authority in the community as a whole. Voegelin is unfailingly perceptive in his analysis of the core of Marsilius's thought as the conception of the *legislator,* which is "the first consistent construction of the intramundane political unity, deriving governmental authority not from an extraneous source but from a specially constructed 'whole' of the community behind its single parts."[10] The problem is that the source of the order actualized by the self-governing *legislator humanus* is nowhere clarified. Despite the invocation of Aristotle, the center of the *Defensor Pacis* does not lie in a conception of *arete.* Nor is there a substantive conception of natural law to provide such guidance, for, although law must follow right reason, it still remains law even without it so long as it is backed by the coercive power of the community. These are familiar tensions within the literature on Marsilius. What Voegelin adds is a sensitivity to the Averroist component of the text's treatment of Christianity as a "cultural curiosity" and its replacement by a vague suggestion of eternally recurring cycles. Order is heavily dependent on government for its realization, hence the concern with the coercive backing of law and the necessity for a monopolistic exercise of authority. What is to form the inner order of the citizens is brushed over in silence, apart from the suggestion that Christianity does not really provide

10. See below, 91.

such order except for the *vulgus*. Marsilius's construction of the autonomous secular state is spiritually nihilistic, and the study of politics has become "a religiously detached, sober, craftsmanlike" analysis of the kind made famous by another Italian thinker.

The problem is of course that such a secular politics and pragmatic political science cannot stand on its own. It remains haunted by the awareness of the degree to which it falls short of the real virtues required to sustain its order and overshadowed by the absence of the inner spiritual renovation that is alone capable of bringing about a lasting political community. This is why, as Voegelin points out, both Machiavelli and Hobbes are such acute analysts of the moral mendacity of their societies and why they undertake their heroic efforts to construct an order on the basis of the minimal expectations of human virtue. Whatever may be gained in the refinement of a science of power calculations, the instability of the constructions is a source of instability all the way up to the present. The existence of political orders whose moral sources can no longer be clearly discerned or clearly articulated virtually guarantees an endless series of attempts to find other means of renewing their vitality. Secular politics is almost by definition bedeviled by the quest for virtue.

The analysis of the assertion of secular political independence follows a generally conventional line. What Voegelin really adds to this perspective is an extraordinarily sensitive analysis of the eschatological impulse that continued largely outside institutional control. He was certainly unique in calling attention to spiritual aspirations that found a new outlet during an era when the conventional institutional carriers no longer proved satisfactory. It was in the period just after his work on the *History* that Voegelin found the theoretical means of analyzing the quasi-religious overtones of social and political movements in the period from the high Middle Ages on. He discovered the overarching significance of Gnosticism as the spiritual and intellectual form assumed by religious idealism outside the limits of institutional compromise and restraints. In many respects the absence of that theoretical identification of the phenomena of spiritual perfectionism in no way diminishes the individual analyses offered in the present volume. Indeed it is preferable that the distracting effect of that often sweeping characterization does not obscure the wealth of concrete details in Voegelin's analysis of John Wycliffe or *Piers Plowman*. Instead he shows himself a master analyst of the crucial but hard to quantify dimension of spiritual enthusiasm that emerges as an independent factor in politics as a result of the disintegration of the *sacrum imperium*.

The pattern begins, as Voegelin pointed out in the preceding volume, with the new consciousness of epoch evoked by Joachim of Fiore (Flora). Joachim's Trinitarian speculation on history explained how the Old Testament age of the Father was followed by the New Testament age of the Son, which was now to be superseded by a whole new dispensation in the age of the Spirit. By rendering the revelation of Christ and the sacramental structure of the church obsolete, Joachim established the pattern that has dominated subsequent history with the vision of an era of autonomous spiritual freedom beyond all institutional supports and restraints. The monastic perfection of human nature had now permeated society as a whole, and a new age was definitively dawning. Mediation and remediation would no longer be required because the fullness of spiritual truth would have been achieved. Voegelin's insight was less in detecting the character of Joachim's construction than in discerning its representative significance. He was able, for example, to recognize its resonances not merely among the Franciscan Spirituals, who regarded their own founder as the prophet inaugurating this new age, but in the character of the saint himself. Voegelin's chapter on Saint Francis is surely one of the most penetrating in his entire corpus, for he can fully acknowledge the rejuvenative contributions of the mendicant founder while sparing none of the critique of the unbalancing dimensions inhering in the order he inspired.

With Saint Francis the imitation of Christ became so complete that it was tempting to see it as a means of social and political transfiguration. Certainly the Franciscans themselves and the church were now to follow the evangelical counsels of perfection with a thoroughness that seemed to suggest that institutional compromise would no longer be necessary. It was an expectation that almost destroyed the Franciscan order in its refusal to establish structures and make the requisite pragmatic adjustments. The debate on poverty and the demand for a total abnegation of all property by the church were experienced as a threat of such seriousness that proponents had to be repulsed with vigor. For no institutional order could survive this pure spiritual exigence, which refused to accept the frailty of all human constructions but insisted that its own transfigurative inspiration be permitted to work its miraculous effect. This factor was still present in the background of William of Ockham, not least in his imprisonment along with Michael of Cesena in the papal foundation at Avignon. For it was the deepest irony of the medieval period, as Voegelin delineates, that it was precisely the efforts to renew its spirituality most decisively that generated the forces of secular independence most completely. If the world has been thoroughly sanctified, then it no longer stands in need of a perfection beyond itself.

This is a process that began at the end of the Investiture Struggle when "the radical spiritualization of the world foreshadowed the rise of the intramundane forces in the following two centuries." The declining ability of the church to contain the new spiritual ferments led to a splintered expression of Christianity, a process that Voegelin identifies as the emergence of "parochial Christianity." This is a perceptive context for recognizing the Reformation as only the culmination of a process long under way in the preceding centuries. While the political factors are skillfully dissected, Voegelin maintains his focus on the inner transformations that constituted the determining reality. This is why an analysis of *Piers Plowman* is worthy of such attention; in it Voegelin finds a potent expression of the eschatological spirit that has been transferred to the humble plowman within the confines of the realm of England. Just as in the profusion of mystical writings during the fourteenth century, Voegelin finds a concentration on eschatological transfiguration without reference to any institutional suggestions for its embodiment. This was the impulse for transformation that found expression in the revolutionary movements of the mystical anarchists of the late Middle Ages. "The civilizational destruction perpetrated by a peasant group fighting for the perfect realm does not differ in principle from the annihilation of the world content in the . . . *Cloud of Unknowing.*"[11]

The great insight of this volume, which in many ways constitutes the center of Voegelin's thought, is that the tension between the transcendent and the immanent cannot be abolished without destroying our hold on both of them. The *sacrum imperium* is of continuing significance because it was one of the most substantial

11. See below, 177.

historical evocations of that tension, and the story of its vicissitudes is of permanent relevance for us. It is Voegelin's achievement here to have clarified the nature of the tension between an order beyond this world and the order of this world, whose balance was the goal that defined medieval civilization. But his study provides more than a historical account of the struggle for that elusive balance. It is rooted in the recognition that the medieval problematic is linked to our own and that any conscientious account must take note of that continuity. The scholar cannot avoid an engagement with the problematic itself. Voegelin's clarification of the central tension is itself a contribution to the unfolding of an order in continuity with it. We recognize in this volume one important phase of a meditative engagement with the past in which the search for a balanced articulation of order came increasingly to appear to him as *the* problem of order.

The medieval volumes of his *History* provide a fascinating perspective on the struggle for a transcendently grounded immanent order within a context in which this was the explicitly declared goal. It is perhaps not too much to suggest that it was in this work that Voegelin developed the main outlines of his understanding of the problem that shaped his approach to the study of order and history as a whole. In some respects the reflections on the *sacrum imperium* drew him to clarify aspects of this endlessly complex relationship that are not so fully presented in his later writings. What is especially evident in the medieval context is the mutuality of the relationship between the spiritual beyond and the temporal embodiment, because it was precisely the effort to bring them into closer relationship that brought about the collapse of the order. The enduring significance of the *sacrum imperium*, as becomes evident in this study, is that its preservation hinged precariously on a recognition of a balance of spiritual and temporal that could never be finally attained.

It is precisely the aspirations of the high Middle Ages to abolish the tension of order that demonstrate its impossibility. Spiritualization of the world was attempted in different ways by the extreme papalists and by the sectarian Spirituals. In each case the project succeeded only in aggravating the disorder of the world; but, more important, the efforts to absorb the transcendent spirit fully into existence served only to undermine its transcendent authority. When the divine reality has been drawn into the existing order of things, then it no longer attracts us with the pull of its ineffable mystery. An intramundane spirituality is in a decisive sense not truly spiritual any longer. Even the fideistic response of Ockham and the *devotio moderna* run the risk of shrinking the divine reality to the inner dimension of faith, a dimension in which God is wholly present or wholly absent. In the former the mystery of the transcendent pull is abolished, and in the latter it can no longer be discerned. We recognize in the effort of the Spirituals to protect the integrity of faith a defensive response that was repeated more widely in the modern civilization that succeeded them. The absorption of divine reality within human experience became indistinguishable from the secular assertion of human independence from all divine connection. Only the tensionally experienced pull of divine reality functioned as the source of order in human existence.

Equally futile was the effort to abolish the tensional struggle from the side of the new secular political constructions. Their inability to ground themselves is fully evident in the effort devoted to establishing the divinely authenticated legitimacy of the territorial monarchs. They had to draw around themselves the divine authorization that attached to the emperor, and the kings of France in particular sought to wrap themselves in the mantle of charismatic and even saintly authority. The monarchs displayed a safer instinct for the nature of political order than did the theorists of secular sovereignty, because they sensed the insufficiency of their authority if it rested on nothing more than themselves and a bare expression of consent. They may have chafed at the existence of an institutionally independent church, but they recognized that they could not construct a political order without reference to a spiritual order that provided the substance of the community bond sustaining it. Their actions and the reflections of such theorists of community as Nicholas of Cusa, with his emphasis on divine *concordantia*, point toward the spiritual dependence of the secular. A wholly secular state remains an impossibility.

The only alternative to the abolition of the tension is the acceptance of the struggle to find an appropriately balanced formulation of its exigencies. The implication that is suggested but not fully articulated by Voegelin in this conclusion is the recognition that freedom too cannot be abolished. It is something of a relief that order cannot be definitively achieved in any historical epoch. Each generation must assume the struggle and in the process exercise the freedom that is alone the way to realizing its humanity. Neither the spiritualization of the world nor the secular evacuation of all spirituality can relieve us of the burden. We are compelled to find again the means of remaining faithful to the pull of transcendent goodness within the conditions of our pragmatic existence. The problem is that to state the problem is not the same as to provide a solution, even a provisional one. The civilizational schism between faith and reason that Voegelin identifies in the high Middle Ages has not disappeared. Modernity as a whole has struggled with its consequences, and they still confront us. When faith has been compelled to migrate to the private world of interiority in the face of the rational critique of science, and secular reason is adrift in the form of technique without guidance, what can be done to bring them together?

In many respects this may be taken as the core question behind Voegelin's work. He is the healer of that civilizational schism, not a spokesman for either side, and it is fascinating to catch his reflections in this volume on the nature of the problematic that first emerged in this era. All of his remarks are informed by awareness of the inadequacy of the various responses developed in the high Middle Ages to the schism that became an open rupture in the modern period. Only Saint Thomas and Nicholas of Cusa emerge as figures who understood and rose to the challenge. Thomas is for Voegelin between the medieval and the modern worlds, as the man who provides a synthetic philosophy of the classic type that preserves the essence of the medieval balance and points toward its transmission into the modern conditions. But Thomas could not change the historical course, and his synthetic achievement remained too bound to the language of a world that would soon be superseded. There is still a need, as Voegelin remarked elsewhere, for a new Saint Thomas, and it is not too fanciful to see his own work as just such an effort. Instead of providing a *cordon sanitaire* separating the spheres of faith and reason as did Ockham, the solution to conflicts such as that represented by the divergent views of Creation would be to recognize that they arise "as a dialectical border-problem that does not permit of an answer in unequivocal finite categories." Voegelin goes on to explain that theological truths "have no meaning if understood as propositions concerning the empirical structure of the world but draw their validity from another source. Kant called this source 'the practical interest'; today we prefer to speak of the expression of fundamental religious experiences in symbols, the symbols drawing their strength from the experiences that they express."[12] This is, by the way, an assessment that indicates that Voegelin had already broken with an approach based strictly on the history of ideas and was beginning to operate with experiences and symbols.

Voegelin's great theoretical breakthrough was intimately connected to his struggle with the civilizational schism that emerged in the late medieval period. He understood that the restoration of order in the modern world was dependent on the discovery of a means of bridging the gap. What he did not sufficiently recognize, in my view, was that the order that was transmitted from the medieval to the modern world was a way of implicitly integrating the transcendent and the temporal, although without rendering their relationship philosophically articulate. This is the constitutional and liberal political tradition whose emergence Voegelin, along with the preponderance of scholarly opinion, locates in the medieval world. In part his failure to recognize the transmission of the philosophic-Christian substance within this tradition may have to do with his reserved estimate of its achievement and prospects. He had, after all, witnessed the transmutation of the Weimar Republic into the Third Reich. It may also have arisen from the pronounced lack of philosophical coherence that has given the liberal constitutional tradition the appearance of greater instability than it in fact has. At any rate his actual treatment of the growth of constitutionalism makes clear both that it is rooted in the medieval synthesis between faith and reason and that it is the major achievement of order transmitted by that world.

The relationship between constitutionalism and the philosophic-Christian synthesis is made clear only in his treatment of Saint Thomas. Voegelin is, in my view, insufficiently cognizant of the extent to which the synthesis is implicitly preserved within the later tradition, but he does state the principle of that relationship with striking forcefulness in dealing with the Angelic Doctor. He recognizes in the Thomasic synthesis the core constellation of sources that go into the formation of the free self-governing individual whose demand for a corresponding political form is the center of the

12. See below, 109.

liberal constitutional tradition. He lists as the main sources "the Aristotelian theory of politics, the Roman constitution, the Israelite primary democracy and kingship, the experience of Italian town democracy, and the sentiment of Christian freedom." They coexist in an unsystematic contiguity, drawing their cohesion from the twin convictions of the participation of all and the freedom of the mature individual. The conjunction of political sources remained, Voegelin acknowledged, an evocative combination that may have had most of its relevance within the Dominican order itself. "It represents, nevertheless, the synthesis of nature and Christian spiritualism in politics, and as the symbol of this synthesis it has dominated, with or without explicit reference to its author, the evolution of Western politics to this day."[13] The political integration effected by Saint Thomas is of course a reflection of the larger synthesis between the freedom of the rational intellect and the illumination of faith that he achieved through the comprehensive elaboration of his underlying conviction "that the order of things in Truth, is the order of things in Being." Faith and reason cannot be in conflict because they reflect the one divine source, and Thomas had found the means of preserving their autonomy within the whole. That example, even though it was not followed, has, in Voegelin's view, "decisively influenced the fate of scholarship in the Western world."

The example of the Thomasic synthesis has provided a tantalizing demonstration of the integration between faith and reason that is possible. As Voegelin recounts the story, Saint Thomas could not have accomplished much more. The forces of disintegration were simply too strong, and the intellectual comprehension of a single individual, no matter how penetrating, could not reverse the direction of history. "The historical literalism of Christianity" could not stand before the emerging "rational critique." It could only be preserved, as Ockham recognized, by firmly enforcing their separation. What Voegelin later came to recognize was that the balance brilliantly articulated by Thomas itself erred by inclining toward a literal or propositional resolution. The ultimate sources of reason and revelation in experience still lay hidden, and the result was that the Thomasic synthesis played into the very collapse it sought to avoid.

---

13. *The Collected Works of Eric Voegelin,* vol. 20, *History of Political Ideas,* vol. II, *The Middle Ages to Aquinas,* ed. Peter von Sivers (Columbia: University of Missouri Press, 1997), 222, 223.

Christian theology has denatured the Platonic *Nous* by degrading it imaginatively to a "natural reason," a source of truth subsidiary to the overriding source of revelation; by an act of imaginative oblivion the revelatory tension in Plato's vision of the *Nous* as the "third god" was eclipsed, in order to gain for the Church a monopoly on revelation. But history has taken its revenge. The nonrevelatory tension, imagined by the theologians as a servant, has become the real antirevelatory reason of the Enlightenment revolt against the Church.[14]

Only a nondogmatic mysticism is capable of apprehending the unity of the two forms in their one source, and it is that quest that marks Voegelin's intellectual heroes in the modern world.

In contrast with this theoretical disintegration of the medieval worldview is the parallel emergence of a new unity in political practice. The development of the constitutional tradition that eventually formed the modern liberal democratic order has long been recognized as a crucial episode in the medieval narrative. We might even go so far as to say that it has now become the dominant perception of the medieval era that it constitutes a prelude to constitutionalism. Voegelin presents this dimension with an insight and depth that compare well with the more recent accounts. Clearly much more is now understood about the emergence of canon and civil law as well as the formation of institutions and ideas of a constitutional nature in the medieval period. But the main lines of Voegelin's analysis are still valid and in overall balance are superior to what is currently available. The already noted defect, which he shares with most of the prevailing scholarship, is the inability to recognize the liberal constitutional tradition as the publicly effective evocation of the philosophic Christian sources of order.

Failure to acknowledge the full significance of the emergence of the liberal constitutional tradition does not, however, obscure the analysis of the process itself. The superiority of Voegelin's account arises from his recognition of the relationship between republican ideas and the formation of a community substance or identity. Most scholars are content if they have traced the development of ideas of liberty and constitutional self-government.[15] But

---

14. Voegelin, *Order and History*, vol. V, *In Search of Order* (Baton Rouge: Louisiana State University Press, 1987), 43.

15. See for example, Brian Tierney, *Religion, Law, and the Growth of Constitutional Thought, 1150–1650* (New York: Cambridge University Press, 1982); Richard Tuck, *Natural Rights Theories: Their Origin and Development* (New York: Cambridge University Press, 1979); and the relevant chapters in J. H. Burns, ed.,

Voegelin insists that ideas are intelligible only in relation to an existing political reality that has motivated their articulation. In this sense his analysis is more historically attuned than are those of contemporary students of the historical setting of political ideas, because Voegelin acknowledges a closer connection between the historical ideas and the political reality that is constituted by them. "The term *constitutionalism*," Voegelin observes, "is not a concept but a symbol signifying a system of articulation as a whole while absorbing into its explicit content only incidental features of the system."[16]

The consequence of this deeper analysis of the constitutional symbols is that Voegelin provides a rich understanding of the institutional development that makes the symbols politically effective. It is a brilliant lesson in the concrete political processes that constitute a liberal democracy. After noting, for example, the emergence of representative assemblies in Spain, Sicily, England, and France from the twelfth century on, he raises the question of the meaning of this phenomenon, which he maintains is to be found in the writs of summons. There the formation of a community consciousness is to be identified. What is new is not the mere sending of delegates but the emergence of communities whose self-articulation requires the sending of delegates. It is no longer that the monarch virtually represents the whole, but that the individual communities must now represent themselves. Later, of course, the process reached its limits in the representation of individuals. Both spiritual and secular spheres witnessed the birth of "this new type of community, consisting of spiritually active and mature individuals, [which] had to become articulate by means of elective processes" within their particular societies.[17]

Representation and its attendant requisites became a feature once the self-consciousness of forming a community had emerged. Voegelin's analysis has the great merit of calling attention to the process by which the emergence of the sense of participating in a larger national or civic community occurred. Representation is meaningful only within the context in which it is accepted that a

---

The Cambridge History of Medieval Political Thought, c. 350–c. 1450 (New York: Cambridge University Press, 1988).
16. See below, 144.
17. See below, 153.

member can make decisions for the whole. Voegelin lays considerable stress on the cumulative and expanding practice of communal deliberation as the incubator for the development of the institutions of self-government. "This formation of communes capable of deliberation and decision is considerably more important than the much discussed incidental development of representation; for the communes are society in form for action, while the representation of shires and boroughs by delegates is an inevitable technique that develops as soon as the substance to be represented is experienced as such."[18] The corollary is that the successful continuation of such institutions is crucially dependent on the presence of mature individuals who view themselves as members of a whole. Self-government begins in community, not in atomistic individuals.

The historical question of what promotes the formation of a sense of community responsibility and prerogatives is handled most skillfully by Voegelin in his analysis of the paradigmatic example of England. Contrary to the widespread conception of an "English tradition" of civil liberties, he shows that such assertions are the result rather than the source of a process long in formation before it became intellectually explicit. It is not that the English were better than most at asserting their rights, but that the development of a strong monarchy permitted the preservation of a range of feudal liberties that could later be asserted as rights against the absolutist royal claimants. Even the celebrated Magna Carta, in Voegelin's interpretation, was less concerned with the rights of the revolting barons than with the royal consolidation of power emerging from the feudal and pointing toward a national constitutional order. A process of royal compulsion of participation in decision making inculcated the habit of self-government that eventually resulted in the assertion of the corresponding rights and privileges to resist the further encroachments of royal power.[19]

The transformation of a *dominium regale* into a *dominium politicum et regale* is well analyzed in the late work of Sir John Fortescue. "The modern constitutional system did not evolve," Voegelin concludes, "on the plane of institutions but through the superimposition of ideas on institutions that had grown in an entirely different

18. See below, 137.
19. Cf. James C. Holt, *Magna Carta,* 2d ed. (Cambridge: Cambridge University Press, 1992), chaps. 10–11.

field of sentiments and ideas. We can state the issue of the relation between medieval and modern institutions in a simplified manner by saying that the institutions that grew in the feudal power field constituted a new fact, and that this new fact contributed to the rise of the sentiments and ideas that determined the further growth and interpretation of institutions in the constitutional direction."[20]

The relation between this intuitive growth of constitutional thought and the larger metaphysical order of reality has remained one of the great questions all the way up to present. Only one thinker in this volume rises to the level of reflection on it, Nicolas of Cusa, whom Voegelin treats in his culminating chronological and philosophical role. Again Voegelin's treatment is unique in detecting the political significance of the mystical dimension of Cusa's work. His role in the Conciliar movement is well known, as are its implications for the development of ideas of representative government. Less well recognized is Cusa's recognition of the inadequacy of the mere institutional forms of representation and consent. Without the underlying spirit of a common order, common responsibility, and *concordantia*, the external forms are of little use, as the Council of Basel demonstrated. Cusa undertook the deliberate search for the source of such universal concordance, *concordantia catholica*, which would supply the substance to the empty vessels of constitutional procedure. This redirected him to the harmony of the order in which man finds himself and which therefore must be the only source of harmony he can find within himself. Just as the cosmos is organized as a hierarchy in which each level is joined by a bond of mutual sympathy with the surrounding levels, so the social cosmos must also be ordered by the reciprocal relationship of love by which the different roles are accepted within the order of the whole. Just as the highest level of concordant unity is the divine Trinity in which the members are perfectly one, so the grace of divine life is what draws all the lower levels toward the corresponding degree of harmony with one another. It is a new evocation of the *corpus mysticum* as the divine-cosmic-human unity of all things in God. Politically this is translated into the vision of an order in which the differences between the wise and the foolish are subordinated to the reality of their deeper community.

20. See below, 135.

The all-important sentiment of trust is the indispensable core of a government of consent. By virtue of that trust the consent of those who participate less directly to those who are in charge is rendered reasonable. Without it, the jurisdiction is simply one of power.

Concordantia is the inspiration that made it possible for Cusa to write the most complete account of a representative institutional order up to that time. Surpassing the fragmented proceduralism and the fideistic religiosity of Ockham, Cusa was able once again to integrate the parts because he was in possession of an integrating vision of the whole. It was, as Voegelin shows, a substantive faith that could simultaneously affirm a realist metaphysics precisely because it was rooted in a recognition of the transcendent openness of both faith and reason. It is difficult not to recognize in the treatment of Cusa's mystical integration the path that Voegelin himself was to follow ever more insistently over the succeeding decades. The unity between faith and reason, which could no longer be found in the formulation of a speculative system, would now be located in the only reality in which it could be found, the prereflective unity of life itself. There in the primal unity of the human soul in openness to the transcendent the underlying unity of all things could be glimpsed and provide the basis for a vision of the eventual return of all things to their common source. Voegelin warms to this mystic-cosmic-historical vision of Cusa in the closing pages of his study of the medieval world. He finds, "Precisely at the moment when the medieval *sacrum imperium* was disassociated into the *societates perfectae* of the church and the nations, precisely at the time when the category of the mystical body was transferred from universal Christianity to the particular national bodies, the new concordantia of mankind was evoked by the Cusanus out of the forces of the new intellectual mysticism. The nations emerging from the *sacrum imperium* did not become a plurality of brute power facts without grace; the mystical faith in the concordantia of mankind was still extended over them as the eternal arc, far outreaching the discord of the times."[21]

In preparing Voegelin's manuscript for publication I have followed the approach of the series as a whole. As far as possible the author's style has been preserved on the assumption that most readers will

21. See below, 266.

wish to hear Voegelin in his own voice. The changes have largely been confined to the minor adjustments of copyediting, a task for which I would like to thank Jane Lago of the University of Missouri Press. I have tried to make the text more usable for contemporary readers by updating the literature cited in the notes, translating the non-English quotations, and using more standard forms of names. In general, Voegelin made his own translations, and these have not been substantially altered. Where he left passages untranslated, I have relied on published translations; otherwise, they are my responsibility. I would like to thank David McGonagle of the Catholic University of America Press for assistance on the more uncertain Latin passages, and Ellis Sandoz for his unfailing advice and encouragement. Research assistance was provided at crucial stages by Tom Lordan.

DAVID WALSH

THE LATER MIDDLE AGES

CONTENTS

D. THE CHURCH AND THE NATIONS

13

Character of the Period

§1. Suspense between the Middle Ages and the Renaissance

The work of Saint Thomas was a triumph of the spirit and the intellect over the forces of the age, but it did not change their course. The sentiments and ideas after Thomas are in complete continuity with those before him. Nevertheless an epoch was marked. It was due not to a radically new factor that might have entered the scene but rather to the cumulative effect of changes that had been in progress for a century; the contemporaries were hardly aware of the revolutionary character of the new forces and sentiments because they developed so slowly.

The slowness of the changes, the lack of a major event that would symbolize the epoch, and the absence of penetrating self-interpretations in this period have caused a variety of opinions concerning its proper characterization. Some historians are inclined to ascribe, at least to its earlier phase, a clearly medieval character; others speak of it sweepingly as the Political Renaissance. In the section "The Structure of the *Saeculum*,"[1] we have given the reasons we set little store by such divisions. What matters is the structure of sentiments and their careful description. We can, of course, classify Dante as a medieval figure because his thought was concerned with the empire and the spiritual church in the Joachitic tradition. But he was also the first man since antiquity to speak to the European public with the authority of a poet; and by virtue of

---

1. *The Collected Works of Eric Voegelin*, vol. 20, *History of Political Ideas*, vol. II, *The Middle Ages to Aquinas*, ed. Peter von Sivers (Columbia: University of Missouri Press, 1997), 103–204.

this authority he may be regarded as a figure of the Renaissance. If, furthermore, we consider that the time of the empire and the spiritual church had passed when he evoked them in his work, we may recognize in him the features of a conservative and a romantic, features that do not belong to the high period of an evocation but appear rather when it is overcome by the twilight of revolutionary changes.

Similar problems arise when we approach the figure of Boniface VIII. The label of the "last medieval pope" still seems to enjoy some prestige. It is justified insofar as Boniface VIII thought of himself in terms of a blend of Gregory VII and Innocent III. When, however, he tried to act on this belief he encountered the French resistance. He discovered that he was just Boniface VIII, the head of a powerful bureaucratic and financial organization that conflicted with the interests of an equally powerful French organization; deeply hurt he complained about the *superbia Gallicana.* Moreover, the characters of his enemies and the forms that the final conflict assumed can hardly be called medieval. Guillaume de Nogaret, this curious French professor of law and royal administrator, storming the palace at Anagni with a gang of soldiers, in company with Cardinal Colonna, and threatening the sick pope in his bedchamber, was certainly not a type provided for in the medieval structure of society. The "terrible day of Anagni" was a savage Renaissance affair in the best style. The public reaction toward the protagonists, on the other hand, was rather medieval. Rarely has a man been vilified like Boniface VIII. The most careful sifting of the evidence shows that he was old, sick, ill-tempered, rash, greedy, exceedingly concerned about the welfare of his family, and endowed with a very good opinion of himself; altogether not a character to make friends. But the venomous flood of accusations concerning his vices, heresy, and generally anti-Christian qualities proves, if anything, that he was a demonic personality, perhaps comparable in some features to Frederick II. The great individual was not yet publicly accepted, particularly not on the papal throne; the time had not yet come of the Borgia, Rovere, and Medici popes. Nogaret, however, had also gone too far. The attack on the pope was more than the opinion of the time could digest; he spent the rest of his life explaining and justifying what he had done.

§2. Shift of Politics to the West

Considering the complexity of attitudes and sentiments, any sweeping categorization of the period as medieval or Renaissance seems inapposite. We have to penetrate to the constituent elements of the situation. Beginning from the periphery of the field of political forces, we have to observe the deterioration of the crusading spirit. The fall of Acre in 1291 could not arouse the European powers to action; the wealth of the princes and the interests of the peoples were absorbed in domestic and European power politics; there were still some minor crusading enterprises, but the great expansive breath of the Crusades had come to an end. In the East began the advance of the Turks. In 1354 they crossed to Europe, by the end of the century they had expanded into Bulgaria and Serbia, in 1453 Constantinople fell, and by the end of the fifteenth century the Balkan peninsula and the Adriatic coast were Turkish.

In the center, the empire had disappeared. More important as a symptom than the Interregnum itself is the fact that no major German prince was greatly interested in becoming emperor. Only under the threat that the pope would appoint an emperor could the election of Rudolph I be achieved in 1273. The new emperor promptly surrendered all claims to Italy. After the short Italian interlude of Henry VII in 1310–1313, which aroused the hopes of Dante, and the expedition of Louis IV (1327–1330), the policy of the German emperors fell into the pattern of dynastic Hausmacht expansion.

In the West, the power of France was in the ascendancy after the fall of the Hohenstaufen; the Interregnum seemed to favor French aspirations of assuming the imperial role that had slipped from the Germans. After the battles of Benevento and Tagliacozzo, Charles of Anjou could as king of Sicily continue the Hohenstaufen policy of European domination through the simultaneous possession of a northern and a southern domain, with France taking the place of Germany. He pursued far-reaching plans for the creation of a Mediterranean empire at the expense of the Greeks, and in 1273 he pushed, though without success, the election of his nephew, the king of France, as German emperor. The imperial policy of France was still a factor at the beginning of the fourteenth century when it expressed itself in the plans of Pierre Dubois for an organization of the Western world and the Near East under French hegemony. By the middle of the century, however, the French resources were engaged in the Hundred Years War with England (1338–1453), resulting in the consolidation of the French national territory. In time the Hundred Years War paralleled the Turkish advance in the East; it ended in the year of the fall of Constantinople.

Finally, we have to consider the great movement that ultimately carried Western civilization around the world, the discoveries of the fifteenth century. These have a direct connection with Crusades insofar as Prince Henry of Portugal, as general of the Order of Christ, used the funds of the order for the equipment of expeditions for the purpose of discovering sea routes by which the Arab and Turkish flank would be turned for Christian attacks from the south and rear. These attempts opened the series of expeditions in the course of which the coast of Africa was explored and in 1487 the Cape of Good Hope was rounded. Since 1410, furthermore, the sphericity of the earth had become topical through the translation of Ptolemy's *Geography*, leading to the attempts at reaching Asia by the western route and the discovery of America in 1492. In the two centuries from 1300 to 1500 the weight of the Western world shifted economically and politically from the central and Mediterranean to the Western powers, and the dynamics of politics was reversed from the Eastern expansion of the Crusades to the oceanic expansion to America, Africa, and the Asia of the sea routes. The foundation was laid for the domination of politics by the Atlantic sea powers in the period from 1500 to 1900.

§3. The Clash between the Church and the Nations

In earlier chapters we had several occasions to guard against the misunderstanding of the temporal power as a political power in the modern sense. In the Roman-Christian time as well as in the *sacrum imperium* the temporal power is always, implicitly or explicitly, understood as the imperial power. The Investiture Struggle was not a conflict between the church and the secular government, but between the two orders of the one imperial unit, represented by the pope and the emperor. We have to be particularly aware that the temporal power, while distinctly not being spiritual, was a charismatic power in the *corpus mysticum*. The great transformation of the charismatic temporal power within the *imperium* into political power in the modern sense was paralleled in the church by the transformation of the papal spiritual power within the imperial order into the ecclesiastical organization as a distinct power unit side by side with the secular political units. We have noted the contraction of the term *ecclesia* to the meaning of the hierarchy with Saint Francis, and the withdrawal of the spiritual power into an organization ranking over the multitude of political units with Saint Thomas. In the hands of the lawyer-popes the formulation of the claims of the church had shifted slowly but irresistibly from claims of a spiritual order to legal jurisdictional claims. By the end of the thirteenth century the church herself had become a power unit organized as an absolute monarchy. The physical maintenance of this power organization on a lavish scale and the perpetration of its political aims necessitated an international tax system and financial administration that clashed with the interests of the growing and closing national political unit. The history of the church in the period after Saint Thomas is the history of the clash with the political powers and of the attempts at finding working relations between the church and the national political forces.

The first phase of this conflict was the open struggle between Boniface VIII and France leading to the affair of Anagni (1303). The second phase is marked by the transfer of the papacy from Rome to Avignon in 1305 and the Great Schism from 1378 to 1417. The third phase is characterized by the Conciliar movement with the three main aims of restoring unity to the church, of reforming the church in the direction of a limited monarchy, and of solving the problem of the new heresies. The fifteenth is the century of the great councils: of Pisa in 1409, of Constance in 1414–1417, of Basel in 1431–1449. The first problem, the unity of the church, was solved through the election and general recognition of Martin V in 1417. The second problem, the internal organization of the church, was advanced considerably in practice through the very procedure of the councils. Parliamentary technique, the evolution of a committee system, the composition of committees by national delegations, and so on, were steps toward the evolution of representative, parliamentary government that had their effects in the secular political sphere, although the reform of church government itself failed. The negotiations over the Hussite question finally produced as an important result the *Compacta* of 1433, the first treaty of the church with a heretical sect. The Hussite question, however, was of comparatively minor relevance, and the negotiations concerning the far more important Greek question failed. Nevertheless, the potentialities of the *Compacta* were unpredictable as they would have opened the way toward dealing with the ever mounting heretical wave along the lines of a federation of the Christian church substance. The Conciliar movement, however, had spent its force. In the Jubilee of 1450 the papacy could celebrate its triumph over the attempt at a readjustment of the church to the new situation; the stagnant policy that finally broke under the impact of Luther and Calvin in the sixteenth century was fixed.

14

The Absolute Papacy—Giles of Rome

§1. The *Unam Sanctam*

The occasion for the clash between the papacy and France is symptomatic of the new world of sentiments in which we move. Boniface VIII had without success attempted a settlement of the dynastic struggles between France and England. As the continued struggle damaged the financial interest of the Curia, the pope issued, in the form of the bull *Clericis Laicos* in 1296, an injunction to the clergy of France and England forbidding them to pay taxes. The answer from France was a royal prohibition to export gold or silver, a measure that cut the Curia off from its French revenue. A compromise was achieved in the following years, but in 1302 a new clash ensued over a royal privilege concerning episcopal appointments leading to the famous bull *Unam Sanctam* of 1302, which asserted the supremacy of the papal spiritual power over all temporal powers. The critical statement runs: "That every human creature is under the Roman pontiff we declare, say and define, and pronounce it necessary for salvation." The two swords, the spiritual and the temporal, are in the hands of the spiritual power, the spiritual to be used by itself, the temporal to be used for it by the princes at the will and tolerance *(nutus et patientia)* of the spiritual. When the temporal power deviates it will be judged by the spiritual. The general formulas are not amplified so that it is impossible to know precisely what they would mean if translated into institutionalized jurisdictions. Nevertheless, the papal claim to a practically unlimited power over the incumbents of temporal government offices is beyond doubt.

a. Imperial Policy and Foreign Policy

The interpretation of the *Unam Sanctam* was obscured in its time, and it still is today, by political emotions. The papal interference in French financial affairs was indirectly an interference in French foreign politics, which already at that time was distinctly tinged by national sentiment. In his resistance the king had public opinion on his side. The bulls *Clericis Laicos* and *Unam Sanctam* have to be seen together as an evolution from the indirect to a direct interference in temporal political affairs. The bull has always been popularly understood in this sense and is still characterized as a notorious document of priestly arrogance. This judgment is understandable from the point of view of established sovereign governments that are not willing to bear outside interference with national politics; the claim of a church to determine the policy of a modern great power most certainly would be politically impracticable. But the historian cannot permit modern political sentiments to cloud his judgment. At the time of Boniface VIII the closed sovereign national state did not yet exist; it was just emerging from the feudal power field. The clash between the pope and France was the very occasion on which the problem of secular national politics, without relation to the interests of the papacy, was discovered. Up to this time the political interests of the spiritual and temporal powers had been, on the whole, parallel. The period of the establishment and expansion of the Western empire had been followed by the period of Western imperialism in the Crusades. Internal Western power politics had begun to cast its shadow with the Gregorian anti-imperial organization of the border states and the imperial counterpolicy of encirclement. But in this phase of power politics the papacy was still a partner to the struggle. Boniface VIII was faced by the entirely new situation of a papacy crowded out of the major political affairs of the Western world. The papal interests were still running in the old grooves of a united Western policy against the Muslim East while the secular political interests were already on their way toward the particularization of the West. The French-English struggle absorbed the resources of the West to such an extent internally that an effective foreign policy of the West as a whole, whose bearer was now the pope alone, became impossible. The vocabulary of the *Unam Sanctam* was still that of the spiritual and temporal powers, but the underlying issue was the transition from a common policy of the Christian West to the secular policy of particular units. "Foreign policy" in the modern sense, as the primacy of concern about the political relations between power units within the West, began to take shape. Under the outworn form of spiritual primacy, Boniface VIII attempted to save the primacy of Western common interests against the particular politics of the Atlantic powers. For this reason he may be said to have been even more than the last medieval pope: he was the last great medieval political figure after the emperors had ceased to be the bearers of Western policy.[1]

b. The Hierarchy of Powers

The excitement about the interference of the spiritual power in temporal affairs has also obscured the fact that the statements of the *Unam Sanctam* are not made bluntly but are reasoned. Even the best presentations of the *Unam Sanctam* overlook the fact that the bull is more than a diplomatic document and contains an important development in the Western rationale of power. Starting from the Pauline dictum that all power is "ordered" by God (Rom. 13:1), the bull analyzes the meaning of "order." An "order" of powers means that the several powers have to be in a hierarchical relation. The inferior power has to be derived by means of intermediate powers from a supreme power that ultimately derives from God. The pseudo-Dionysian theory of the hierarchies is adduced in support of the construction. "For according to the order of the universe things cannot be equal or immediate but the lowest will be brought into order by the intermediate, and the lower by the higher." From the premise, which is assumed as evident, that the spiritual power ranks higher in dignity than the temporal it follows, in combination with the pseudo-Dionysian theory of the hierarchy of powers, that the spiritual power institutes and moderates the temporal.

We have met with the pseudo-Dionysian theory of the hierarchy before, in the treatise of Bertrand of Bayonne, when it was used to construct the papal absolutism within the ecclesiastical hierarchy.

---

1. On the changing pattern of politics and its connection with the problem of taxation see the excellent survey in T. S. R. Boase, *Boniface VIII* (London: Sherrer Ross, 1933), 131 ff. On the general context see K. Pennington, *Pope and Bishops: A Study of Papal Monarchy in the Twelfth and Thirteenth Centuries* (Philadelphia: University of Pennsylvania Press, 1984).

The construction of the *Unam Sanctam* does no more than expand the argument of Bertrand beyond the ecclesiastical order into a general theory of power including the temporal. The criticism of Gerard of Abbeville is equally valid against this enlarged theory: the constitutional theory of the *corpus mysticum* is replaced by a new doctrine of power. In the theory of the *sacrum imperium* the charismata are given by God directly; the functions within the *corpus mysticum* are exercised freely; the members are held together by mutual love in the Pauline sense (1 Cor. 13). The hierarchical theory of power is a new element, incompatible with the Pauline doctrine as well as with the Gelasian. It rationalizes the older Christian evocation in the direction of a hierarchical system with an absolute power at the top of the pyramid.

The political failure of the attempt must not deceive us about its function in the history of Western constitutional theory. The theory of the charismata and of the Gelasian balance of powers was applicable only as long as the temporal power was represented by the more or less uncontested single imperial head. When the unity of Christian mankind split up into national bodies politic, the absolutist construction of the power hierarchy was one possible means of saving the spiritual unit of Western mankind. If the attempt failed the alternative would be a disintegration of the spiritual power paralleling and following the disintegration of the imperial power. The several temporal political units would tend to acquire the status of separate spiritual units, as they actually did with the rise of nationalism as the spiritual determinant of the Western political communities.

§2. Giles of Rome (Aegidius Romanus)

The ideas of the bull have to be placed in an environment of intellectual discussion of which the most important document is the treatise *De ecclesiastica potestate* of Giles of Rome.[2] It is generally assumed that the treatise of the papal counselor, preceding the bull only by a few months, had a strong influence on the *Unam Sanctam*. Most of the decisive formulas of the bull seem to be taken literally from the opening chapter of the treatise. Through the

---

2. The edition used is Giles of Rome, *De ecclesiastica potestate*, ed. Richard Scholz (Weimar: Böhlau, 1929).

work of Giles the origins and implications of the absolutist theory become indeed fairly clear. We may distinguish between two main roots: the mysticism of Hugh of Saint Victor and a new conception of power originating in the pathos of the intellectual who, in his capacity of counselor to the powers that be, is willing to shoulder the burden of governing the benighted inferior subjects.

a. The Mysticism of Hugh of Saint Victor

From Hugh, a German mystic who flourished in the school of Saint Victor during the middle of the twelfth century, seem to stem two cardinal ideas of Giles of Rome and, in consequence, of the *Unam Sanctam*. In his *De sacramentis fidei Christiana*, Hugh had evoked the idea of the militant Christian people, the *ecclesia* of Christ, united through faith and the sacramental dispensation and divided into the corporal and spiritual orders of laymen and clergy, the *sacerdotium* in the unit having the spiritual, sacramental, and jurisdictional supremacy over the *regnum*. The evocation is symbolistic and does not enter into the institutional delimitation of the two powers. This evocation of a symbolic indeterminate spiritual supremacy is paralleled by Hugh's interest in the pseudo-Dionysian treatise on the hierarchy of angels.[3] The application of

---

3. Hugh of Saint Victor, *De sacramentia Christianae fidei* (Migne, *Patrologia Latina*, vol. 176). The decisive passage from this treatise, which influenced the *De ecclesiastica potestate* of Giles and determined the formulations of the *Unam Sanctam*, is the following:

"Quanto autem vita spiritualis dignior est quam terrena, et spiritus quam corpus, tanto spiritualis potestas terrenam sive saecularem potestatem honore ad dignitate praecedit.

"Nam spiritualis potestas terrenam potestatem et instituere habet, ut sit, et judicare habet si bona fuerit. Ipsa vero a Deo primum instituta est, et cum deviat, a solo Deo judicare potest, sicut scriptum est: spiritualis dijudicat omnia, et ipse a nemine judicatur (I *Cor*. II). Quod autem spiritualis potestas (quantum ad divinem institutionem spectat) et prior sit tempore; et major dignitate; in illo antiquo veteris Instrumenti populo manifeste declaratur, ubi primum a Deo secerdotium institutum est; postea vero per sacerdotium (jubente Deo) regalis potestas ordinate" (Lib. II, pars II, c. IV, p. 418, C, D).

("To the extent that the spiritual life has greater dignity than the earthly, and the spirit than the body, by as much does the spiritual power precede in honor and dignity the earthly or secular power. For spiritual power has also to establish earthly power in order to exist, and it has to judge it, if it has not been good. Indeed, it itself was established first by God and when it goes astray it can be judged by God alone, just as it is written: 'The spiritual man judgeth all things; and he himself is judged of no man' (1 Cor. 2). Now, it is manifestly declared among that ancient people of the Old Testament where the priesthood was first established by God that spiritual power, in so far as it looks to divine institution, is both prior in time and greater in

the hierarchical idea to the relation of supremacy of the spiritual over the temporal power has the earlier noted effect of sharpening the institutionally indeterminate symbolic supremacy to a relation of delegation and control.4

b. The Intellectual and His Will to Power

The other root of the absolutism of Giles is the will to power of the intellectual. This new element in political doctrine is exemplified particularly well by Giles because in his earlier years, when he was the tutor of the later Philip the Fair, he had written his *De regimine principum* (1285), in which absolute monarchy was presented as the most desirable form of government while the question of submission of the temporal power to the spiritual was barely touched.

---

dignity; afterwards indeed royal power was arranged through the priesthood at God's order. Wherefore, in the Church sacerdotal dignity still consecrates regal power, both sanctifying it through benediction and forming it through institution"; *Hugh of Saint Victor on the Sacraments of the Christian Faith*, trans. Roy J. Deferrari [Cambridge, Mass.: Medieval Academy of America, 1951], 256.)

Hugh of Saint Victor, *Expositio in Hierarchiam Coelestem S. Dionvsii Areopagitae* (Migne *Patrologia Latina*, vol. 175). The mystical, institutionally indeterminate character of the theory of the hierarchy appears in the following passage on p. 931: "Summa ergo potestas, et prima secundam, et tertiam potestatem post se constituit in angelis, et hominibus, ut ei et conformes participatione virtutis, et cooperatrices consortio potestatis sint. Et divisit dona virtutum, et secundum divisiones donorum distribuit officia potestatum; et omnia dona de uno, et omnia potestas sub uno; et unum in omnibus, et omnia ad unum, et in uno" (Therefore the highest power, and the first, establishes the second and the third power after it in the angels and in men, in order that they be conformed to it by participation in virtue and sharers with it in an association of power. And he divided the gifts of the virtues, and according to the divisions of the gifts he distributed the offices of the powers; and he gave very many gifts and established many powers, and all the gifts were from the one, and all the power was beneath the one; and the one was in all, and all were toward the one and in the one). The Trinitarian division of every hierarchy, which dominates the argument of the time, is discussed in 1.IX, chap. 10: "Synagogae angelicae ordinationis repetitio" (The synagogues of the angels are divided in a repetition of the order). The text from Dionysius quoted there on p. 1099 runs: "Et omnem hierarchiam videmus in primas, et medias, et ultimas virtutes divisam" (And we see every hierarchy divided into highest, middle, and lowest virtues). We remember that this idea also determines the Thomistic conception of the three necessary orders of society. When the division is transferred to the problem of the spiritual and temporal powers and their relative order in a hierarchy, it does not fit too well because after all there are only two powers. The difficulty is dodged by Giles of Rome and by Boniface VIII through the classification of the temporal power as the lowest, the lower spiritual offices as the middle, and the pope as the supreme rank in the hierarchy.

4. I cannot do more in this context than touch on the complex problem. The question has never been treated, as far as I can see, though most certainly the origins of our modern idea of the hierarchy of power, of delegation of power and control from the top of a governmental pyramid, would deserve a monograph.

Carlyle expresses his surprise at the development from the earlier work to the later: "The earlier work is significant especially . . . for its abnormal assertion of the principle that the monarch should be above the law. The later work is almost wholly occupied with the superiority of the Spiritual over the Temporal Power, in terms which are not only extreme, but even in some respects contradict the judgement of the most important ecclesiastical writers." "It must be confessed that the development is arresting, and even startling."[5] The development loses its enigmatic character if we recognize that Giles was less interested in spiritual or temporal power than in power as such. He was willing to advocate any power as absolute as long as he was associated with it. If Giles were placed in a modern environment we would have to say that he was a Fascist by temperament. His fundamental position is perhaps best revealed in this remark: "it is natural that those who are superior in intellect and excel in industry should rule." This is the confession of an intellectual activist.[6]

We have used the word *Fascist* advisedly in order to characterize an intellectual atmosphere that seems to have baffled earlier interpreters who lacked the experience we have today due to contemporary events. We find expressions of surprise similar to the one just quoted in the work of the Carlyles concerning also single theoretical tenets: "The position of Egidius Colonna [Giles of Rome] is remarkable, and different from the normal medieval tradition" (p. 71); "It is curious that Egidius should have departed so far from the normal medieval conception" (p. 406); etc. The common cause

---

5. R. W. and A. J. Carlyle, *A History of Medieval Political Theory in the West*, vol. 5, *The Political Theory of the Thirteenth Century* (Edinburgh: Blackwood, 1950), 403.

6. *De Renuntiatione Papae* XVI.1, ed. Roccaberti, Bibliotheca maxima Pontificia, vol. II (Rome, 1698). It should be noted, however, that not everybody would be inclined to agree with the interpretation given in the text. Jean Rivière in his *Le problème de l'église et de l'état au temps de Philippe le Bel* (Louvain and Paris: Spicilegium Sacrum Lovaniense, 1926), 226, does not see any conflict between the earlier and the later work. Professor C. H. McIlwain, *The Growth of Political Thought in the West* (New York: Macmillan, 1932), 257 ff., agrees with Rivière and argues that Giles may have suppressed his opinions concerning spiritual supremacy in his earlier work precisely because they were the same as those he published later. There is a point to the argument, but I prefer the interpretation given in the text because it fits well with the general style of the politics of Giles as presented in the following paragraphs, and because the absolutism of the earlier work fits well into the atmosphere of French politics at the time of Charles of Anjou, about which I shall say more in the following chapter.

of the various features that make the theories of Giles seem "abnormal" by the standards of medieval tradition is the new sentiment of power. As soon as the idea of the spiritual unity of mankind is translated from the free coexistence of Christians as members of the body of Christ into terms of a spiritual unity controlled by the holder of supreme power, the outlines of a form of government appear that today we are accustomed to calling totalitarian. The work of Giles is of particular historical importance because our popular opinion of the Middle Ages as being dark and oppressive of liberty is mainly determined by these new overtones that are *not* medieval, but rather modern.

c. Theory of Power

Medieval theory proper has a doctrine of powers in the plural, but no doctrine of power in the singular. The *De ecclesiastica potestate* is the first Western treatise on power as such. Power is defined as the potency of an agent to produce certain effects (II.6, p. 61).[7] There are four types of power: the natural forces, the arts, the sciences, and the domination of men. Significantly the natural forces are the first; for now, with the beginning of natural science, the universe becomes the model of a system of powers having causes and effects. The possession of the second power, the *potestas artificialis*, enables its owner to produce artifacts; the third, the *potestas scientifica*, is the possession of right reason in speculative considerations. By the *potestas principatum*, finally, princes are made potent, materially and spiritually, to exert dominion over men. A distinction between spiritual and material powers is expressly denied except for the superordination of the one to the other (II.6, p. 62).

Corresponding to the powerful ruler appears, at the other end of the scale, the powerless subject, obedient and completely subservient, having no natural rights, but only such rights as are derived from his status in the power organization and granted by the absolute holder of all power. The subjects are *servi ascripticii, servi empticii, censuarii, tributarii*; they are in a state of servitude *(servitus)*; and they have no total dominion over earthly goods, but

---

7. "Quod nihil aliud est potestas, nisi per quam aliquis dicitur esse potens" ("By way of describing power, then, let us say that power is nothing other than that through which someone is said to be powerful"; *Giles of Rome on Ecclesiastical Power*, trans. R. W. Dyson [Woodbridg, Suffolk: Boydell, 1986], 57).

only a *dominium particulare* with obligation of tribute to the power (II.10, p. 95). This harsh doctrine is aggravated by the theory that God, who might have exerted the dominion of the world without earthly rulers, has given power to the princes because he wanted the creatures to participate in his dignity; the creatures should not be idle but have a sphere of power and action of their own (II.15, p. 137). This human dignity in the image of omnipotent divinity is given to the rulers only. It does not become clear whether the subjects share in this dignity; the creation of man in the image of God becomes dangerously close to being a privilege of those who hold power.

d. Papal Power

The general theory of power, which in itself might be applicable to any instance of political power, is elaborated upon with regard to the power of the Roman pontiff. The plenitude of the spiritual and material powers belongs to the pope. Both swords are in the hands of the church, but they are not held in the same manner. The church has the spiritual sword to use herself, and she has the material sword to be used at her command *(ad nutum)* by the secular princes. The princely power is completely subordinate to the papal (I.1–9).[8] Secular power has the function of "ordering matter at the disposition of the ecclesiastical power" (II.6). All organs and instruments of government, the arms, the earthly goods, and the laws have to be administered in obedience to, and at the will of, the church (II.6, p. 69). All laws specifically, imperial as well as those of other princes, are invalid if they are in conflict with ecclesiastical laws; and confirmation by the spiritual power is required for their validity (II.10, p. 92). These technical rules make Christian mankind a closed governmental system with respect to legislation, administration, and the use of the instruments of coercion.

---

8. The symbolization of the two powers by the two swords goes back in continuity to Bernard of Clairvaux, who used the symbol in his *De consideratione libri V ad Eugenium Tertium*. In the spiritual atmosphere of the twelfth century, however, the material sword is only perhaps *ad nutum* (by the nod) of the spiritual power, and if so, at the same time *ad jussum imperatoris* (by the order of the emperor). The Gelasian coordination is preserved. See J. A. Watt, "Spiritual and Temporal Powers," in J. H. Burns, ed., *Cambridge History of Medieval Political Thought* (New York: Cambridge University Press, 1988), chap. 14.

Within the ecclesiastical hierarchy itself, the power is concentrated at the apex of the structure in the pope. The church practically disappears behind the pontiff. "What the pope does may be said to be done by the church" (II.12, p. 109). We are very close to the *L'état c'est moi!* The church substance has been transformed into a hierarchical governmental organization with an absolute head, representing the whole.

e. The Sacrificium Intellectus

The same tendency toward a rigidly controlled and closed political system appears in the theory concerning matters that today we should call ideological. Giles has the dubious distinction of having evolved the theory of a hierarchy of sciences. Hierarchy as a general category of social order also extends to the various sciences in such a way that theology is the mistress of all sciences *(domina scienciarum)* and science, including philosophy, is the servant *(ancilla et famula)* of theology. Philosophers must not destroy the castle of theology by their arguments, but have to adapt them to the service of theology and the church (II.6, p. 64). A generation after Saint Thomas, who could establish the freedom and independence of the intellect because he was a great spiritualist, there appeared in Giles the first modern political intellectual to use the intellect as a subservient instrument for the support of a dogmatic position in much the same manner as do our contemporary leftist and rightist intellectuals. Considering the popularity in our time of atrociously incorrect opinions about the Middle Ages, it is worthwhile to state explicitly that the *sacrificium intellectus* (which is spoken of with the greatest horror by those who invoke it most abjectly) is not demanded by the free Christian spirituality of Saint Thomas but by the intellectual in power politics.

f. Ecclesiastical Totalitarianism

Finally, we have to consider a doctrine that illuminates the new attitude particularly well because it does not follow of necessity from the axioms of the theories of power and hierarchy but is rather a voluntary addition conflicting strongly with the traditions of Christian thought. The idea of Hugh of Saint Victor, modeled on the events of Hebrew history—that the royal authority has to be instituted by the sacerdotal—is interpreted to mean that no princely power can be properly called royal unless it is thus instituted. No rulership can be just unless it is instituted by the church. Any so-called kingdoms of the pre-Christian time were nothing but *magna latrocinia* in the Augustine sense. This doctrine is a flagrant mis-interpretation of Saint Augustine, and it breaks with the tradition that pagan governments might have a high civilizational rank, like Rome in the argument of Saint Augustine, though these govern-ments would be deficient in justice in the Christian sense because they do not render God his due. Such non-Christian governments are organized, according to Giles, by the "civil power" only and have no claim to be recognized as legitimate political organizations (I.5, p. 15). This political theory is extended to a doctrine of property rights. Only he who lives in obedience to a temporal power, which in turn is obedient to the Christian spiritual power, can justly hold any property at all; pagans and excommunicated Christians have no property rights. No title to property can be established naturally through occupation or inheritance; the supposed owner must also be a member of the church. Through the Fall men have lost all their rights; such rights as they have, they receive through their status in the sacramental order of the church, which has total dominion over all things. The whole sphere of natural law is abolished, and the legal status of men is made dependent on their obedient integration into the absolute governmental machine headed by the pope. The outlines of a totalitarian organization become recognizable.

The main elements of a political theory are thus developed for the case of the absolute church; these elements could be transferred to the secular political sphere when the particular national units had reached a degree of concentration that would permit the raising of spiritual claims in addition to the legal claims. The first great theory of this style appears in the national sphere after the Reformation in the *Leviathan* of Hobbes. More immediately the work of Giles had far-reaching effects on the course of history because he was the general of the Augustinian Order, and his extreme papalism became the school doctrine of the order. Within the order the opposition against the doctrine formed the intellectual environment that gave support to Martin Luther.

15

French Kingship

§1. The Problem of Royal Power

It is not easy to give an adequate and clear account of the French
position in the conflict with the papacy. The cause of the difficulty
is obvious. The symbols of the spiritual and temporal powers refer
implicitly to the pope and the emperor as the representatives of
the two orders in Christianity. A transfer of the system of symbols, and of the universe of arguments connected with it, to the
relation between the pope and a particular kingdom in Christianity
must lead to complications. On the side of the *sacerdotium* nothing essentially new need occur; but on the side of the *regnum* a
clarification of the meaning of temporal power will necessitate a
theory of royal power with regard to its relation not only to the
spiritual but also to the temporal imperial power. Moreover, the
transfer of the argument from the sphere of Christian mankind to a
particular political subdivision will arouse the thorny question of
the relation of the ecclesiastical organization within the boundaries
of the particular unit to the center of the church organization that
is located geographically outside the particular unit. The theory of
royal-temporal power will have to deal, therefore, with the three
main questions of (1) the relation of royal power to papal power,
(2) the relation of royal power to imperial power, and (3) the relation
of the church within the kingdom to the central church organization, the Gallican and Anglican questions. If we add to the main
questions the special problems of Christian poverty and church
property, and correspondingly of the property of the citizen and
the royal power of taxation, we are faced by a field of problems
that could be ordered systematically only by a masterful political
thinker. No such thinker of superior stature appeared at the time.

The principal questions were treated competently by able lawyers and clerics, but not in systematic form. The literary production of the time has the character of political pamphlets written on the occasion of specific conflicts with special political aims in view. John of Paris can be singled out perhaps as the one thinker who approaches a penetrating analysis of at least some questions; his privileged position is due to the fact that he could use the *De ecclesiastica potestate* as the object of attack, injecting thus the order of Giles of Rome into his own work. If we do not wish to be submerged by a flood of materials relevant to one or the other of the problems we have to practice a severe economy and confine ourselves to an outline of the historical forces and the types of argument presented by them.

§2. Independence from Imperial Power

The simplest argument is concerned with the character of the royal power of France in relation to the imperial power. In principle the problem had to arise with the increase in power of the border states of the empire favored by Gregory VII. The first indication that a French claim to power independent of the imperial existed is contained in the decretal *Per Venerabilem* of Innocent III (1202), which declares that the king of France does not recognize a superior in temporal matters. At the same time a canonist, Alanus, forwarded the general principle that every king has in his realm the same rights as the emperor in the empire; he refers to the origin of the rule in the international law of the time insofar as the division of the realms *(divisio regnorum)*, introduced by *ius gentium*, is approved by the pope.[1] About the middle of the century the claim was expressed by Louis IX in the formula that the king holds power from God only and from himself, the formula that, in slight variation, is still the symbol of French princely sovereignty in the theory of Bodin.[2] For variations of the formula in the later thirteenth century we can refer to the excellent literature on the subject.[3]

1. Rivière, *Le problème de l'église et de l'état*, appendix IV.
2. *Les établissements de Saint Louis*, ed. Paul Viollet (Paris, 1881), 2:135.
3. Hellmut Kaempf, *Pierre Dubois und die geistigen Grundlagen des französischen National bewusstseins um 1300*, Beiträge zur Kulturgeschichte des Mittelalters und der Renaissance, ed. Walter Goetz, vol. 54 (Leipzig and Berlin, 1935), and the literature quoted there. See also McIlwain, *Growth of Political Thought*, 268, and the

§3. John of Paris—*Tractatus de Potestate Regia et Papali*

The problem of French independence was treated systematically by John of Paris in his *Tractatus de potestate regis et papali* of 1303.[4] The title indicates the two political fronts: the treatise does not deal with secular power in general, but with the royal power of France specifically; the independence of the secular royal power has to be guarded against the empire as well as against the papacy. By its date it is placed at the climax of the struggle between Boniface VIII and France, at the time of the convocation of the Estates General, as a riposte to Giles of Rome.

As in the case of Giles we have to penetrate through a surface of formal argument that is concerned with the respective rights of the spiritual and temporal powers to the underlying sentiments, which have little to do with the Gelasian imperial problems. For the sentiment itself has become secular in the sense that it is bent toward an elimination of the spiritual power from the substance of the polity and no longer toward its limitation in a mixed spiritual-temporal community. The instrument for the expression of this sentiment is found in Aristotelian political theory. John was a Dominican and consequently influenced by Saint Thomas, but slight shifts of emphasis made it possible for him to weight the artfully balanced system of Thomas in favor of the secular national government. With Saint Thomas it had remained in suspense which type of polity should take the place of the polis as *communitas perfecta*; John of Paris decided for the *regnum* as the perfect type; a smaller unit would not be sufficient, a larger would make governmental control and law enforcement difficult. For him, the perfect community does not arise, as with Thomas, out of the free cooperation of the

---

literature quoted there. One formula of particular importance should be mentioned. It is to be found in the *Speculum Judiciale* of Guillaume Durant, dating from the early years of Philip the Bold (1270–1285). In bk. IV, pt. V, par. 2 of this treatise the absolute sovereignty of the king is affirmed in the formula of the *princeps in regno suo*. The treatise remained an authority up to the seventeenth century. See Ernst Kantorowicz's classic *The King's Two Bodies* (Princeton: Princeton University Press, 1957) for a survey of the context of the growth of royal power; for a more recent summary see K. Pennington, "Law, Legislative Authority and Theories of Government, 1150–1300," *Cambridge History of Medieval Political Thought*, chap. 14.

4. In Melchior Goldast's *Monarchia Sancti Romani Imperii, 1612–1614* (Frankfurt, 1614; photographic reprint, Graz, 1960), 2:108 ff.

spiritually mature men, but needs the ordering power of the king for giving social coherence to the naturalistically understood inclinations and skills of men. The argument for the superiority of spiritual aims in life over the temporal is refuted by the assertion that the king himself has a spiritual power because he does not simply order men corporally but guides them toward the "common civil good" consisting in a life of virtue. In order to avoid the equivocation of the term *spiritual* we may say that John develops the idea of a culturally closed polity under royal leadership, relegating religious life to a separate department that may be added to the secular polity but does not form an essential part of it. The clear separation of the secular sphere from the religious is then elaborated upon by an array of arguments asserting the royal power as immediate under God and refuting all papal claims to a right of interference in temporal affairs because of a hierarchical superordination of the spiritual over the temporal power.

The specific arguments for the case of the French *regnum* reveal the extent to which the idea of the mixed spiritual-temporal *imperium* was destroyed. John tries to show that no claim of papal superiority over France can be drawn from the Donation of Constantine. The donation did not transfer to the pope the Western empire nor the imperial insignia but only certain provincial territories not including France. The donation was, furthermore, legally invalid. And under no circumstances, finally, could a title be established over the Franks because they were never subject to the empire. The argument proves that the original meaning of the *translatio imperii* is completely lost. The God-willed transition of the *imperium* of Christian mankind to the West is reduced to a lawyers' squabble about territories and the validity of acts. The imperial idea is dead, and the realm with its secular national culture under the leadership of the king rises as the new political center.

§4. Thaumaturgic Kingship

While the problem of royal power is a general European problem, it was formulated for the first time in the French case. In England it appeared only toward the end of the fourteenth century, in the reign of Richard II.[5] There is more than one reason that the king

---

5. McIlwain, *Growth of Political Thought*, 268.

of France became the model of national kingship independent of the empire, and France the model of the sovereign self-contained nation. The general causes of the peculiar French development have been set forth earlier in the analysis of the Migration.[6] The comparatively stable and continuous evolution of the kingdom of the Franks, its remoteness from the control of Byzantium, the Christian enhancement of the Merovingian sacred bloodline through the conversion of Clovis to orthodox Christianity, the alliance of the Carolingians with the papacy, and the transfer of imperial dignity to Charlemagne, the *rex et sacerdos*,[7] laid the foundations on which the Capetian kings could grow into the role of sacred rulers of their realm, rivaling in rank the emperors.[8]

One of the most important factors contributing to the distinction of the Capetians as the *reges Christianissimi* was their power to heal various diseases, in particular scrofula. It is not absolutely certain to which reign the miraculous power can be traced in continuity. It is testified for Robert II (996–1031), but he was a saint and could do miracles whether being a king of France or not. Of his successor, Henry I (1031–1060), we know nothing. For Philipp I (1060–1108) and Louis VI (1108–1137) the healing of scrofula is reported as a customary achievement connected with the royal house. From this time up to the French Revolution the tradition

6. See vol. II, *The Middle Ages to Aquinas,* chap. 2, pp. 41–51.

7. Addressed as such at the Synod of Frankfurt, 794, by the bishops of northern Italy, MGH, *Conc.* II.i.142.

8. The fate of Charlemagne in the rivalry between the French and the Germans would merit special attention. The data for the critical period are assembled in Gaston Zeller's "Les Rois de France candidats à l'Empire," *Revue Historique* 173 (1934). The title *rex Francorum,* indicating the heritage of Charlemagne, was used by the German emperors up to Henry IV (1056–1106), while the title *emperor,* added by Charlemagne to *rex Francorum,* is attributed by chronists to some of the early Capetians. In the twelfth century a determined drive began to build the figure of Charlemagne into the ancestry of French kingship. Louis VII (1137–1180) was married in 1160 to the daughter of the Comte de Champagne, who derived from the Carolingians. Their son, Philipp Augustus, is hailed as the *Carolide.* Philipp Augustus (1180–1223) married the daughter of the Comte de Hainaut; a genealogy was circulated that made her a descendant of Charles of Basse-Lorraine, the Carolingian who was superseded by Hugh Capet. With their son, Louis VIII (1223–1226), the crown of France reverted, according to contemporary chronists, to the Carolingians. Counteracting this policy, Frederick Barbarossa had Charlemagne canonized in 1165, the year of the birth of Philipp Augustus, in order to capture him for the empire. Up to that time Charlemagne has been in the German tradition mainly the "butcher of the Saxons." This earlier tradition, however, has never quite died out in Germany and was strong enough to become a major object of discussion with the advent of National Socialism.

does not seem to have suffered an interruption. The period in which the custom consolidates is significant; it is the time between the Gregorian anti-imperial organization of the border states and the first reliably reported expression of French national sentiment by Suger de Saint Danis in 1124.[9]

The thaumaturgic, sacred kingship received its full effectiveness through Louis IX (1226–1270), the saint. To the healing power as an emanation of the charismatic bloodline, the flavor of a non-Christian miracle seems to have attached itself. Godfort of Beaulieu, the biographer of Saint Louis, stresses that the king added the sign of the cross to the pronunciation of the magic formula used by his predecessors "so that the healing should be attributed rather to the power of the cross than to the majesty of the king."[10] The charisma of the king had become Christian down to the physiological sphere. The function of Saint Louis for the growth of the French royal and national consciousness can hardly be overrated; France was symbolized by a saint at the time when the empire was headed by the anti-Christian figure of Frederick II. The influence of the saintly king, who died in 1270 while conducting a crusade, on the formation of the French monarchy increased toward the end of the thirteenth century with his canonization in 1297. We have to see the rallying of the nation around Philip the Fair in his struggle with Boniface VIII against the background of the charismatic prestige of the royal house.

§5. Charles of Anjou

A further factor in the rise of France to predominance in Europe was the personality and policy of Charles of Anjou, the brother of Saint

---

9. The corresponding English custom is derivative. The healing power of the king seems to have been established by the time of Henry II (1154–1189), though Henry I (1100–1136) may have made the first attempts. The healings were still practiced by James II; William II refused to perform the rite; Queen Anne resumed it; the last healing occurred on April 27, 1714. The Prayer Book dropped the rite only after 1732 in the English edition; in the Latin, after 1759. For details on the healing power and its history see the treatise by Marc Bloch, *Les Rois Thaumaturges: Etude sur le caractère surnaturel attribué à la personne royale, particulièrement en France et en Angleterre,* Publications de la Faculté des Lettres de l'Université de Strasbourg, 19 (Strasbourg, 1924). English edition: *The Royal Touch: Sacred Monarch and Scrofula in England and France,* trans. J. E. Anderson (London: Routledge and Kegan Paul, 1973).

10. *Histoire de France,* quoted by Kaempf, *Pierre Dubois,* 37.

Louis. The legal formula that "the king who does not recognize a superior is emperor in his realm" originated with Italian lawyers in the thirteenth century. But it was coined under the impact of the de facto imperial position of Charles of Anjou.[11] His fantastic rise was possible because of the broad and sound foundation laid by the French penetration into the eastern Mediterranean following the Fourth Crusade. Baldwin, the count of Flanders, became emperor in 1204; the counts of Flanders were followed by the Courtenays in 1216. The La Roches became dukes of Athens; Achaia was held by the Villehardouins. The occasion for Charles of Anjou to embark on his Mediterranean policy came with the summons extended by Pope Clement IV for the Crusade against Manfred of Sicily. The battles of Benevento (1266) and Tagliacozzo (1268) established the Anjou power in Sicily and Naples. From his Italian position Charles conquered Corfu in 1267, and, from the new military base, he started to extend his influence into the Despotate of Epirus and proclaimed himself king of Albania, after the death of Michael II of Epirus in 1271. By the treaty of Viterbo (1267) he acquired the claims of Baldwin II to the Byzantine empire; by the marriage of his son to the heiress of the Villehardouins he became suzerain of Achaia; by the marriage of another son to the heiress of the Arpads he established his house in Hungary; alliances with the Serbs and Bulgars extended his influence over the Balkans; the last crusade of Saint Louis to Tunis in 1270 was part of the general policy and reveals plans concerning North Africa and perhaps Egypt. The culmination of this policy of French imperial expansion was the candidacy of his nephew Philipp III for imperial dignity in 1273. The reasons advanced by Charles of Anjou in favor of the project show to perfection the pathos that the French monarchy had acquired through the life of Saint Louis. The royal race of France was so visibly distinguished by God through King Louis that from now on it would devote itself completely to the service of God and the increase of his power. The son would show himself the true heir of the great father who died the death of a martyr. And the only way to serve God entirely was to carry the dignity of the empire; the *rex*

11. See Francesco Ercole in Archivio Storica Italiano, ser. VII, vol. XVI; Rivière, *Le problème de l'église et de l'état*, 424 ff.; Kaempf, *Pierre Dubois*, 23–26. For an extensive account of the Italian discussion see Quentin Skinner, *Foundations of Modern Political Thought*, vol. 1, *The Renaissance* (Cambridge: Cambridge University Press, 1978).

Christianissimus needed the united power of Christian mankind to fulfill his service.[12] The union of the empires of the West and of the East in the hands of the royal house of France was a great dream.

§6. Pierre Dubois

This policy received its first great setback in the Sicilian Vesper of 1282; in 1285 Charles of Anjou died. While his program was never realized fully, the impetus imparted by Charles to French policy survived him. The expansion into Italy and the Mediterranean continued; the claims to the throne of Byzantium and the candidacies for the imperial dignity of the West were renewed; and the transfer of the papacy to Avignon in 1305 may be understood as a formal completion of the close relations between the French popes of the thirteenth century and the French princes.

In this atmosphere of imperialistic exuberance could grow the literary curiosity of the *De recuperatione terre sancte*, of 1306, by the French lawyer Pierre Dubois.[13] The treatise is a curiosity insofar as it has its roots neither in a philosophical or theological position nor in a realistic political partisanship, but in the mind of an intellectually and politically irresponsible personality with an astonishing sensitivity to the climate of the age and an equally astonishing insensitivity to the more stable forces that determine the steady course of history and are only slowly influenced by the climate. As a consequence, the work of Dubois has sometimes been taken too seriously as an expression of French hegemonic ambitions, and sometimes it has been underrated and estimated as utopian. Langlois is probably right when he says: "It is not surprising that, at the beginning of the 14th century, the heads of some people in France were turned by all the events. . . . Irresponsible advisers were

12. MGH, *Constitutiones et acta publica imperatorum et regnum*, vol. 1 (Hanover: Hahn, 1893), 585 ff. See the relation and interpretation by Kaempf, *Pierre Dubois*, 47 ff.

13. Pierre Dubois, *De recuperatione terre sancte*, ed. Ch. V. Langlois (Paris, 1891). On Dubois see, besides Kaempf, *Pierre Dubois*, Richard Scholz, *Die Publizistik zur Zeit Phillipps des Schoenen und Bonifaz' VIII* (Stuttgart: Enke, 1903); Fritz Kern, *Die Anfänge der französischen Ausdehnungspolitik bis zum Jahre 1308* (Tübingen, 1910); Eileen E. Power, *Pierre Dubois and the Domination of France*, in F. J. C. Hearnshaw, *The Social and Political Ideas of Some Great Medieval Thinkers* (London, 1923; rpt. New York: Barnes and Noble, 1967); Peter Klassen, *Zur Geschichte der europaischen Idee I*, Die Welt als Geschichte, Zeitschrift für universalgeschichtliche Forschung, vol. 2 (Stuttgart, 1936).

bound to arrive at a kind of optimistic intoxication and at visions of a universal monarchy held by France for the benefit of mankind."[14] The political impracticality of most of the ideas of Dubois does not impair, however, his flair for the tendencies of the time. If he is "intoxicated" as far as his projects are concerned, he is perfectly sober in his perception of everything that is "progressive" in his environment. By his clear-sighted constructivism, unhampered by sentiments of tradition, ruthless in the pursuit of a policy, he is representative of the new type of royal lawyers like Nogaret and Flotte.[15]

The principal purpose is indicated by the title as the reconquest of the Holy Land. The universal political idea of the expansive Christian West is resumed, but it will have to be pursued now by the king of France, for the empire is in decadence and the pope by the nature of his office cannot be the war leader in the crusade. The policy is medieval in inspiration and will soon be completely superseded by the national struggle for existence in the Hundred Years War; but the means for its perpetration as envisaged by Dubois are most distinctly postmedieval. The old imperial sentiment is dead. The emperor is seen as a German king who will have to receive a compensation in form of hereditary kingship and independence from the electors for his consent to the French predominance in Italy. The papacy will have to be shorn of its temporal appurtenances. The possessions of the Holy See in Italy as well its suzerainty over England, Sicily, and Aragon have to be ceded to France. The wealth of the great orders, and particularly of the Templars, has to be confiscated for the king as a war chest for the great enterprise. The church will be supported by the state, the pope will be a French pensioner. The surrender of the temporal power will confine the papacy to its spiritual functions; and this restriction will substantially contribute to a purification and spiritualization of the church.

When the question of the church is settled and the French position guaranteed through the domination of Italy and the establishment of a French secundogeniture for the East in Cyprus, Europe will be ripe for a new political order, assuring internal peace and the

---

14. Ch. V. Langlois, in *Medieval France*, ed. Arthur Tilley (Cambridge, 1922), 102.
15. [Pierre Flotte, one of the royal apologists in Philip's dispute with Boniface VIII, rejected papal claims with the retort: "Your power is verbal, ours however is real." Quoted in Burns, ed., *Medieval Political Thought*, 347.]

concentration of power that is necessary for a policy of conquest in the East. The construction proposed by Dubois is a league of European sovereign states, to be constituted by a council of the temporal and spiritual princes, convoked by the king and pope at Toulouse. Conflicts between the members will be arbitrated by a proper tribunal: the council will appoint a panel of judges, and the judges will chose six of their number to decide cases.[16] An appeal may be carried to the pope, thus securing the ultimate influence of France. In cases of breaches of the peace or a refusal to abide by the decision of the tribunal, sanctions are provided in the form of a blockade of food and supplies against the offender, and ultimately

16. This formulation glosses over an obscurity of the source that is of some importance for students of international organization. Dubois expresses himself in the following terms on the composition of the tribunal of arbitration (*De recuperatione terre sancte*, ed. Langlois, 11): "Sed cum iste civitates et multi principes superiores in terris non recognoscentes, qui justiciam faciant de ipsis secundum leges et consuetudines locorum, controversias movere captabunt, coram quibus procedent et litigabunt? Responderi potest quod concilium statuat arbitros religiosos aut alios eligendos, viros prudentes et expertos ac fideles, qui jurati tres judices prelatos et tres alios pro utraque parte *(eligant)*, locupletes, et tales quod sit verisimile ipsos non posse corrumpi amore, odio, timore, concupiscentia, vel alias, qui convenientes in loco ad hoc aptiori, jurati strictissime . . . testes et intrumenta recipiant, diligentissime examinent" ("But what of those cities and the many princes who recognize no superior authority on earth possessing the power to judge them in accordance with local laws and customs? When these cities and princes engage in controversies, before whom shall they institute proceedings and conduct litigation? One may reply that the council should decide that arbitrators be chosen, religious or others, prudent men, experienced and trustworthy, who being sworn, shall select three prelates as judges and three others for each party to the controversy. They should be men of substance, and of such character that it would be unlikely that they could be corrupted by love, hatred, fear, greed, or by other means. They should assemble in a place suited to the purpose, and be bound by the strictest oaths. The several articles of complaint and defense should be submitted to them in brief and simple form before they assemble. After first rejecting what is superfluous and irrelevant, they should receive the testimony and documentary evidence and examine them most diligently"; Pierre Dubois, *The Recovery of the Holy Land*, trans. Walther I. Brandt [New York: Columbia University Press, 1956], 78–79.)

The word *eligant*, put in parentheses, is missing in Dubois's text; and even if it is supplemented, the passage does not give a clear sense. The following conjectures concerning the intentions of Dubois are possible: (1) The council will either appoint a board of arbiters itself, or cause it to be appointed by some other agency. (2) The board of arbiters will consist of religious and secular persons indifferently, or it will have to be composed de jure of a group of ecclesiastical and another group of secular arbiters. (3) The arbiters will select the judges from their numbers, or they will select persons who are not members of the board of arbiters, or they are free in their choice. (4) The arbiters will select the judges not at all, but the parties to the conflict will select judges from the board of arbiters, or the judges will be selected in agreement between the arbiters and the parties, from the board or outside the board. (5) The tribunal will consist of twelve judges, six ecclesiastical and six secular. Or, it will consist of nine judges, three ecclesiastical and three secular for each of the parties to the conflict. Or, it will consist of six judges, three ecclesiastical and three

of war. The defeated violator of the order and his supporters will be bundled off to the Holy Land where their fighting energies can be employed usefully against the infidels.

This machinery has attracted much attention because of the obvious parallel with modern ideas for a league of nations. The importance of the idea and of the parallel should not be diminished, but neither should it be overrated: if the technical problem is given of constructing a constitution with orderly procedures for the relations between sovereign states, any good lawyer would have to develop some such model; he could hardly do anything else. The parallel should be rather a warning that the construction of an international constitution is the easiest thing in the world and has no bearing on the feasibility of the project. More important than the content of the construction is the fact that at the time there existed already intellectual, progressive lawyers for whom the Christian imperial idea had so completely lost its evocative force that a reconstruction of Europe out of the forces of the particularized nations under a hegemon seemed advisable. The idea of the hegemonic league of nations and the intellectual creed that the unity of Western mankind can be produced synthetically by lawyers have remained ever since an important strain in the political ideas of the West. The dawn of a new age can also be felt in the practical reasons advanced by Dubois in favor of his project and in corollary suggestions. World peace is desirable for the undisturbed flow of commerce. The crusade is, in the true spirit of later mercantilistic wars, an instrument of economic and colonial policy; expensive Oriental products will become cheaper, and trade routes in the Mediterranean will be safer. Coinage should be a royal monopoly and the value of money should be stabilized. A system of public education is proposed, under the supervision of the state; schooling has to be primarily practical in order to increase the economic power of the nation. Textbooks will have to concentrate and simplify the enormously swollen body of knowledge. Women are admitted to the schools. Judicial procedure has to be simplified,

---

secular. For various interpretations see Jacob Ter Meulen, *Der Gedanke der Internationalen Organisation in seiner Entwicklung, 1300–1800* (The Hague: Nijhof, 1917), 104; Christian L. Lange, *Histoire de l'Internationalisme* (Oslo: Aschehoug, 1919), 1:104; Frank M. Russell, *Theories of International Relations* (New York: Appleton-Century, 1936), 108.

the law codified, and the courts made accessible to the people at large through reduction of the cost of litigation.

The economic considerations and the suggestions for education and judicial reform reveal the same sentiments as the general political construction: the ruthlessness of political and administrative rationalism and the willingness to override the traditional institutions in favor of a reorganization in the service of the national monarchy. It will not be necessary to go into a detailed discussion of the suggestions; the parallels with, and anticipations of, later developments are obvious. But we should be aware that the work of Dubois as a whole is the most convincing symptom of the new force of the national monarchy that was to compel in the following centuries the political reform with its culmination in Renaissance absolutism.

16

Dante

§1. The Isolation of the Political Thinker

With Dante a new type of political thinker entered the Western scene, and with the attitude expressed in his work a new dimension was added to the pattern of Western political thought. Dante (1265–1321) was the first Western thinker who had no status in a social group that would give representative authority to his word and form the audience for what he had to say. He was neither a cleric, secular or monastic, nor a lawyer, papal, imperial, or royal. He tried to be a man of politics but fell victim to the struggles of Florence, because he was to the roots of his personality in disaccord with the strife of passions that was the substance of Italian town politics. He was a party for himself, speaking by authority of the *majestas genii*.

The isolation of the political thinker that became manifest in Dante had been in the making for the preceding two centuries. During the Investiture Struggle the participants were still firmly bound by the social framework of the *sacrum imperium*. Immediately afterward began the loosening of social ties. The vision of Joachim of Fiore (Flora) called for a new dispensation, doing away with the structure of feudal society; but the abbot of Fiore was embedded in the narrow social reality of the Cistercian and later of the Florensian Orders. Saint Francis had to break with the social reality of his origins; and even the reality of his creation, the Franciscan Order, was overshadowed by the time of his death by the problem of an institutionalization conflicting with his ideas. Saint Thomas could grow in the environment of the Dominican Order, but the resonance of his political work on the wider theater of European affairs was practically nil. Siger de Brabant was a cleric, but his ideas carried him beyond the institutional fold and to his death in jail.

Giles of Rome shows the alternative to the threatening isolation of the free spirit. He was in no danger of isolation or of going to jail, for he had thrown his intellectual weight deliberately on the side of power. As a consequence his ideas had a sounding board in the *Unam Sanctam* that left nothing to be desired. But his success reveals the price the thinker has to pay for public status in the new order of power politics: he had to sacrifice the spiritual and intellectual independence that was as dear to Saint Thomas as it was to Siger de Brabant. For a man like Dante who experienced the reality of the spirit strongly, this alternative was unacceptable. With a sure touch that testifies to the personal distance he had won, he placed Siger and Thomas, the two antagonists of the preceding generation, side by side in the Fourth Heaven because the *veri* of Siger, though *invidiosi,* originate just as the orthodoxy of Saint Thomas in the honest striving for truth and are justified before God, if not before man.[1] In his own age the transcendental guides

---

1. *Paradiso* X.136 *ff.:* "Essa é la luce eterna di Sigieri, / Che, leggendo nel vico degli strami, / Sillogizzo invidiosi veri" (That is the eternal light of Siger, / Who, while lecturing in the Streets of Straws, / Syllogized resented propositions). The juxtaposition of Thomas and Siger in the *Divina Commedia* is one of the thorniest problems of the Dante interpretation. Two recent contributions to the question merit particular attention: Herbert Grundmann's "Dante und Joachim von Fiore," *Dante-Jahrbuch,* vol. 14 (1932), and Martin Grabmann's "Siger von Brabant und Dante," *Deutsches Dante-Jahrbuch,* vol. 21 (Weimar: Böhlaus Nachfolgr, 1939), 109–30. Grundmann shows convincingly that Dante tried to harmonize the conflicting tendencies of the age, not by proving that they were compatible, but by understanding the conflicts of doctrines and attitudes as the surface of an underlying unity of the spirit and the intellect. Grundmann deals specifically with the juxtapositions of Joachim of Fiore and Bonaventure, of Thomas and Siger, and with the mutual praises of Bonaventure and Thomas. Grabmann, in the later article, summarizes the results of Fernand Van Steenberghen's *Siger de Brabant d'après ses oeuvres inédites,* Philosophes belges, textes et études, vols. 12–13 (Louvain: Editions de l'Institut Supérieur de Philosophie de l'Université, 1931). Van Steenberghen is of the opinion that the personal conflict of Thomas and Siger was not so strong as is sometimes supposed: they had great respect for each other. The later *Quaestiones de Anima* of Siger show, furthermore, a tendency to approach the Thomasic theory of the soul. In the treatment of the question, it seems to me, it has been taken too much for granted that Dante himself was unconditionally orthodox and that Siger had to appear to him as a heretic who under no condition could be placed side by side with the pillar of orthodox doctrine. The recent changes in our general picture of Dante, and the better understanding of his own Joachitic and Averroist leanings, let the whole Siger-Thomas question appear in a different light. See for these questions the treatment of the *Monarchia* and the *Divina Commedia* in this chapter. In general see Étienne Gilson, *Dante the Philosopher,* trans. David Moore (New York: Sheed and Ward, 1949); Giuseppe Mazotta, *Dante's Vision and the Circle of Knowledge* (Princeton:

of spirit and of intellect had disappeared. He, who by his nature was urged to follow them, found himself lost in the dark thickets of rampant passions. This is the opening theme of the *Divina Commedia:*

> "Nel mezzo del cammin di nostra vita
> Mi ritrovai per una selva oscura
> Che la diritta via era smarrita."

> (Midway in the journey of our life
> I found myself in a dark wood,
> For the straight way was lost.)

It takes a long journey to see again the guiding Stars, the keyword on which each of the three parts of the *Divina Commedia* closes, and God who moves them by his love (*Par.* 33.145).

§2. The Separation of Spirit from Politics

Since the time of Dante the spiritual realist has been faced with the problem that the surrounding political reality of the Western world no longer can adequately absorb the spirit into its public institutions. The incision in Western history corresponds to the time of Heraclitus in Hellenic civilization. We can discern three main phases of the process in which the spirit and politics drifted apart. The beginning of the first phase is marked by Dante and by his discovery of the new spiritual loneliness. The two centuries after Dante have been characterized as the "waning" or the "twilight" of the Middle Ages because all over Europe they showed signs of decomposition, in some countries earlier and in others later, in some more catastrophically and in others less so. The internal disorder in France ensued after the lost battles of Crécy (1346) and Poitiers (1356) and lasted until the reform of the army in 1445. The corresponding disorder in England, with the Peasant Revolt equivalent to the French Jacquerie of 1358, came somewhat later in the reign of Richard II (1377–1399); after a short recovery under the Lancasters, the complete breakdown followed in the Wars of

---

Princeton University Press, 1993); Alison Morgan, *Dante and the Medieval Other World* (New York: Cambridge University Press, 1990). [On Siger, see vol. II, *The Middle Ages to Aquinas*, 178–204.]

the Roses (1455–1485). A new level of dynastic consolidation and of mastery of the conflicting domestic forces was reached only in the second half of the fifteenth century: in France by the time of Louis XI (1461–1483), in England through the Tudors (1485), and correspondingly in Spain through the reigns of Ferdinand of Aragon and Isabella of Castile (1479), in Portugal under John II (1481), in Russia through Ivan the Great (1462), in the German territories with the accession of Maximilian I (1493). During the period of decomposition of medieval society, that is between the time of Dante and the sixteenth century, no first-rate political thinker rose to dominate the chaotic scene.

The second phase is marked by the appearance of the religious reformers and of the secular spiritual realists. The religious reformers, represented by Luther and Calvin, tried to re-create spiritually determined political institutions out of the fading church substance. The attempt, resulting in the split of the church, failed grossly; the spiritual movements were absorbed into the particular Western political spheres. The secular spiritual realists—Machiavelli, Bodin, Hobbes, Spinoza—tried, each one according to the powers of his personality, to find the place of spirit in a world of particular political units. Machiavelli attempted the evocation of the demonic leader; Bodin envisaged the state as the starting point for a contemplation that would lead to the *fruitio Dei*; Hobbes created the psychological analysis of political passions and evoked the totalitarian spiritual power to subdue them; Spinoza tried to find a construction of government that would make the world livable for the intellectual mystic. All four of them were isolated as political thinkers, covered with vituperation for their atheism, or their immorality, or their impartiality.

The third phase again brings the two types of thinkers to a new level. To the earlier reformers corresponds the politico-religious activist, represented by Karl Marx, who tried to rejoin the spirit and the social institutions by a revolutionary destruction of existing society in order to make room for the guiltless New Man, the proletarian. To the spiritual realists of the sixteenth and seventeenth centuries corresponds the completely isolated free spirit of Friedrich Nietzsche, whose analysis of European nihilism is the last judgment of the postmedieval Western world as the *Divina Commedia* was its first.

§3. Spiritual Realism—The Earthly Paradise

The wider perspective permits a more intimate understanding of the problems of Dante. The two approaches to the problem of Western mankind losing its spiritual unity—reform and revolution on the one side, the attempt to find the proper relation of the individual spiritual realist to the political structure of the age on the other—are still undifferentiated in Dante. He has the hope of a new spiritual church in the Joachitic tradition, as expressed in the *Divina Commedia.* This same type of hope reappears in Luther and the revolutionaries of the nineteenth century. Dante's profound experience of the reality of the spirit, on the other hand, determines his personal negative attitude toward a field of politics that he sees as ruled by the spiritless, destructive passion of material power. It is the type of negativism that reappears in the attitudes of the realists from Machiavelli to Spinoza and later of Nietzsche.

We have used the term *spiritual realism* in order to signify Dante's own sentiment as well as that of the later thinkers. The use is necessary in order to avoid a terminology that can touch only on secondary phenomena surrounding the fundamental attitude. Dante has been called an idealist because he believed in the ideals of spiritual order, peace, and the common good of Christian mankind as the guiding principles of politics. There is no objection against this classification except that the "belief in ideals" is a secondary phenomenon requiring in every instance an investigation of the ulterior structure of sentiments that determine the belief. A thinker may express a belief in certain ideals because they are conventional in his time and he has not enough personal substance to do anything but follow a convention; or he may do so because he has an active insight into a hierarchy of ethical values handed down by tradition; or he may do so because he is moved by the spirit and is able to produce an order of values out of his immediate spiritual experiences. The distinction between the primary sphere of sentiments and the secondary sphere of ideals is of special importance because spiritual sensitiveness and strength need not express themselves at all in the advocacy of what commonly are called ideals. Except for his dream of the Italian nation, few historians would be inclined to call Machiavelli an idealist; but certainly the man who understood the problem of religious reform and evoked the demonic master of politics as a substitute, who at least would create external order, was strongly touched by the spirit. Hobbes was metaphysically a materialist; but nobody can penetrate the fake spiritualism of certain political sectarian types of the seventeenth century as he did unless a true spiritual experience has enabled him to see the difference. Hence we shall use the "spiritual realism" in order to designate the attitude of the political thinker of the fourteenth century and after, who has to detach himself intellectually, and sometimes also practically, from the surrounding political institutions because he cannot attribute to them representative function for the life of the spirit that he experiences as real within himself. Dante is the first thinker to be clearly conscious of the gulf that separates the spiritualist from the forms of postmedieval political existence.

Again, Dante has been called a conservative and a romantic. And again, the classification has its truth if we reflect on the overt contents of his political theory alone and do not take into account the motivating sentiments. To evoke the idea of world monarchy as the constitutional form for a Christian world at peace certainly had a touch of the romantic at a time when the continuity of the empire had been interrupted by the Interregnum and when the restored imperial power was on the way toward the Hausmacht policy. Nevertheless, we should miss the most important aspect of the *Monarchia* if we saw nothing in Dante but a belated imperialist, just as we should miss in Giles of Rome the new philosophy of power if we excerpted from his work only the passages that make him appear a belated papalist.

We have placed Dante at the beginning of an evolution that leads through the realists of the Renaissance to Nietzsche, and we have to stress that his plan of a *monarchia temporalis*, of a temporal monarchy, is not medieval in principle but looks rather toward the future: it stands at the beginning of the series of plans that try to construct a political organization of the Western world as a superstructure over the particular political units. The formula of the temporal monarchy is not a medieval heritage but was evoked by Dante; he was conscious and proud of the achievement because he believed he had found the convincing symbol for the new order of eternal peace that should supersede the political misery of the time. Dante's idea of the monarchy is not an idea of restoration. He does not want to bring back an earlier dispensation of forces, but looks rather to a new dispensation though in the imperial form.

His monarchy has the eschatological touch of the Third Realm of Joachim of Fiore; it is related to later ideas concerning the organization of a peaceful order even by his vocabulary: the state of temporal felicity he wishes to bring about is symbolized *(figuratur)* by the mythical conception of the Earthly Paradise, the symbol that was still employed by Lenin to designate the Communist Realm *(Mon.* 3.16). The *Divina Commedia* states explicitly that the Earthly Paradise is the same symbol that was expressed by ancient poets in the myth of the golden age *(Purg.* 28.139–41). Considering the eschatological element in Dante's monarchy, which runs counter to the medieval compromise of Christianity with the world, we have to rank his conception, in this respect at least, rather with the plans for a Western reorganization after the breakdown of the empire. We must not forget that it is contemporary with Dubois's plan for a European organization under French hegemony.

§4. Literary Forms and Symbols of Authority

For the public utterances of a private individual Dante had to develop literary forms and symbols of authority suitable to the new function. In the earlier phase of his political writing he adopted as his literary medium the letter, which had been evolved by Frederick II and used by Saint Francis. The open letter, as a political manifesto, becomes the instrument of expression for the individual that has no institutional public but rather appeals to "public opinion." The question of the authority by which he writes his *Letters* is answered by Dante through the various roles that he assumes in these manifestos.[2] In the *Vth Letter,* addressed to the princes and peoples of Italy, he designates himself as the *humilis Italus;* in the *VIth Letter,* addressed to the Florentines in the town, he speaks as the *Florentinus;* in the *VIIth Letter,* addressed to the Emperor Henry VII, as the *Florentinus* in company with all Tuscans who desire peace. In all three of these letters he designates himself as

2. Dante Alighieri, *Epistolae,* ed. Paget Toynbee (Oxford: Oxford University Press, 1920). On Dante's relationship to the political order see Donna Mancusi-Ungaro, *Dante and the Empire* (New York: Peter Lang, 1980); Joan M. Ferrante, *The Political Vision of the Divine Comedy* (Princeton: Princeton University Press, 1984); C. Grayson, ed. *The World of Dante: Essays on Dante and His Times* (Oxford: Oxford University Press, 1988); Alessandro Passerin d'Entrèves, *Dante as a Political Thinker* (Oxford: Oxford University Press, 1952); John A. Scott, *Dante's Political Purgatory* (Philadelphia: University of Pennsylvania Press, 1996).

the "undeservedly in exile." In the *Monarchia*, which elaborates systematically the doctrine of the *Letters*, he returns to the conventional form of a political treatise.[3] But at last, in the *Divina Commedia*, he achieves the great innovation of a political poem in the *lingua volgare*, addressing himself by this medium to the Italian-speaking people at large.[4]

The symbols of authority do not appear in a time sequence but have to be distinguished as simultaneous elements in a more complex whole. Three sources of authority are to be discerned. The first is indicated by the self-designations of the *Letters* and by the use of the *lingua volgare* in the *Divina Commedia*. Dante speaks as the Italian and the Florentine to his people; his withdrawal from party groupings does not deprive him entirely of political status; as a member of the political community he could assign himself the representative function of a speaker. The second source of authority was Joachitic spiritualism. Dante, as a Christian spiritualist, could assume, with regard to the realm of peace and to the spiritual church that is to come, a prophetic function similar to that of Joachim. And, finally, Dante could speak by virtue of his poetic genius, his most personal but at the same time most problematic source of authority. The source is problematic because in the Christian order the poet had no specific divine authority to speak as a seer. Dante was conscious of the question and supported, therefore, his own authority by that of Virgil and the four other pagan poets in limbo who receive him honorably as the sixth of their company (*Inf.* 4.64–105). The authority of Virgil is of special importance as that of the author of the fourth *Eclogue*, predicting the golden age and the divine child, and of the *Aeneid*, announcing the imperial mission of Rome. Nevertheless, the poet who is touched by the god has never held convincing authority in the Christian world

3. Dante Alighieri, *De Monarchia Libri III*, ed. Ludovicus Bertalot (Gebennae, 1920). English and Latin edition: *Monarchia*, ed. Prue Shaw (New York: Cambridge University Press, 1995).

4. Tommaso Casini and S. A. Barbi, *La Divina Commedia di Dante Alighieri*, 6th ed. (Florence: Sansoni, 1926). English edition: *The Divine Comedy*, translated with commentary by C. S. Singleton, 6 vols. (Princeton: Princeton University Press, 1970–1975). Recent relevant studies include Ferrante, *Political Vision*; Jeffrey Schnapp, *The Transfiguration of History at the Center of Dante's Paradise* (Princeton: Princeton University Press, 1986); Richard Kay, *Dante's Christian Astrology* (Philadelphia: University of Pennsylvania Press, 1994); and Steven Botterill, *Dante and the Mystical Tradition: Bernard of Clairvaux in the Commedia* (New York: Cambridge University Press, 1994).

with the exception of Germany, where, since Hölderlin, the poet as the divine voice of the nation has a function that is strange and practically unintelligible to the Western nations.[5]

§5. The *Letters*

The *Letters* are important in the work of Dante as an orgy of symbols reflecting the eschatological atmosphere of his politics. A time is impending that is the golden age of the ancients as well as the *tempus acceptabile* of Deutero-Isaiah and of 2 Corinthians. Dante appears as John the Baptist announcing the *agnus Dei*, as Virgil announcing the child and the Saturnian age, and as Samuel admonishing Saul to smash the Amalakites. The emperor, Henry VII, is Caesar confounding his enemies, Augustus introducing the *pax romana*, Aeneas founding the new Rome, the second Moses leading his people to Canaan, and the David who smites Goliath. The Italians are exhorted to give up their stubbornness; the Lombards specifically are admonished to remember their Trojan bloodline and to accept the emperor, to forget the barbarism of their Scandinavian descent and submit to the prince of peace who rises like the sun and comes like the apocalyptic Lion of Judah. The easy showering of this wealth of symbols is overwhelming; it indicates that we are no longer in the time of the laborious and conscientious symbolistic art of a Joachim. The symbols have not spent their force, but their use is distinctly literary and at the service of a new evocation of a peaceful world quite beyond the Gelasian problems of the *sacrum imperium*.

§6. The *De Monarchia*

The difficulty of distinguishing between the medieval language of Dante and the sentiments that meet a new, postmedieval situation has been touched upon. It is a severe handicap in the adequate interpretation of the *De Monarchia*. We isolated earlier the conception of the *temporalis monarchia* and its function in bringing about the terrestrial paradise. The actual content of the treatise is less relevant since the potential project, the restoration of an emperor of the West, was indeed an anachronism. In this respect the critical

5. See Max Kommerell, *Der Dichter als Fuehrer* (Berlin: Klostermann, 1928).

evaluation of the work as conservative, reactionary, and romantic is quite justified.

a. The Universal Intellect: Averroism

There are, however, some special points that merit attention in a history of ideas. Book I of the *Monarchia* deals with the general structure of society, derived from the nature of man, which requires the temporal monarchy as the adequate form of community order. The theory is Aristotelian in principle, but the conclusions differ widely from those of the *Politics.* The transformation that the theory undergoes at the hands of Dante is revealing for the limitations of Hellenic political theory as well as for the specifically Christian problems. The basic question arising with regard to Aristotelian politics in any non-Hellenic environment is the question of the criterion of the *societas perfecta.* For Aristotle it was axiomatic that the polis was perfect. Already in the system of Thomas we noticed the appearance of the *regnum* as the perfect society. Dante raises for the first time the theoretical question on principle. The framework of political society has the purpose of serving as the field of operations for fully developed human faculties. For Dante the specifically human faculty is the universal *potentia intellectiva.* According to Dante it is incompatible with the universality of human nature that man should find a completely sufficient existence in any particular realm *(regnum particulare).* To the universality of the intellect, the *universitas hominum* organized under the world monarch has to correspond. Hence the Aristotelian chain of social forms has to be continued through the family, village, and city to the realm and world empire before we arrive at the perfect form in accordance with the nature of man. Concerning the origin of Dante's conception, a clue is furnished by the fact that in the decisive passage *(Mon.* 1.3) on the *virtus intellectiva* as the essence of man, Dante refers to the commentary of Averroës on the Aristotelian *De Anima* in support of his position. As this is the only source mentioned in the context, we may assume that Averroist ideas were the predominant influence in Dante's construction. His derivation of the world monarchy from the universality of the intellect would fit well, indeed, into a political system evolved by Siger de Brabant.[6]

---

6. I find that the suggestion in the text agrees with an opinion, expressed without reservations, of Karl Vossler: "Den 'möglichen Verstand' in seiner ganzen

b. Intellectual and Hegemonic World Organization

Dante's argument for the world monarchy is unanswerable, if the anthropological approach to a science of politics is taken seriously and if the essence of man is placed in the *virtus intellectiva*. Dante as a theorist is on this point superior to Thomas as well as to Aristotle. A discussion will have to meet the argument on its own anthropological ground. The construction of Dante is no longer acceptable—not because the idea of a world emperor is medieval and, therefore, obsolete, but because our modern anthropology is enriched by insight into the historical structure of the human mind. It is no longer possible to identify the essence of man with ahistoric intellect—though it is done, of course, quite frequently. The unity of mankind is not intellectually static; it is an open field in which the possibilities of the human mind unfold historically and manifest themselves in the sequence of civilizations and of nations. To stop history at any point of time, and to elevate a civilizational crosscut, or more frequently a fragment of the crosscut, to the rank of an absolute and to call it the nature of man has become impossible. With this insight into the historicity of the mind the idea falls that a static "organization" can be the political answer

---

Ausdehnung, das heisst bei der Gesamtheit der Menschen, zu aktualisieren, die Mitteilung and Verwirklichung der überweltlichen Universalintelligenz in weitestem Masstab zu organisieren, aus der ganzen Menschheit einen einzigen, kollektiven averroistischen Philosophen zu machen, darauf läuft schliesslich alle politische und ausserkirchliche Anstalt und Arbeit hinaus" ("To actualize the 'possible intellect' in its complete extent, i.e., in the universality of humanity, to organize the communication and realization of the global universal intelligence in the widest sense, to create out of the whole of humanity a single collective Averroist philosopher, would finally be to provide that from which every political and extra-ecclesiastical institution and effort would flow"; *Die Göttliche Komödie,* 2d ed. [Heidelberg: Winter, 1925], 1:340 ff.). In agreement with Vossler is Helene Wieruszowski, "Der Reichsgedanke bei Dante," *Dante-Jahrbuch,* vol. 14 (1932). Furthermore, I should like to draw attention to a curious coincidence. Dante's idea of a world monarch as an analogue to God's government of the world is very close in its conception to the Mongol principle of "One God in Heaven, One Emperor on Earth," as pronounced in the Mongol state documents of the period 1245–1255. The most important of the missions to the Mongol court were conducted by Franciscans, and it is not absolutely improbable that Dante should have had knowledge, through his Franciscan connections, of the reports of the missions and of the principal Mongol political ideas. Beyond the coincidence that Dante's idea appeared sixty years after the Mongol ideas could have become known to the West, there is, however, no evidence to support the connections. Cf. for the Mongol ideas my essay "The Mongol Orders of Submission to European Powers, 1245–1255," in *Byzantion* 15 (1940–1941), reprinted in Voegelin, *Anamnesis: Zur Theorie der Geschichte und Politik* (Munich: R. Piper and Co., 1966), 179–223.

to the idea of man. The drama of human history cannot be caught in a governmental power organization, imperial or otherwise, and cannot be submitted to the rules of a trial in court. The defect of Dante's theory is its intellectualism, though he did not go so far as to propose a world state, but left the particular political organizations intact, reserving to the world monarch the functions of an umpire. Historians have felt instinctively that plans of world organization like those of Pierre Dubois, or the later ones since Sully, which originate in the will to power of a particular nation or group of nations, are better in accord with the forces of history because they are frankly hegemonic. Nevertheless, the approach of Dante cannot be neglected for this reason as having no further consequence. Intellectualism is not dead, and probably never will be; insight into the historical structure of the human mind is far from being a common possession of the political thinkers of our time. Our modern plans for world organization are, as a rule, hegemonic; they are historically realistic insofar as they are based on the principle that political conceptions of order originating in a particular area should be made preponderant over the whole of the Western world, if not over the globe. But they are also, as a rule, intellectualistic insofar as they are based on the assumption that the particular idea of order is not particular but universally human, and that all men of goodwill and good reason are, therefore, ready to submit to it. Disappointment has to result from the blend. The conflict between hegemonic power politics and intellectual dreams of a politically organized *universitas hominum*, personified in the early fourteenth century by Pierre Dubois and Dante, is not yet solved and still seems rather far from a solution.

c. The Myth of the Italianità

The second book of the *Monarchia* deals with the questions of whether the Roman people had the right to assume the office of the world monarchy or whether the Roman imperial position was due to usurpation. The details of the investigation are not relevant in our context, although they constitute a model case for the religious and philosophical analysis of the symptoms by which the will of God in history can be known. Important for us is the entirely new situation in which it is not the claim of the emperor that is defended against encroachments of the spiritual power but the claims of the *populus romanus*—and that is, for Dante, the contemporary Italian people in continuity with the Romans of antiquity—against all competitors, such as the French. The Italian people is the imperial people *kat' exochen* by virtue of the civilizational work and the order of peace re-created by the Roman empire, and by virtue of the distinction that the empire received through the fact that Christ permitted himself to be tried by a Roman court. It would be rash to interpret these sentiments as nationalistic. The national consciousness is stirring strongly in Dante, but his imagination is not captured by the vision of an Italian national state emulating the French as was Machiavelli's. He hopes for the end of internal strife and the ejection of foreigners, but the regeneration should make the Italian people fit to assume again their function as the empire people. We have to remember that the emperor in whom Dante puts his hope is not an Italian but a Luxembourg. What emerges from the pages of Dante is the myth of the *Italianità,* which was to remain a permanent element in Italian political thought through the vicissitudes of modern Italian history up to the ideas of fascism. In the eighteenth century, in the mind of Giambattista Vico, it gained the consciousness of a specific distinction of the Italian before all other nations because she is the only modern Western nation that has a great cycle of history before the Migration. Today it expresses itself in the less distinguished *ressentiment* of Italian intellectuals against Anglo-Saxon barbarians who stalked the woods as primitive savages when Italy was the leader of mankind.

The third book leads back to the relation of the imperial authority with the ecclesiastical. The argument is imperialist, asserting the direct derivation of imperial authority from God against the hierarchic construction; it receives its importance from the implications of the theory of the temporal monarchy and the terrestrial paradise that were discussed earlier.

§7. The Vision of *Purgatorio* 29–33

The *Monarchia* is not Dante's last word in politics. The stages of his personal maturation are reflected in the hierarchy of souls in the third part of the *Divina Commedia.* In the Fourth Heaven (*Par.* 10–14) we find the theologians, in the Fifth (*Par.* 15–18) the warriors fighting for God, in the Sixth (*Par.* 18–20) the just rulers, and in the Seventh (*Par.* 21–22) the contemplative biography, the period in which he stood under the influence of the Franciscan Spirituals, his active political life in Florence, his hope for the emperor, Henry VII, as the bringer of the new age of peace, and, finally, the withdrawal into the contemplative attitudes of the *Divina Commedia*.

The economy of a general history of ideas does not permit a detailed analysis of the political philosophy of the *Divina Commedia*; we have to concentrate on the decisive apocalyptic vision of *Purgatorio* 29 and 32–33. The vision is expressed in spiritual symbols, and a consensus on every single point can, therefore, hardly be achieved. But the main lines have become clarified through the assiduous work of centuries of interpreters; we have a guiding rule for the interpretation through the better insight into the Joachitic roots of Dante's evocation. Joachitic is the distinction between the corrupt feudal and the poor spiritual church; and Joachitic is the expectation that the period of iniquity will be followed by a purified church and realm to be inaugurated by a savior personality.

The vision of the *Purgatorio*, though, is not a simple reception of Joachim's prophecy of the Third Realm of the Spirit. The eliterian spiritualism of Joachim was a movement away from the spiritual-temporal unity of the empire; by its reduction of history to spiritual process it surrendered the secular life of mankind; its narrow conception of a brotherhood of the perfect was incompatible with the idea of the organized Christian people. Dante lived in the wider horizon of the imperial problems of his time. He saw the decadence of the church and its *renovatio evangelica* in connection with the decadence of the secular power. The present of the *sacrum imperium* is recognized in the full extent of its misery; the papacy in Avignon and the predominance of France in the affairs of the West are the two aspects of the dissolution. The reconstruction of the *imperium* will have to extend to the temporal as well as to the spiritual power. The resumption of the idea of the spiritual-temporal condominium is not, however, a return to the pre-Joachitic problems of the Investiture Struggle. The old empire is dead. It is even doubtful whether Dante had any hope of renovation in the immediate future; while he is not explicit on the point, there are indications that he considered the event as far distant as five centuries. The problem of the empire is taken out of its setting of contemporary power politics and transposed into the categories of symbolistic history.

The basic symbols, as we said, are Joachitic. The empire will be inaugurated by a Dux,[7] who is, however, a temporal imperial figure and not, as with Joachim, a spiritual one. Only on the second plane appears a spiritual leading figure, designated as the *Veltro*. In Joachitic categories the double headship of the empire is restored.[8] But this is an empire of the future; it will not be brought about by actions of the now living incumbents of the papal and imperial thrones; and it will not be brought about at all by political action in the mundane sense, because the empire is one of the periods in a divinely ordered course of history and the saving figures will appear in their due time as ordained by God. If we compare this

7. See *Pur.* 33.37 ff. The leader is announced as the *cinquecento diece e cinque;* five hundred, five, and ten, written in Roman numerals, give the word DVX. The pronunciation of *Duce* could not fail to appeal to Fascist intellectuals; an illuminating study by Domenico Venturini, *Dante Alighieri e Benito Mussolini,* 2d ed. (Rome, n.d.), exploits the predictions of the *Divina Commedia* for the Fascist regime.

8. For the *Veltro* see *Inferno* I.100 ff. It should be noted, however, that the temporal leader is so predominant in the *Divina Commedia* that some authorities are inclined to identify the *Veltro* with the *Dux* and believe that Dante had only one leading figure of the empire in mind. The predominance of the *Dux* is undeniable, but the identification of the two figures seems due rather to a neglect of the Joachitic element in Dante. On the details of the question see the excellent commentary of Casini and Barbi, *La Divina Commedia,* and the bibliography given therein. Since the publication of the Casini and Barbi commentary of 1926, the discussion of the Veltro question has developed unexpectedly. Alfred Bassermann has ventured early in this century the thesis that the figure of the Veltro was inspired by legends of the Great-Chan of the Mongols ("Veltro, Gross-Chan und Kaisersage," *Neue Heidelberger Jahrbücher* 11 [1902]). The verse of *Inf.* 1.105 relating to the Veltro—"e sua nazion sera tra feltro e feltro"—was supposed to refer to a birth between the felt walls of a Mongol tent. This thesis was accepted none too well by other Dante authorities. In the late 1920s the discussion revived because one of the foremost authorities on medieval symbols of rulership, Fritz Kampers, became inclined to accept the thesis of Bassermann. A heated debate followed that the interested reader will find in volumes 11, 12, and 13 of the *Dante-Jahrbuch;* the participants were Fritz Kampers, F. Frh. von Falkenhausen, Albert Bassermann, and Robert Davidsohn. An anticlimax came in the form of the concluding paper of Robert Davidsohn, "Ueber den Veltro" (*Dante-Jahrbuch,* vol. 13 [1931]). Davidsohn had found that the word *feltro,* which means *felt,* does also exist in the older language of the mountaineers of Tuscany, and there it has the meaning of a *woolly fleece.* If, as is quite probable, this was the meaning that Dante had in mind, the verse in *Inf.* 1.105 would simply mean that the Veltro will be born among shepherds, in good Christian fashion.

In the preceding footnote I have mentioned the attempt of Venturini to relate the prediction of the *DVX* to Mussolini. When Hitler came into power, Bassermann hurried to see in him the fulfillment of the Veltro prediction (Alfred Bassermann, *Für Dante und gegen seine falschen Apostel Streifzüge* [Buhl-Baden, 1934], 7 ff.). It is worthwhile to note the reception that the idea found in the memorial article for Bassermann, written by Josef Hermann Beckmann: "Es war Bassermann ein beglückendes Erlebnis, als mit der Machtergreifung Hitlers für ihn dieser Sehnsuchtstraum eine Wirklichkeit fand in der Person des Führers. Er fand den Dreiklang 'Veltro—Sonnenmuthus—Hitler'. Die Eigenschaften, die Dante dem kommenden Erretter zusprach, findet er in Adolf Hitler erfüllt, er sieht den Veltro

conception with the prophecies of Joachim we may say that the elements of fatalism reappear that are an inevitable ingredient of every philosophy of history that tries to evoke a fixed pattern of the course of events extending into the future. Dante's fatalism is even stronger than Joachim's because Dante does not assume the function of a prophet whose appearance prognosticates the future realm; his prophetism is not existential but, under the apparatus of symbolism, intellectual, as we noted on the occasion of the play of symbols in the *Letters*. His fatalism approaches rather the submission to a course of history under an eternal law that was characteristic of Siger de Brabant and the Averroists.

In another respect the evocation of Dante may be ranked with that of Saint Augustine. Dempf has remarked correctly that Dante's vision is the counterpart of the *Civitas Dei* insofar as it brings to its completion the evocation of a Christian realm that had remained a torso in the work of Saint Augustine.[9] The comparison can be driven beyond the question of content into the sphere of sentiment. The *Civitas Dei* marks the end of the Roman-Christian period because it accepts the defeat of the idea of a Christian empire; the *saeculum* is *senescens*; no hope is left in the world of history, and we have to wait for the second appearance of Christ, which will put an end to the essentially senseless course of human events. The situation and the sentiments of Dante are in some respects similar to those of Saint Augustine. Again the empire has failed and there is no hope

---

nicht kosmopolitisch, sondern volkisch. Hitler tragt darum auch vollkommen die Zuge des Veltro, als des Erneuerers, Wiederherstellers, Lichtbringers nach der furchtbaren Nacht des Unheils . . . jeder neue Erfolg (Hitlers) predigt . . . die frohe Botschaft, dass die alte Weissagung vom Weltkaiser kein Traum ist, sondern mit der grossen Weltwende Wirklichkeit zu werden sich anschickt. Und auch Dantes grosse Perspektive gewinnt damit . . . die Bestätigung ihrer wahren Deutung und ihre letzte beglückende Weihe" ("For Bassermann Hitler's seizure of power was a happy event. For him this yearning dream found a reality in the person of the führer. He found the triple chime, 'Veltro–Solar Myth–Hitler.' The qualities that Dante ascribed to the future savior he found fulfilled in Adolf Hitler; he saw the Veltro not in a cosmopolitan but in a folk way. Hitler perfectly bore therefore the mark of the Veltro, as the renewer, restorer, illuminator after the frightened night of wickedness . . . each new achievement of Hitler proclaimed . . . the joyous message, that the old prophecy of the world emperor was no dream, but was destined to become a reality with the great turning point of the world. And moreover Dante's broad perspective won thereby the confirmation of its true meaning and its final happy inauguration." Hermann Beckmann"; Alfred Bassermann, Ein Leben fur Dante," *Neue Heidelberger Jahrbücher*, n.s. [1938]: 18).

9. Alois Dempf, *Sacrum imperium: Geschichts- und Staatsphilosophie des Mittelalters und der politischen Renaissance* (Munich and Vienna: Oldenbourg, 1929; 4th ed., 1973), 482.

of restoration in the immediate future; there is a time of waiting ahead comparable to the *saeculum senescens.* The individual can do nothing but withdraw into the attitude of religious contemplation; he can pass judgment on the inequities of the time, but time will pass over him. And again, the *saeculum* will come to an end by divine intervention, with the important difference, however, from the Augustinian conception that the end will not be the advent of the heavenly realm but a new imperial dispensation in the history of Christian mankind. We are faced for the first time in the *Divina Commedia* with the sentiment of hopeless hope that some deus ex machina will abolish the centrifugal and destructive tendencies of the intramundane forces and at the same time establish a perfect intramundane Christian realm. The categories of Dante are medieval insofar as his image of the perfect realm is the perfect medieval empire; but his sentiment is modern insofar as it has absorbed the reconstruction of the *saeculum* that had been the work of the twelfth and thirteenth centuries. The hope is hopeless because the intramundane forces are with us as legitimate forces in a Christian world that has become God's world into the material substratum; they will always be centrifugal and destructive; they cannot be abolished, they can only be bent to the aims of a Christian spiritual order. But the dream of their abolition is the great force in our modern world that makes their suppression at least possible when they threaten to disrupt the Christian order entirely.

17

Marsilius of Padua

§1. The Beginning of German Constitutional Development

The papal interference in the reign of Louis IV (1314–1347) became the occasion for the settlement of relations between the empire and the papacy as well as for a new penetrating analysis of the relations between secular and sacerdotal power. The papal refusal to recognize Louis IV as emperor aroused the national sentiment of the German princes, with the result that by a series of acts the constitutional position of the emperor was made independent of the pope. In 1338 the *Kurverein* of Rense was formed, which declared valid the election of an emperor by the majority of electors, without papal confirmation; the subsequent Diet of Frankfurt, without reference to the pope, declared the electors competent to choose an emperor, thus divorcing the imperial institution completely from the papacy; finally, the Golden Bull of 1356 laid down the regulations for imperial elections without papal intervention. This remained in force until 1806. Following France and England, the German territories started on the process of national contraction and the evolution of national institutions, replacing the older Gelasian constitution of the Western empire. With the *Kurverein* of Rense and the Golden Bull the evolution of German imperial constitutional law may be said to have begun. The form of a federation of the German princes, with the emperor as their elected head, which was created at the time, remained in principle the German constitutional form through the vicissitudes of the centuries. Its tradition was so strong that it was carried over even into the foundation of the empire in 1871. The leading authority on the Bismarck constitution, Paul Laband, interpreted the form of government of the German empire as an aristocratic republic of the German princes under the presidency of the emperor.

§2. The *Defensor Pacis*

Of the flood of partisan literature that the struggle produced on both sides, the antipapal *Defensor Pacis* stands out as the first treatise that evoked the idea of a supreme secular state organization, in the same radical fashion in which the *De ecclesiastica potestate* of Giles of Rome had evoked the idea of supreme papal power. The treatise has long been recognized as one of the most important theoretical essays of the late Middle Ages, but until recently its precise position in the history of ideas was exposed to misunderstandings for a number of reasons.

Of minor importance for reaching a correct understanding is a question that has occasioned much brilliant argument, the question of authorship. The treatise goes under the name of Marsilius of Padua, but in 1326, two years after its completion, Marsilius had to flee from Paris together with his colleague in the Faculty of Arts, John of Jandun, because they were considered coauthors. The attempts to attribute parts of the book to one author or the other on the basis of internal evidence have not led to a consensus, although the stylistic differences between the *Dictio Prima* and the *Dictio Secunda* (parts I and II) make it plausible that at least the original drafts of the two parts were not written by the same man. The work as it stands is well knit; no breaks are perceptible that might be attributed to the inevitable imperfections of a cooperative effort. Although a knowledge of the respective shares in the work of the two authors would enable us to draw their intellectual profiles more clearly, it is hard to see in what way such knowledge could improve our understanding of the contents.

The more serious obstacles to an adequate understanding can be reduced to three main points. A critical edition of the text has been accessible only since 1928.[1] Earlier editions happened to be

1. *The Defensor Pacis of Marsilius of Padua*, ed. C. W. Previte-Orton (Cambridge: Cambridge University Press, 1928). English edition: *The Defender of the Peace*, trans. and intro. Alan Gewirth, 2 vols. (New York: Columbia University Press, 1951–1956); for a recent study see Cary Nederman, *Community and Consent: The Secular Political Theory of Marsiglio of Padua's Defensor Pacis* (Lanham, Md.: Rowman and Littlefield, 1995). A translation of Marsilius's other writings is available in *Writings*

defective in the most important passage of the whole book, I.12.3, so that the isolated defective passage could induce the belief that Marsilius had evolved a theory of popular sovereignty and majority rule. After the publication of the restored text, this misunderstanding has become impossible. It was, however, unnecessary even before the restoration because chapter 13 of *Dictio Prima* gives seven pages of clear and unequivocal explanation of precisely the critical passage so that a balanced reader was not compelled to fall into this error.[2] The inclination to read modern ideas into a medieval treatise at all costs was due rather to the second cause of misinterpretation; that is to the willingness of historians of the progressivist age to enhance the greatness of an earlier thinker by letting him brilliantly "anticipate" later ideas because "later" ideas are supposedly more advanced and enlightened so that their "anticipation" is a particular merit. This tendency is wearing off now; the more scientific attitude of placing the ideas of a thinker properly into his own environment is beginning to prevail.[3] The difficulties encountered by the historian in his endeavor to place the ideas of Marsilius properly are the third source of misunderstandings. The *Defensor Pacis* is based largely on the *Politics* of Aristotle. The relation to Aristotle again raises the problem that we had to discuss earlier in regard to Thomas Aquinas:[4] the "reception" of Aristotle does not mean an adoption of his theory of the polis; it means rather a selection of isolated Aristotelian theories to be fitted into a system based on entirely different principles. The references of Marsilius to Aristotle have too frequently been taken at their face value; a comparison shows that in decisive points they are unwarranted; in the fundamental points the relation to Aristotle is less intense than the apparatus of references would suggest. A still greater obstacle for an adequate interpretation was, until recently, our insufficient knowledge of Latin Averroism. Marsilius as well as John of Jandun were Averroists. If the *Defensor Pacis* is taken as an isolated document in its time, it must surprise the reader by

---

on the Empire: Defensor minor and De translatione Imperii, ed. and trans. Cary Nederman (New York: Cambridge University Press, 1993).

2. That excellent historians and otherwise careful analysts could make the mistake is evidenced by its appearance in Dempf's *Sacrum imperium*, 435. For a good presentation of the correct view see McIlwain, *Growth of Political Thought*, 303 ff.

3. See on the tendency to read modern meanings into medieval concepts the amply justified strictures of McIlwain, *Growth of Political Thought*, 303 ff.

4. See vol. II, *The Middle Ages to Aquinas*, chap. 12, pp. 207–32.

its modernisms. If the antecedent history of Siger de Brabant and Boetius is known, the treatise appears much less anachronistic. It should not be regarded primarily as a first pronouncement of ideas to be developed more fully in later times, but rather as the last step of a development, covering more than seventy years, and for the moment reaching a dead end in the *Defensor Pacis*.

§3. The Relation to Aristotle

The treatise is organized in three parts, called *Dictiones*. The *Dictio Secunda* is the longest, containing the detailed polemic against sacerdotal power in general and papal power in particular; it reduces the *sacerdotium*, as far as its coercive powers are concerned, to a subdivision of the secular polity, acting exclusively by sufferance of the law laid down by the secular government. The briefer *Dictio Prima* contains the exposition of the principles of politics from which the applied rules of the *Dictio Secunda* are derived. The short *Dictio Tertia* consists in the main of an enumeration of forty-two rules summarizing the argument of the preceding *Dictiones*. The most important part for the history of ideas is the *Dictio Prima* with its exposition of principles.

Throughout the *Dictio Prima* run references to the "divine Aristotle" as the ultimate authority on political theory. Nevertheless, Marsilius like Thomas substitutes for the polis the *civitas* or *regnum*, including as a *communitas perfecta* the national territorial polity that was excluded by Aristotle. The position of Marsilius in his political environment is, furthermore, the very opposite of that of Aristotle. Aristotle could take the century-old polis for granted; he was interested in the life of men and citizens in an unquestioned political form. The creation of a particular polis could be a problem for him, but never the existence or structure of the polis as such. Hence he could start with the assumption that man is destined "by nature" for life in the polis, and had only to investigate the conditions of this life. The systematic centers of his theory were, therefore, the *eudaimonia* as the meaning of human life and the *arete* as the virtue of the citizen. The secular political community of Marsilius, on the other hand, is not a form of life with a venerable tradition, but a new type of organization divorcing itself in an embittered struggle from the old empire. The *Politics* of Aristotle is the last word of the dying polis; the *Defensor Pacis* is the first word of the secular state. Marsilius has only incidental use for the conception of man as destined for life in the secular state. His first topic is the coming into existence of the state, under severe travail, through the efforts of the secular king with the aid of his expert lawyers and financial administrators, ordering and regulating the social groups of the realm and particularly reducing an overweening priesthood to its proper position in a body politic. The problems of *eudaimonia* and *arete* are forced into the background. The title of the treatise indicates its primary interest: the establishment of peace and tranquillity in the community through the subordination of the disturbing sacerdotal power under the monopolistic secular power as the ultimate guarantor of political and legal order (III.3: *De titulo huius libri*).

§4. The Organic Analogy

The *Defensor Pacis* is an inquiry into the conditions for tranquillity in the polity. Marsilius finds the starting point for his analysis in the comparison of the *communitas perfecta* with a healthy animal. Tranquillity is for the *regnum* what health is for the animal. "The *civitas* is like an animal nature" (I.2.3); tranquillity will reign in the realm if all its parts are well ordered to their tasks (I.3.1); the well-ordered community is an analogue to the well-proportioned, and in all its parts well-functioning, animal (I.2.3). For the organic analogy Marsilius refers to the authority of Aristotle's *Politics*, 1254a and 1302b. A reading of these and other passages reveals that, indeed, one of them, 1302b, compares the parts of the political community to the members of an animal body. But the systematic place of the analogy is not the same with Aristotle as with Marsilius. In the *Politics* the analogy appears in the context of the theory of revolutions; disproportionate growth of the rich or the poor element will disturb the peace of the community and may become one source of revolutions among several others. The comparison of the polis to the animal is entirely incidental to this specific cause of revolutions, while in the theory of Marsilius it becomes the centerpiece of a theory of the state. In the other passage, 1254a, the organic analogy has a vastly different function. The structure of the polis is compared, not to the proportions of the animal body, but to the relation between the soul and the body in a living being. The soul is the dominant part, controlling the functions of the body. Aristotle draws the political conclusion that the better man, corresponding to the soul, should dominate slaves by nature, corresponding to the body; the argument is intensified by the suggestion that the better men should rule over the lesser like men rule over animals. Obviously, the organic analogies in the two contexts have nothing to do with each other; there is no coherent organological theory in the system of Aristotle.

Hence, in the system of Marsilius, the organic analogy has a function that cannot be derived from Aristotle; it is related to the *Politics* by more or less superficial associations only. For its antecedents we have to look rather in the direction of the pre-Aristotelian organic analogy in the work of John of Salisbury. The *Policraticus* tried to constrict intramundane governmental power as representative of the particular commonwealth within the old empire. The attempt could not be completely successful at the time because the commonwealth was not yet evoked with sufficient strength to make the function of the king as representative of the "whole" quite plausible. The organic analogy was used by John of Salisbury in order to make the existence and internal structure of the commonwealth intelligible. A good deal of these evocative difficulties had disappeared by the time of Marsilius; the intramundane political units had gained impressive reality; nobody needed much persuasion to believe that England or France existed. But the difficulties of the theoretical construction has barely been touched. Marsilius had to take up the problem almost where John of Salisbury had left it. The organic analogy was for him as for the earlier thinker the means of establishing the commonwealth as an entity in the field of political powers so that he could proceed to the solution of the problem of how the ruling individual or the ruling group in the commonwealth, the *pars principans* in his terminology, could exert its function of ordering the life of the community with representative authority.

§5. The Problem of Intramundane Representative Authority—The *Legislator*

The organic analogy is an aid to the evocation of the commonwealth as a whole; it is not of much help, however, for the solution of this second problem, the problem of representative authority. If the authority of rulership is not derived from divine ordination but is supposed to be rooted in the commonwealth itself, the problem arises of where to locate the source of authority within the intra-mundane polity. The comparison with the animal body does not furnish an answer, for the ruler is one of its members and cannot derive his authority from the other members of the functioning unit, whom, on the contrary, he has to regulate. The source has to lie somewhere back of the single members in the comprehensive "whole." In modern language: back of the constitution, and of the political society functioning under it, lies the constituent power of the people, which may be institutionalized in a constitutional convention or assembly. Marsilius has the historical distinction of having attacked this problem of political speculation in principle for the first time in the modern West. His analysis is penetrating and clear; we may even say it gives the perfect answer to the problem for its time; but because it is the perfect answer for the time it cannot be a theory of popular sovereignty. The source back of the legally organized functioning commonwealth from which the ruler derives his authority is called by Marsilius the *legislator*. The term cannot be rendered in English simply by "legislator" because our modern legislative function is *under* the fundamental law; the *legislator* of Marsilius, a translation of the Aristotelian *nomothetes*, on the contrary, is the intramundane agent authorizing the constitutional order under which the ruler executes his functions, including rule making. The *legislator* and his function are defined in the famous passage I.12.3: "We define in accordance with the truth and the opinion of Aristotle, *Politics* III.6 (III.11 in the modern counting) that the *populus* or *civium universitas*, or its socially relevant part *[pars valentior]* is the *legislator* or prime and proper effective cause of the law, through its choice or will expressed in articulate terms *[per sermonem]* in a general assembly of the citizens, commanding or determining that something be done or not done concerning civil actions of men, by temporal punishment or penalty. When I say 'the socially relevant part' *[valentior pars]* I mean relevant by the quantity as well as the quality of the persons in the community for which the law is given; whether the aforementioned *universitas civium* or its socially relevant part makes itself the law, or entrusts its making to one or more persons who, of course, are not and cannot be the *legislator* himself but act only for a definite purpose, at a definite time and in accordance with the authority conferred on them by the original *legislator*" (I.12.3).

The evaluation of this definition depends on the meaning of the terms *universitas civium* and *valentior pars*. The earlier assumption that the *universitas* means the people in the modern constitutional sense of the population of voting age and that the *valentior pars* is the majority of the people has become impossible today even philologically. The earlier text defined *valentior* as *considerata quantitate*; the emendated critical text adds *et qualitate*. I have also discarded other translations, such as "prevailing part" or "dominant part"; they are literally correct but convey no meaning unless elaborated upon. Instead I have used the translation "socially relevant part," taking the term from Max Weber; it means all members of the community who cannot be neglected politically without causing revolutionary instability of the social order. The translation is justified insofar as it corresponds to the intentions of the Aristotelian *Politics,* on which the idea of Marsilius is based, as well as to the intentions of Marsilius himself as elaborated in chapter 13 of the *Dictio Prima*. From both texts it appears that members of the community can be socially relevant to the degree that their weight cannot be politically neglected, either because of their numbers or because of their qualities. The poor usually will be relevant because of their numbers, while those who are relevant because of their qualities of character, education, and property usually will be the few rich, though Aristotle envisages the possibility of a class of rich who may be relevant because of their numbers. For Marsilius the dividing line between quantity and quality seems to run between a lower class of peasants, artisans, and merchants and an upper class of priests, military men, and lawyers (I.5); in the context of I.13 the men of quality are distinguished as the educated, prudent, and legal experts from the mass of the uneducated *(indocti)*.

Marsilius presents an elaborate scheme for the procedure of the *legislator* (I.13), destined to guarantee the initiative of the educated few and at the same time to preserve a power of approval for the mass of the uneducated. C. W. Previte-Orton is of the opinion that the scheme reflects the procedure actually used by the Italian communes of the time. But setting aside the actual procedure, which for technical reasons cannot in a large territory like France be the same as in an Italian town, we may say that the picture of the social structure with its hierarchy of status groups as outlined by Marsilius is valid in general for late medieval society. His *legislator* is simply the stratified medieval society in any political unit. The point is important because there is no *absolute* necessity even at the time of Marsilius to conceive the "whole" of a community in these terms. It would not have been at all impossible for political theory in the thirteenth and fourteenth centuries to take the turn toward a construction of popular, democratic government. We have noticed tendencies in this direction in the ideas of Thomas Aquinas. The social forces that could have formed the material basis for an evocation of popular government were present in the religious communal movements of the Italian and, to a lesser degree, the western and northwestern European towns. History, however, did not favor this development at the time. The religious popular revolt was suppressed as heretical; it achieved its irruption into the institutional sphere only in the sixteenth and seventeenth centuries. Marsilius was not interested in the spiritual forces that lived in these movements; in the *Defensor Pacis* there is no trace of the idea of spiritually free, mature Christians forming the substance of the polity as in the theory of Thomas Aquinas. Such populist elements as actually can be discerned in the conception of the *legislator* are not due to any evocative effort on the part of Marsilius but are, as Previte-Orton has remarked correctly, descriptions of actual town institutions.

Summarizing this part of the doctrine of Marsilius, we may say that the theory of the *legislator* is the first consistent construction of the intramundane political unit, deriving governmental authority not from an extraneous source but from a specially constructed "whole" of the community behind its single parts. The construction of Marsilius is related to the theory of popular sovereignty insofar as this latter theory has the same purpose of constructing an intramundane political unit. But apart from the identity of purpose, it is a genuinely medieval idea, using the materials of the medieval stratified society for the conception of the "whole," without regard to the possibilities of a populist construction that were present in the politico-religious town movements.

§6. Limited Government—Italianism

In the preceding analysis we have stressed the elements that determine the place of the *Defensor Pacis* in the general history of medieval ideas. When we proceed now to the details of the position and function of the ruler, we have to be aware that the surface of common Western problems has worn thin while the substratum of national particular problems has gained in thickness. At the time of the Investiture Struggle an antipapal treatise was as a matter of course pro-imperial; by the time of the fourteenth century the tension between the papal and the imperial powers had shifted to the tension between the papal and the plurality of national secular powers. The theory of Marsilius, while antipapal, bears the distinctive marks of Italian problems that were not valid in the same manner for other national regions.

This point has to be taken into account when we consider the power of the *legislator* over the *pars principans.* The ruler is instituted by the *legislator,* and he is submitted to his corrective power even to the point of suspension and deposition in case of gross abuse of authority (I.18). The idea of deposition by the *universitas* is, indeed, a solution of the problem that had worried John of Salisbury; the unbalanced solution of the earlier thinker, the correction by means of tyrannicide, is now replaced by action in due form on the part of the commonwealth. The internal logic of the intramundane construction of the polity through identification of the "whole" with the *universitas* leads toward ideas of a limited government. It would be rash, however, to hail Marsilius as the precursor of constitutional government and limited monarchy, as sometimes has happened, for the development of ideas and institutions is not uniform over the Western world and there is no one ideal form toward which it tends. The problem that was solved by Marsilius is strictly the construction of the intramundane polity; the "limitative" feature is incidental to the solution of the primary problem; and the primary problem permits alternative solutions that do not at all imply limitations on the ruler. For it is not necessary to identify the "whole" of the commonwealth with the *universitas* of its living members, be they understood as medieval stratified society or modern people. It is equally possible to shove the "whole" back into an immaterial substance of the community beyond the multitude of the living so that the governing authorities become the direct representatives of the immaterial substance back of all empirical groups within the community. The result would be the unlimited authority of the ruling elite or the ruling leaders as we have observed it in Russia and Germany. As theoretical constructions the alternatives can be separated; in the governmental practice of our modern communities they will be found operative

simultaneously in varying strengths. It is hard to imagine that
a government could operate permanently against the consent of
the empirical people even if its authority were entirely unlimited;
and it is equally hard to imagine that a representative government
should not find itself occasionally under the necessity to act in
defiance of the opinion of the living because deference to the higher
authority of the immaterial entity of the commonwealth requires
such action.

With regard now to the technical possibilities and the effectiveness of control of the *universitas* over the ruler, the size of
the commonwealth is an important factor. It is not an accident
that a plebeian citizen from Padua should develop the idea of a
government limited by the *universitas*. The theories of Aristotle
regarding this question were eminently useful to Marsilius because
he could amalgamate them with the political experience of the
Italian town. The *Defensor Pacis* is the first treatise on politics
that reveals the specific affinity between the Hellenic theory of
the polis and the problems of the Western towns. The extension
of Aristotelian categories beyond the scope of the town remains
a permanent source of embarrassment; Rousseau went so far in
his *Contrat Social* as to exclude expressly the transfer of his ideas,
which were meant for the model of Geneva, to a national realm like
France. Marsilius was not yet aware of these difficulties; we have
seen that he substituted without scruples the *regnum* alternatively
with the *civitas* for the polis. Nevertheless, his theory has its full
meaning only in the context of Italian town politics.

The point is important for the interpretation of the *Defensor
Pacis* because a good deal of its supposedly anticipative character
will disappear if we regard the theory of the *legislator* and his powers not as early in relation to later ideas of limited government but
as Italian and simultaneous with the transalpine ideas originating
in the large national *regna*. The ineffectiveness of the treatise in
its time was in part due to the fact that the political evolution
in western Europe went in a far different direction, culminating
in the absolute monarchy in England and France. The turn toward
limitation of government and popular sovereignty north of the Alps
came only when the forces of the popular movements were released.
The idea of limiting the government by the medieval *universitas*
developed in the Italian environment with its tradition of Mediterranean town politics; but the idea of limiting the government by

the people developed in the West and extended its sway over Italy only with the national rebirth of the nineteenth century.

§7. Averroist Naturalism

From the internal structure of the secular polity we return to the general level of problems. This general part of the Marsilian theory is esoteric in character, and its presentation is, therefore, surrounded by certain hazards. The authors were Averroists; to publish an Averroist treatise on politics implied the practical certainty of personal unpleasantness. The Averroist tendencies can be sensed in the decisive parts of the book, but they are neither stressed nor integrated into an explicit system. It is fair to assume that the authors, while not suppressing their views, did not care to advertise them aggressively but deliberately left it to the knowing reader to complete a pattern of theory that they themselves did no more than suggest.

The chief aids in obscuring the Averroist contents are the twisted references to Aristotle. In I.4.1 the impression is created that the Aristotelian theory of the good life has been simply taken over: men congregate in a community in order to satisfy the needs of life, and they combine in the perfect society for the sake of the good life, consisting in the liberal occupation of the practical and speculative soul. But the passage is no more than the inconsequential quotation. In the Aristotelian system the doctrine of the good life is elaborated into the theory of the good man and good citizen and his virtues; in the system of Marsilius this elaboration, or an equivalent, is missing. Instead we find a naturalistic philosophy of society. The division of agricultural, artisan, mercantile, military, sacerdotal, and ruling functions in the community is due, for Marsilius, to the providence of nature. Nature has endowed men with different inclinations or habits in order to furnish the human material for the life of the perfect society (I.7). Marsilius mentions specifically the naturally determined habits of military action and governing prudence, of operative and speculative inclinations. The unit of man is broken up into a gamut of natural endowments, with the result that Marsilius has no personalistic anthropology, Christian or otherwise, but a typically Averroist collectivist philosophy of natural man. The naturalistic radicalism of the doctrine becomes apparent when we compare it with the parallel Aristotelian theory in the *Politics* VII.8–9 (1328a–1329a). Aristotle, too, pays attention to the natural inclination of man, but he also takes into account the occupational problems and the idea of the perfect personality. Husbandry is assigned to slaves and barbarian *perioeci* because it leaves no leisure for the life of a citizen; the slaves and barbarians are an inferior kind of man and, hence, are not candidates for the perfect personality. Mechanics and tradesmen are not necessarily slaves by nature, but their occupation is ignoble, and, therefore, they cannot be full citizens; the question of whether they are by nature unfit to be citizens remains in suspense. The perfect citizens, finally, are not differentiated according to natural inclinations; everyone has to fulfill the functions of warrior, ruler, and priest in succession at the proper time of his life. The polis, thus, is organized around an ideal of man; at least the members of the upper class fulfill the conditions of a well-rounded personality, and through their integral human qualities they are able to form the substance of the community.

§8. The *Pars Principans*

Marsilius has no idea of man comparable to the Aristotelian. Out of the diversification of human habits a *civitas* can be built, but it cannot grow. In the language of Marsilius: the natural habits are the *causae materiales* of the state, but not its *causae formales* or its *causae efficientes*. The formal cause of the social order is to be found in the fundamental laws issued by the *legislator* and its effective cause is the *legislator* himself. The state is not an organism, but an organization; its parts are *officia* in the sense of obedient fulfillment of an order issued by an instituting authority (I.7.1). In this connection the function of the *pars principans*, of the ruler, becomes of prime importance. The *legislator* cannot do more than draw the general outlines of the social order. It falls to the ruler to order and coordinate continuously the other parts of the *civitas*. Excesses have to be corrected; equity and proportion have to be maintained (I.5.7). This function is characterized as *judicialis et consiliativa* (I.5.7) and as *executiva* (I.15.4); it includes also a rule-making power *(praecipere)* (I.15.6); and it falls specifically to the ruler to issue regulations concerning the numbers and qualifications of men who may join the one or the other social group so that the due proportions are preserved (I.15.10). The ruler is the *pars prima* because he institutes, determines, and conserves all other parts (I.15.14).

Since in the conception of Marsilius the *civitas* does not grow historically from the free converging efforts of its members but depends for its existence on the ordering activity of the ruler, it cannot be stable unless the ruler has a power monopoly. If the size of a realm requires a plurality of regional governing authorities, they have to be strictly subordinate to the regulative and corrective power of the central authority. A multitude of men becomes by definition a *civitas* insofar as it has a ruler with ultimate secular authority (I.17.11).[5] This accentuation of the sovereignty of the ruler as determining not only the unity but also the unit of the state is not a complete reversal of the theory of the *populus* or *universitas* as the primary substance of the commonwealth, for the ruler still remains instituted by the *legislator*; but it shows how slender the basis is for the assumption of a sovereign *universitas*. The weight lies heavily on the governmental organization, which has yet to perform a unifying work of centuries before modern nations reach a degree of coherence that enables them to function as the sovereign.

§9. The Plurality of Warring States

The political theory proper of the intramundane state is completed by a few remarks concerning the question of a universal monarchy. Marsilius considers a political organization of mankind under one supreme ruler undesirable. There should be a plurality of states corresponding to the regional, linguistic, and cultural diversification of mankind, for it seems to be the intention of nature that the propagation of men should be moderated by wars and epidemics so that limited space would be sufficient for the process of eternal generation. As the effects of war and disease might be diminished by world peace, attempts at political organization should not go beyond the plurality of natural polities (I.17.10). The Averroist eternal process of generation is the ultimate principle of political philosophy.

---

5. *Defensor Pacis* I.17.11: "Sic quoque unius civitatis aut provinciae homines dicuntur una civitas aut regnum, quia volunt unum numero principatum" ("Similarly, the men of one city or province are called one city or state because they wish one government in number"; *Defender of the Peace*, trans. Gewirth). See Marino Damiata, *Plenitudo potestatis e universitas civium in Marsilio da Padova* (Florence: Studi francescani, 1983).

§10. The Law

The theory of law corresponds to the theory of politics. The systematic difficulties of Saint Thomas are now easily overcome because only one of the various meanings of the term *law* is accepted as relevant for the secular state. Law is defined as a general doctrine concerning the just and useful and their opposites in civil matters, from which are to be derived coercive rules, sanctioned by temporal punishments or rewards (I.10.3–4). The law combines right content with temporal sanction, but the coercive element outweighs the right content. Marsilius acknowledges the possibility of a jurisprudence as the science of the just and unjust, of the useful and the injurious (I.10.4), but he does not acknowledge a natural law as such. A *vera cognitio* of the just (the term *lex* is carefully avoided) is not a law (I.10.5); a *falsa cognitio*, on the other hand, is a law if equipped with temporal sanction; it is deficient as far as rightness is concerned, but it is a law nevertheless (I.10.5). An exposition of the contents of natural law is significantly missing in the *Defensor Pacis*.[6] The *potentia coactiva* (I.10.4) dominates the theoretical scene as in the *De potestate ecclesiastica* of Giles of Rome.

§11. Christianity and the Church

Compared with the positive theory of the state, the argument directed against the sacerdotium is an anticlimax, though it fills the main body of the book and is its principal practical purpose. The attitude of Marsilius toward Christianity is Averroist: the truth of the faith is recognized on every occasion, while its contents are treated with such indifference that the position of Marsilius can hardly be characterized as even fideistic; not the faintest attempt is made to

---

6. In *Defensor Pacis* II.12.7 Marsilius enumerates, in the form of a quotation from Aristotle, *Ethics* V.7, a conventional contents of a natural law. The passage is followed, however, by the sentences: "Quae licet sint ab humana institutione pendentia, transumptive *iura* dicuntur *naturalia*. Quoniam eodem modo creduntur apud omnes regiones licita et eorum opposita illicita, quemadmodum actus naturalium non habentium propositum conformiter apud omnes proveniunt, velut *ignia* qui sic *ardet hic* sicut *in Persia*" ("Although these depend on human enactment, they are analogously called 'natural' rights because in all regions they are in the same way believed to be lawful and their opposites unlawful, just as the acts of natural beings which are devoid of will are everywhere uniform, like fire, which 'burns here just as it does in Persia' "; Gewirth trans.). The *ius naturale* is identical with a *ius gentium*. My attention was drawn to this passage by Professor Friedrich von Engel-Janosi.

achieve harmony between faith and reason in the Thomistic sense. The meaning of life and of the good life is a topic for the philosopher, and Aristotle is the authoritative guide for mundane problems; on questions of the eternal life no consensus has been achieved, and it is beyond rational discussion (I.4.3). Christianity is treated as one religious "sect" among others, though it is formally opposed as the one true religion to the multitude of false ones. The detachment reaches the grotesque in I.6, where the tenets of the Christian faith are summarized in an elementary textbook fashion as if the treatise were written for readers who had never heard of Christianity before. This chapter could have been written only by a man to whom Christianity had become a cultural curiosity and did not appeal to any more profound sentiments. This assumption is confirmed by Marsilius's evaluation of religion as being a holy terror for the vulgar whose morality of conduct is fortified by the expectation of punishment in the beyond for deeds that escape the mundane judge (I.6.11). The punishment lies in the beyond, in the *saeculum aeternum*; under no circumstances can the priesthood acquire coercive power over men independent of secular authority. Christianity specifically is interpreted as an otherworldly religion that must not be institutionalized in the form of a church having a *potestas coactiva* over its members. To Christ himself are denied the functions of a king and judge except in the *saeculum aeternum*; while in this world he has the function of a "physician" who can inform, order, prognosticate, and express judgments concerning a life leading to eternal health or damnation but not support his advice, through priests, by compulsion in this life (II.9.2; also II.7.5). In this context appears a curious passage, which unfortunately is corrupt, but can have, if restored, only one meaning: Christ in his mercy is withholding punishment "to the end of each period" in order to give men time for meritorious conduct and penitence.[7] The phrase "to the end of each period" can hardly mean anything else but that Marsilius accepts the Averroist theory of eternally recurring world cycles and that Christ assumes his function as judge at the end of each cycle as he is born and crucified in each cycle.

---

7. *Defensor Pacis* II.9.1: "Voluit enim ex sua misericordia Christus usque ad extremum cuiusque periodum concedere mereri, et de commissis in ipsius legem poenitere posse" ("For in his mercy Christ wished to give every person the opportunity to become deserving up to the very end of his life and to repent of sins committed against Christ's law"; Gewirth trans.).

The principles governing the relations between the church and the secular polity flowing from this position can be anticipated. I select only some of the main rules. The church has no coercive power but is subject in every respect to the authority of the human legislator who ordinates the life of man toward his mundane happiness (II.4–5). Church penalties, including excommunication, can be applied only with permission of secular laws (II.6). The clergy is not exempt from the secular courts (II.7). The internal hierarchical organization of the church has to be abolished because all priests are equal; the position of the Roman pontiff has historical, not spiritual, reasons (II.5). Only Scripture itself has to be believed by all Christians; its interpretation is a function of a general council of the church (II.19). The general council is to be composed of delegates from all provinces of the world, chosen by the community of the faithful according to the provisions of the human legislator; due weight has to be given to quality; laymen, as for instance the kings, are included as much as churchmen (II.20).

§12. The Esoteric Creed

From the preceding presentation of the *Defensor Pacis* it should have become clear that its doctrine cannot be reduced to a simple formula. Too many theoretical and practical problems are interwoven, too many streams of sentiment flow together, and too well hidden are the principles of the authors who tried to elude papal censorship. In spite of the esoteric character of the fundamental doctrine it is possible for us, however, as it was for the papal censors, to penetrate to the core of the sentiments and ideas and to place them in their time. We have said that the political theory is Averroist; but this statement requires an important qualification. In the chapter on Siger de Brabant we have seen that the collectivism of Averroist theory is not unequivocal.[8] Mankind is a collective unit through the oneness of the *anima intellectiva* in which single human beings participate, as well as through the natural process of eternal generation that embraces them all. If these two levels of human collectivity are taken singly as the basis for theoretical construction, the resulting political ideas obviously will be widely divergent. The *anima intellectiva* lends itself to the evocation of a

8. See vol. II, *The Middle Ages to Aquinas*, chap. 11, pp. 178–204.

world empire of mankind, the universality of the political organization corresponding to the universality of the collective mind. If the natural process becomes the determinant of theory, the idea of an unending stream of successive and simultaneous polities may be evoked, each having for its basis the communities produced by nature. The first possibility is realized in Dante's idea of a world monarchy; the second in Marsilius's idea of a plurality of closed secular states, at war with each other. The *Defensor Pacis* has to be ranked, therefore, with the *Monarchia* of Dante; the two treatises together represent the potentialities of Averroism in politics.

The esotericism of the *Defensor Pacis* makes it difficult to decide whether the treatise as a whole may be called a system of politics. The prevailing opinion seems to be that the theory of the secular state, as evolved in the *Dictio Prima,* is incompatible with the church policy of the *Dictio Secunda.* This opinion can be supported by good reasons. A merely fideistic attitude toward Christianity would already impair its vitality as a community-shaping force. But Marsilius goes farther: he expressly considers religion as an opium for the people, and Christianity is deprived of all meaning if Christ becomes a figure that appears and disappears rhythmically in the eternal sequence of world cycles. For the naturalistic intellectual, Christianity must be just one illusion more and cannot be integrated consistently into the system of secular politics. It is possible, however, to take another view of the matter. We remember that the Arabic philosophers had arrived at an attitude of toleration with regard to Islam.[9] The multitude would be granted indulgence in an orthodox religion because it cannot rise to higher levels of reasoning and insight, and the creed of the intellectual would remain the possession of an unobtrusive group of philosophers. It is quite probable that the authors of the *Defensor Pacis* adopted this attitude. Their church policy would be, in this case, a quite consistent way of dealing with the convictions of the vulgar, leaving them their faith and even, through the general council, a form of institutionalized expression, while curbing the influence of the priesthood on the polity where the intellectual experts should reign supreme. We cannot decide in favor of the one or the other opinion because a key part of the Marsilian doctrine is probably missing. The *Dictio*

9. See ibid., 183–86.

Prima evolves an institutional theory of the secular state, but it avoids touching upon the question of the intellectual and spiritual community substance. We hear some vague talk about the good life, about the just and useful, and about the liberal occupation of the practical and speculative soul; but we hear nothing of a code of ethics and natural law and nothing of a central purpose of life like the Aristotelian *bios theoretikos.* As Christianity does not furnish the community substance either, we may suspect that back of the revealed political theory the authors have had some intellectual creed determining their conduct of life, leaving them free to bless the mass of the people with a utilitarian mundane policy. Through the substantial emptiness of the *Dictio Prima* we can see the blank spot; but we do not know what was written on it invisibly.

§13. Political Technicism

The attitude is spiritually nihilistic as far as the polity is concerned, though there may be an intellectual creed in the background. As a result of these sentiments, the approach to political problems becomes technical in the sense of an understanding of power problems without personal participation on the part of the political thinker in the loyalties and the faith of the community. The treatment of revolutions and their prevention is the part of Aristotle's *Politics* in which Marsilius is most interested. This technical approach of Marsilius has always been recognized as being related to the politics of Machiavelli. Marsilius has not concentrated his will to secular statesmanship in an evocation comparable in grandeur to Machiavelli's Prince; this is hardly to be expected if we consider the opprobrium that became attached to the name of Machiavelli even two centuries later and is still attached to it in public opinion. But the position is preformed in all essentials; and a good share of the fame that is Machiavelli's as the first representative of postmedieval secular politics should go to Marsilius. The relationship should be stressed because it gives an insight into the antecedents of Machiavelli's position and permits us to trace at least one of its component factors back to Averroist naturalism.[10] It should be stressed, furthermore, because both Marsilius and Machiavelli were Italians.

10. [See Antonio Toscano, *Marsilio da Padova e Niccolo Machiavelli* (Ravenna: Longo, 1981).]

Under the impact of the sad experiences with the church in Italian politics, the Italian climate of sentiment became favorable to a religiously detached, sober, craftsmanlike approach to problems of politics. This distinctly Italian form of political thought, which is noticeable even in its recent great representatives, in Mosca and Pareto, had already taken shape in the early fourteenth century.

18

William of Ockham

From the analyses of Giles of Rome, John of Paris, Dante, and Marsilius of Padua emerges a pattern of political theory that is characteristic of the fourteenth century. It is necessary to consider this pattern for a moment and to distinguish it from that of the preceding centuries because its clarification will be of help in the analysis of William of Ockham, the most complex thinker of the age.

§1. A Pattern of Theory—The Problem of William

At the end of the Investiture Struggle the radical spiritualization of the world foreshadowed the rise of the intramundane forces in the following two centuries; the system of Saint Thomas Aquinas, at the end of the thirteenth century, achieved the grandiose synthesis of the forces for the moment; but we see them reappear afterward in full strength, and only then do they become recognizable in the vastness of their problems, which could not be mastered by any single thinker of the following period. The first important characteristic of the late Middle Ages is, therefore, the absence of a classic philosophic system that could be accepted as the representative symbol of the age. Instead, we find an open field of theoretical expressions, every one of them a fragment of meaning not yielding a complete understanding of the age if taken singly. They have to be seen together, in their interrelation, if one wishes to draw a true picture of the problems that occupied the thinkers of the period. In this respect the century after Saint Thomas resembles the preceding: in order to appreciate the extent of the pre-Thomistic intramundane upheaval we had to review the secular individualism of John of Salisbury and the spiritual of Saint Francis, the imperial pathos of Frederick II and the intellectual of Siger de Brabant, the historical consciousness of Joachim of Fiore and the incipient legalism of action of the popes and emperors. The same forces are present in the fourteenth century, but their expression can no longer be identified with a clear series of representative personalities. The revolutionary work of the twelfth and thirteenth centuries is done; the intramundane forces are established, which means that they have expanded into bodies of doctrine and sometimes into institutions that add their own momentum as a factor to the situation. The elemental character of the preceding period has disappeared; we are faced now with considerably more complicated cross-patterns of determinants.

If we try to unravel the complexes of sentiments and ideas and so reduce them to the determining factors, we have to place first the differentiation of Western mankind into the particular collectivities that have given the title to this segment ("The Church and the Nations"). On the one side, the spiritualism of the church has developed into the ecclesiasticism of Boniface VIII and Giles of Rome, and on the other side we can observe the national sentiments reaching the stage where they inject problems of national institutions into general political theory. We noticed the reflection of the French monarchy in John of Paris and of Italian town institutions in Marsilius of Padua, and we shall observe presently the traces of the English background in the theory of William of Ockham. In no case, however, is the collective unit the exclusively determining factor of a theory. The expression of the collective intramundane forces blends with that of the personal forces of the earlier period. The Joachitic expectation of the Third Realm reappears in combination with the hopes of Dante for a regeneration of the Roman-Italian imperial mission, the Averroist intellectualism of Siger and Boetius Dacius in combination with the Italian republicanism, anticlericalism, and political technicism of Marsilius. The imperial dreams of the Hohenstaufen are transformed into the imperialism of Charles of Anjou and the French hegemonic ideas of Pierre Dubois. And in William of Ockham the element of English institutions is a minor factor in an attitude that draws its strength from the spiritualism of the Franciscan Order.

The same forces are at work, but the new ideas are more than a reshuffling of old motives. The ideas of the twelfth and thirteenth centuries, having gained their own momentum, produce a set of problems that can be distinguished as a new factor common to the otherwise widely divergent ideas of the fourteenth century. In the work of Giles of Rome we could observe the dissociation of power from the spirit, both precariously linked again through the evocation of a hierarchy with the substances of power and spirit concentrated in its head. In the vision of Dante the spirit has receded from the contemporary field of powers and passions, and their reunion becomes a hope for a distant future. In the *Defensor Pacis* the secular power structure has become a closed unit and Christianity is a creed for the people, while in the half-veiled background there appears an Averroist creed for the intellectual. The trend is clear. The acceptance of the "world" as part of the divine creation since Cardinal Humbert and the *York Tracts* made possible the rise of the intramundane forces. The forces of the world, having established themselves, now threaten to cut loose from Christian spirituality and to find a new balance in an intramundane order. The thinkers of the fourteenth century are concerned either, like Marsilius of Padua, with the establishment of the new intramundane order or, like Giles and Dante, with the development of a formula that will preserve the Christian transcendental order and at the same time integrate the structure of the world.

In dealing with the situation, William of Ockham has the distinction of having penetrated it thoroughly and of having developed, with the resources of Franciscan spiritualism, a theoretical position that was to recur later in the history of modern ideas. The fixed data of his problem were the following: Christian spiritualism and Christian theology had to be preserved intact. The principal danger to such preservation was the reality of the world and the preoccupation with it in the form of science. Science, however, had become one of the established facts in Western civilization and could not be abolished, hence an ontology and epistemology had to be developed that would permit a critical, free exploration of reality without endangering the theologoumena. The great intellectual opponent to this task was Aristotelianism in its Averroist form; hence the new metaphysics had to be a radical counterposition to the Averroist naturalism and determinism of the human personality. Thomism itself was a danger because the assumption of the harmony between faith and reason would lead through the practice of rational, philosophical inquiry to tensions between natural and supranatural theology that ultimately might undermine the integrity of the dogmatic system.

§2. Nominalism and Fideism

I have stated the problem advisedly in terms of data as if it were to be solved by a method of calculation because the metaphysics of William of Ockham is, indeed, a brilliantly calculated system of answers to the given questions while an existential center determining the philosophical attitude is missing. William is the first of a distinguished line of modern philosophers who philosophize on problems that do not originate in a radical philosophical experience but are offered by the environment for an intellectual solution. There is nothing in William of the sublime certainty of Saint Thomas that the order of the world is a manifestation of the divine intellect and that it is to be re-created by man in the order of truth. The order of the world is, for William, created by God, but it is not a revelation of the *ratio aeterna;* the world as it is owes its structure not to the divine substance but to an act of the divine will; the omnipotent God could have made it different if he had wanted to do so. The world does not have an essential structure, but realizes of the infinite possibilities the one that was God's choice.[1] Using the distinction of Duns Scotus between the *potestas absoluta* and the *potestas ordinata* of God, William conceives of the order of nature as a hypothetical order determined by the *potestas ordinata;* it is a stable order so that, on the basis of empirical knowledge, we can formulate general notions and rules with regard to temporal sequences of events under equal circumstances, but God at any moment can irrupt into the order by action of his *potestas absoluta* and change the expected course of events. The order of nature does not have a structure of real universals; we cannot know, therefore, any substance in itself but can know it only by its accidentals. The causality in the order of nature is not denied, but, being dependent on the will of God, who may change it, it does not have the character of necessity. This conception of nature as a hypothetical order is the basis of Ockham's nominalistic theory of knowledge.[2]

---

1. The presentation of the problem has to be brief. The reader should be aware that the insistence on the differences from the theology of Saint Thomas overstresses heavily the voluntaristic element. For a balanced understanding an extensive analysis would be necessary. In this context we endeavor to bring out the distinctive overtones.

2. See on these questions Erich Hochstetter, *Studien zur Metaphysik und Erkenntnislehre Wilhelms von Ockham* (Berlin and Leipzig: De Gruyter, 1927), esp. chap. 2,

The implications of the construction are of the greatest consequence for the system of Ockham as well as for the later history of ideas. If the substance of nature is inaccessible, our knowledge of the external world becomes a problem of organizing empirical materials by means of the conceptual instruments of the human mind. The object of knowledge is not the *real* object, but the object as it appears and is thought of ("intentio in anima naturaliter significans omnes illas res de quibus praedicatur" [intention in the soul naturally signifying all those things about which it can be predicated]).[3] The way is opened for empirical science and for the Critique of Reason, culminating in the system of Kant. The establishment of a critical theory of knowledge is undertaken not, however, primarily in order to secure the progress of science but in order to restrict science critically to its field of possibilities. The substance of the world, including man (Kant's *Ding an sich*) and God, cannot be reached by science. The critical confinement of science to the accidentals has the purpose of saving faith from its encroachments. In the realm of revealed faith and of theology reigns the *potestas absoluta* of God; it is the field of the completely irrational, defying attempts at a rational theology. The revealed religion is a miracle of God, not to be caught in the categories of science; its content cannot be penetrated by natural reason and, hence, its acceptance is possible only through the miracle of faith operated by God in man. The irrational content of the dogma is believable because God has, through his *potestas absoluta*, infused faith in man, compelling the sacrifice of intellect. William gives the first construction of a strictly fideistic religious position, accepting the rationally impenetrable dogma by an act of faith that is worked in man by a miracle of God.[4]

"Metaphysische Voraussetzungen." See also Sytse Ulbe Zuidema, *De Philosophie van Occam in zijn Commentar op de Sententien*, 2 vols. (Hilversum: Shipper, 1936); vol. 1 contains the treatise just cited, vol. 2 selections from the *Commentary*; see esp. 1:452, on Ockham's conception of God as an *Uebermensch*, as the *agens fortissimum*. The passage on the *agens fortissimum* is to be found in Ockham's *Commentary on the Sentences* II.19.L (Zuidema's *Supplement*, 210). In general see Gordon Leff, *William of Ockham: The Metamorphosis of Scholastic Doctrines* (Manchester: Manchester University Press, 1975) and *The Dissolution of the Medieval Outlook* (New York: New York University Press, 1976) as well as Heiko Oberman, *The Harvest of Medieval Theology: Gabriel Biel and Late Medieval Nominalism* (Cambridge: Harvard University Press, 1983).

3. On intention and signification see Ernest A. Moody, *The Logic of William of Occam* (New York, 1934; rpt. New York: Russell and Russell, 1965), esp. chap. 2, "The Logic of Terms," 47–50.

4. See Zuidema, *Philosophie van Occam*, 1:pt. 6 on *God en zijn werk*.

It is difficult to catch the atmosphere of sentiment surrounding this position, precisely because it is an atmosphere and the sentiment does not go to the roots of existence. The Christianity of William is most certainly not based on the *pistis* in the Pauline sense of "the substance of things hoped for," or of an active openness to the transcendental reality. We can understand the sentiment perhaps best as an evolution of Franciscan Christianity; the intramundane imitation of Christ by Saint Francis implies, as we saw, a concentration on the suffering Jesus to the extreme of stigmatization, but it is not very sensitive to the rich pneumatic experience of faith that constitutes the substance of the Christian community. In the case of Saint Francis, his intense experience of creaturely humbleness could blot out with its radiance the impoverishment of other dimensions of Christian experience; in the case of William of Ockham, intramundane Christianity is reduced more clearly to the sincere acceptance of the creed. This reduction to a lower level of intenseness has other characteristic consequences. In the existential experience of faith the sentiment has its dimensions of certainty and wavering, of hardening and opening, of degrees of the *metanoia* and oscillations of its preservation, and so on, but even in the extremes of doubt and rejection the movement of the soul is still determined by the impact of transcendental reality. The attitude of Ockham gives no room to doubt, but it implies a profound understanding of the possibility of unbelief. Faith for man has become a possibility; if God did not work the miracle there would be no faith; the sense of creative, active faith is lost. Ockham can understand that, without the interference of the divine *potestas absoluta*, he might as well not believe.[5]

The term *skepticism*, sometimes used in connection with William, does not characterize the sentiment adequately because it beclouds the historic significance of the phenomenon. In William

---

5. See for this problem Nicola Abbagnano, *Guglielmo di Ockham* (Lanciano, 1931), chap. 9, "La Personalità di Ockham," esp. 340 ff.: "Il vecchio motto 'Credo ut intelligam' perde qui veramente il suo significato, in quanto per Ockham non si tratta più di procedere dalla fede alla ragione, di, esprimere e formulare in, un sistema di concetti il *credo* ecclesiastico, ma si tratta di effettuare l'elaborazione concettuale dei dati che l'esperienze offre" (The old motto, "I believe that I may understand," here truly loses its own meaning insofar as for Ockham it is not so much a question of proceeding from faith to reason, of expressing and formulating in a system of ideas the ecclesiastical credo, but rather of carrying out the conceptual elaboration of the data that experience offers). In this context see Leff, *William of Ockham*.

a great cycle of Western Christianity comes to its end, the cycle that began with the realism of the *York Tracts* and now peters out in the nominalism of the late scholastics. The world has been integrated into the realm of God spiritually, but its structure could not be integrated into the rational system of faith intellectually. The harmonization of the spirit and the intellect had failed. We are not surprised, therefore, to find in William's ominous effort to save faith, out of a wreckage that faith itself had not the strength to save, the very symptoms of the destruction that he tries to counteract. The Averroist conflict between the authorities of faith and reason is overcome, but at the costly price of the admission that the philosophers' argument in such decisive questions as for instance the eternity of the world against creation in time is irrefutable. William admits, in this case, that the argument of Duns Scotus against the assumption of an indefinite series of *causae* and for the necessity of a *causa prima* in time is untenable. He solves the difficulty by confining the intellectual analysis to the natural sphere and exempting the supranatural from its competence. The correct intellectual solution would have been the recognition of the problem of the indefinite series as a dialectical border-problem that does not permit of an answer in unequivocal finite categories. It belongs in the class of problems that were treated by Kant under the title of the "Antinomies of Pure Reason." This solution entails, however, the admission that the theologoumena of this class have no meaning if understood as propositions concerning the empirical structure of the world but draw their validity from another source. Kant called this source "the practical interest"; today we prefer to speak of the expression of fundamental religious experiences in symbols, the symbols drawing their strength from the experiences they express. The solution was probably possible, even at the time of Ockham, considering the tendencies in the Averroist movement supporting it, though it was developed fully only at the end of the nineteenth century, under the pressure of the comparative science of religions, in the modernist movement.

§3. Secular Civilization and the Withdrawal of the Church

But Ockham had to deny himself this solution, and the Catholic Church has ever since refused even the slightest step in this direction. The refusal of William marks the beginning of a withdrawal of the church from the compromise with the world, a withdrawal that was necessitated by an enrichment of the content of the world that threatened to engulf the substance of faith. With the addition of free intellectual activity to the modes of expression of intramundane man in the forms of critical speculation, of critical empirical science, and later of critical history, a new system of ordinates was created that reduced the absoluteness of the creed to a historically relative religion. The critique of reason is existentially compatible with a dogmatic intellectual mysticism; it is not compatible with a historical religion. The historical literalism of Christianity cannot be abandoned at any point without endangering its center: the historical Christ and his reality as the savior of mankind. The attitude adopted by William is symptomatic of the momentous situation that the Christian penetration of the "world," progressing since the foundation of the Western empire, has now to be stopped. Factors have grown in the world that have to remain in the world; the period of imperial Christianity with its, at least attempted, complete integration of the life of man in the life of the *corpus mysticum* had come to an end. An intramundane civilizational process would now run parallel with the Christian civilizational process as organized in the church. The split between the secular world of Western civilization and the Christian became ever wider until it found its great formulation under the pontificate of Pius IX. The *Syllabus Errorum* of 1864 branded it as an error to believe that the Roman pontiff should reconcile himself to, and agree with, "progress, liberalism and contemporary civilization"; furthermore, among others, naturalism, nationalism, indifferentism, socialism, and communism were declared as errors.

The separation of the two streams, the secular and the ecclesiastical, has consequences that are already visible in the work of William and other thinkers of the early fourteenth century. We have noticed in Giles of Rome the demand for the *sacrificium intellectus* in the form of a subordination of intellectual activity to the dogma of faith. In William the demand reappears more cautiously in the form of the recognition of a supranatural sphere beyond the categories of intramundane knowledge. In both cases the question of spiritual authoritarianism also becomes visible, as closely related to the new problem in the life of the church. With Giles the spiritual authority of the church is concentrated in the pope. In the system of William the conception is extended beyond the human sphere into the transcendental: he develops the idea of an absolute authoritarian God who posits the content of faith at his will.

The tension between the independent intellect and the authority of faith changes fundamentally the relations between the church and the temporal sphere because from this point on the temporal sphere becomes increasingly identified with secularism and laicism, in the precise meaning of a realm of human existence that is organized under the authority of the critical intellect. The coordination of the two powers as orders within the one body of Christian mankind gives way to a new order in which the church is on the defensive as an enclave within the process of secular civilization. The result for the church is a hardening and drying up of its intellectual life, for any movement that might touch the dogmatic sphere involves the risk of shaking the system on principle and opening it to the destructive invasion of the secular intellect and, therefore, has to be shunned. As George Santayana has aptly put it in his essay "Modernism and Christianity":[6] the age of partial heresy is past; the age of total heresy has succeeded. With the *Professio Fidei Tridentina* of 1564 the dogmatic movement of the church was practically closed. The first dogma added after the Council of Trent, promulgated by Pius IX in 1854, without support of conciliar authority, was the dogma of the Immaculate Conception. The first council, after three hundred years, was the Vatican Council of 1869–1870, proclaiming the dogma of Papal Infallibility. At the height of the progressive civilizational exuberance of the nineteenth century, an evolution reached its stage of formalization in institution and dogma that was foreshadowed in the sentence of Giles of Rome: "What the pope does may be said to be done by the church." On the secular side we can observe the movement of analogues to the ecclesiastical evolution. The absolute God, the absolute pope, and the absolute faith of Giles of Rome and William of Ockham are followed by the absolute prince, the absolute people, and the absolute enlightened reason; the infallible pope of the nineteenth century is followed by the secular analogues of the leaders who cannot err, in the twentieth. The civilizational schism made necessary, finally, an ordering of the relations between the representative

6. [*The Works of George Santayana* (New York: Scribners, 1937), 7:24–49.]

institutions of the two processes. The problem of the relations between the church and the states as the secular power units became
increasingly important, producing the various phenomena of the
established church, the disestablished church, the free churches
and sects, religious toleration, freedom of worship, the subordination of the churches to the law of the states, the concordats, and
so on. Through the whole evolution of the schism the Catholic
Church, however, maintains its claim to be the arbiter of Western
civilization and insists on its demand to eliminate the process of
secular civilization from history. The principal events marking this
attitude of the church are the foundation of the Society of Jesus
(1540), the organization of the Universal Inquisition (1542), the
Index Prohibitorum Librorum since 1559, the formulation of the
papal right to interfere in temporal matters by Cardinal Bellarmine
(*De potestate summi pontificis in rebus temporalibus*, 1610); and,
after the eclipse of the late eighteenth century, the reestablishment
of the Jesuit Order, the Inquisition and the *Index* in 1814, and the
earlier mentioned *Syllabus Errorum* of 1864 claiming for the church
the control of culture, science, and the educational system, rejecting the idea of toleration and freedom of conscience, and claiming
the independence of the church from the control of the state.[7]

§4. The Last Phase of Franciscan Spiritualism

From the work of William we have isolated the authoritarian strain
and given considerable attention to it because it is so frequently
overlooked. The ideas of the period are so complex that the temptation to simplify is almost irresistible. In the case of William there
is a great temptation to overstress his achievement as a critical

---

7. This chapter was written before the publication of the papal encyclical *Divine Afflante Spiritus*, of September 30, 1943. It would be premature to speculate at this time on the probable practical consequences that the encyclical will have for the relations between the church and secular civilization, but it should be clear that this momentous document reverses in decisive points the attitude of the Catholic Church that has contributed to the widening gulf. [This note seems to have been added to the manuscript by Voegelin at a later date. He was apparently struck by Pius XII's encyclical that reversed the church's opposition to modern methods of biblical scholarship. It was notable as one of several early indications of the shift in attitude toward the modern world that culminated in the work of the Second Vatican Council. The most representative statement from the council was *Gaudium et Spes*, or *The Pastoral Constitution in the Modern World*, in which a sympathetic engagement with the modern world was proposed in place of an earlier defensiveness.]

philosopher and to see in his work primarily the beginnings of an agnostic secular critique of reason. The temptation is great because William was not a papalist but, on the contrary, was opposed to the very tendency toward papal authoritarianism that we indicated in the preceding paragraph. The interests of the Franciscan Order drove him into the opposition, and the ideas he evolved for an institutional reorganization of the church even make it possible to classify him as a forerunner of the Conciliar movement. But the authority that he denied to the ecclesiastical hierarchy and its head, he arrogated for the trained, intellectual theologian, that is, to the type produced in an exemplary manner by the mendicant orders. We have to realize that the medieval political tensions do not run only between the spiritual and temporal powers as embodied in the hierarchical church and the temporal territorial princes, but that the militant orders, military as well as mendicant, constitute a third, though minor, power that potentially may clash in open rivalry with the other two. By the beginning of the fourteenth century in two instances the tension had reached the breaking point: in the earlier discussed clash between the Templars and Philip the Fair and, almost contemporaneously, in the clash between the Franciscans and the papacy. The result was the same in both cases. The sovereign military order had to give way to the national monarchy, and the intellectual authoritarianism of the Franciscan theologians succumbed to the authoritarianism of the church.

The immediate conflict between the Franciscans and the papacy originated in the renewal of the struggle over the idea of poverty on a new level of argument. The strictly spiritual idea of Franciscanism had burst out again, and for the last time, in Peter Olivi. His *Postilla in Apocalypsim* of 1295 was the last great attempt to understand the *novum et solemne saeculum* that was to follow the abolition of the feudal church in Joachitic categories and to see its content in the evolution of the Franciscan Order, as the new *corpus mysticum*, toward victory over the dying world. It is probable that the ideas of Olivi influenced Dante in the years 1287–1289 when Olivi was a lecturer in Florence; the Joachitic *renovatio vitae evangelicae* and Dante's *vita nuova* are closely related. The broader effectiveness, however, made itself felt after Olivi's death, in 1289, when he was worshiped as a saint by spiritual groups in Provence. To the church the movement seemed serious enough to warrant a ruthless struggle of extermination, ending in the condemnation of Olivi.

After this defeat a group of Franciscan Spirituals, led by the general of the order, Michael of Cesena, resumed the discussion of poverty, but now on the level of juristic argument. The struggle assumed European proportions when Michael of Cesena and William of Ockham escaped from the papal prison in Avignon in 1328 and sought the protection of the emperor in Pisa. The struggle about Franciscan poverty became part of the struggle between John XXII and Lewis the Bavarian. The new debate was opened by a 1331 circular letter by Michael of Cesena, in which he declares heretical twelve articles of the papal bull *Quia vir reprobus*. Some of the principal articles found heretical were the following: Christ had the *universale dominium omnium rerum temporalium* as a true king and lord temporal; he had also particular property; he had never counseled to the apostles the complete renunciation of all property; he had left to the apostles private property and common property in immovables; he has never taken a vow of poverty; the vow of the orders living without private property does not extend to the necessities of life. The articles of the pope as well as the protest of the general show that the discussion of poverty had definitely become a legal dispute. The Christian substance was getting thinner and thinner; in the great process of despiritualization of Christianity we have seen the hand of God in the translation of empire change into a legal transaction, we have seen the spiritual reform of the church hardening into ecclesiastical legalism, and we see now the life of Christ and the apostles discussed in terms of private and communal property. Both partners to the struggle were wrong; neither is the kingdom of Christ a temporal principality bristling with regalia as the papal legalist wanted it, nor is the eschatological indifference toward property of the early Christians a form of communism as the general of the Franciscans would have it in the interest of the intramundane poverty ideal of his order. Nevertheless, the struggle has in the history of ideas the importance of having started the debate over early Christian communism that is going on even today.[8]

<hr/>

8. For the controversy and for the data concerning Ockham's life see Abbagnano, *Gugliemo di Ockham*, chap. 1, "La Vita e le Opere." See also C. K. Brampton's introduction to *Gulielmi de Ockham Epistola ad Fratres Minores* (Oxford: Oxford University Press, 1929). More recent light has been shed by Jürgen Miethke, *Ockhams Weg zur Sozialphilosophie* (Berlin: De Groyter, 1969); A. S. McGrade, *The Political Thought of William of Ockham* (Cambridge: Cambridge University Press,

§5. William's Method of Politics

The circular letter of Michael of Cesena was answered by a papalist, and this answer in turn provoked a great critical commentary by William of Ockham, the *Opus Nonaginta Dierum* of 1332. Before we enter, however, on the analysis of this and the further voluminous works of William, a word is necessary concerning the proper approach.[9] William did not develop a system of politics but dealt with the political questions of his time incidentally to the larger theological problems. His great effectiveness was due less to his political positions—against the papal *plenitudo potestatis* or for a conciliar construction of church-government—than to his methods of dealing with problems of law and government; a listing of his opinions is, therefore, considerably less important than an understanding of the reasons that induced him to adopt them.

His method in politics represents the same combination of nominalism and fideism that characterizes his general philosophical position, but only on the occasion of its application to political questions does it reveal its full significance. The appearance of nominalism in politics presents us with a problem similar to that of the appearance of psychology in the period of Greek disintegration. Psychology proved, with regard to the phenomena of the mind, an approach that became specifically important when the substance of a community dissolves and, as a consequence, the anxiety of man is set free and finds its expression in a predominance of individual reactions and urges in human conduct. Nominalism, while always

---

1974); C. Dolcini, *Il Pensiero Politico di Michele da Cesena, 1328–1338* (Ravenna: Faenza-Fratelli Lega, 1977).

9. The following editions of Ockham's works have been used: (1) *Dialogus*, in Melchior Goldast, *Monarchia S. Romani Imperii*, 2:394–957 (*Pars Prima*, 394 ff.; *Pars Secunda*, 740 ff.; III.I *De Potestate Papae et Cleri*, 772 ff.; III.II *De Potestate et Iuribus Romani Imperii*, 868 ff.); (2) *Opus Nonaginta Dierum*, in ibid., 2:993–1236; (3) *Octo Quaestiones de Potestate Papae*, in *Guillelmi de Ockham Opera Politica*, ed. J. G. Sikes (Manchester: University of Manchester Press, 1940), vol. 1; (4) *Guillelmi de Occam Breviloquium de Potestate Papae*, ed. L. Baudry, Etudes de Philosophie Médiévale, ed. Étienne Gilson, XXIV (Paris, 1937); (5) *The De Imperatorum et Pontificum Potestate of William of Ockham*, ed. C. Kenneth Brampton (Oxford: Oxford University Press, 1927); (6) *Gulielmi de Ockham Epistola ad Fratres Minores*, ed. with notes and an introduction by C. Kenneth Brampton (Oxford: Oxford University Press, 1929). More recent translations: *A Short Discourse on Tyrannical Government* and *A Letter to the Friars Minor and Other Writings*, ed. Arthur Stephen McGrade, trans. John Kilcullen (New York: Cambridge University Press, 1992, 1995).

a theoretical possibility, gains its importance, just as psychology, as an interpretation of political reality when the substance of the community is losing its force and, as a consequence, the relational aspects come to the fore. The clearest symptom of the change in legal theory is the shift of accent from the content of the just order to the question of ultimate interpretation. As long as the members and groups of a community accept in fundamental agreement an objective order, the inevitable dissensions may lead to serious clashes, as we have seen in the Investiture Struggle, but there is no disruptive doubt that they all live *under* the order and are equidistant to it. If, however, the sentiment of the common bond is disturbed by tensions arising from the growing sentiments of particular communities—such as the church, the national kingdoms, the sects, and the orders—the decisional element of authority is experienced with a new sharpness, and the question becomes paramount of who will have the final decision in a conflict and why. In the theories of William the relational outlook is all-pervasive, in the same manner as in the controversy between John XXII and Michael of Cesena; still more important than the questions of *what* is heretical and *who* is a heretic is the question of who will *decide* who is a heretic. The answer for Ockham is clear; the ultimate decision rests with virtuous and expert theologians who cannot be moved from a recognized truth by any argument, even if an angel from Heaven tried to persuade them *(Dialogus)*. The most interesting problem for a nominalistic theory of law is not the normal functioning of the order, but the emergency case of its disruption and the emergency power that will make the decisions to hold it together.

The theory of William, however, is not a case of pure nominalism. His nominalism has the purpose of preserving intact the structure of the faith against Averroist naturalism and even against such elements in Thomism as seemed to endanger the orthodox doctrine. As a consequence, we find side by side with the acute analysis of customary law and of decisionism pieces of doctrine that had been pushed into the background by the rationalism of Saint Thomas. In many respects the theory of William appears more "medieval" than the Thomistic theory. This mixture of a post-Thomistic nominalism and a pre-Thomistic dogmatism has frequently puzzled historians to the degree that they found the "real" opinion of William unascertainable, while a more recent

study arrives at the conclusion "that no really essential difference exists between Ockham and Aquinas" on the questions of
natural law, and "that it is on the whole erroneous to extend the
nominalistic-realistic schism to embrace their respective theories
of natural law."[10] Both attitudes reflect the despair that Ockham is
not as nominalistic as he should be, and insofar they are justified;
but we cannot accept either the thesis of the obscurity of Ockham,
or the thesis that there is no essential difference between his legal
theory and the Thomistic.

§6. Theory of Law

Ockham has, indeed, a theory of natural law—which he could not
have if he were a strict nominalist who deems the substance of
reason inaccessible—but it is not the Thomistic theory of a natural
rational order of human relations. He never develops his theory in a
clear systematic form, but we can notice unmistakably the revival
of the older idea of "relative natural law" that governs the state
of fallen man, in contrast with the absolute order of reason that
governs the paradisiacal state. The idea is implied in Ockham's
assumption that the actual order of human relations is obligatory,
as willed by God, though it is not the ideal order. In addition we
can notice a revival of Seneca's critique of civilization in the more
radical manner of *Epistola XC*, which views the actual order as
the product of human depravity. Under this second aspect the legal
order is man-made and consists, at least predominantly, of human
positive law as distinguished from natural law.

From the blending of the two ideas result complications of terminology that are all the more confusing because of the incidental
treatment the problems receive. The paradisiacal state of innocence
is a state of reasonable *dominium* over the world *(temporalia)*
without resistance; it is a state without violence and, therefore,
without private property rights, which ultimately would require
defense by force. The state of fallen man, governed by a variety of
laws, is opposed to this state of natural equity. The *Opus Nonaginta
Dierum* distinguished between the *jus fori* (right in law court) and
the *jus poli* (right of heaven or natural right). The *jus fori* is the

10. Max A. Shepard, "William of Occam and the Higher Law," *American Political
Science Review* 26 (1932): 1005–23 and 27 (1933): 24–38.

property order after the division of the originally common *tempo-ralia;*[11] it is a stratum of law preceding in time and ranking higher in order than the civil law enacted by rulers. Insofar as the property order precedes the political order, it is *jus gentium* in the specific sense of a customary law binding the princes; it can be broken only in an emergency by the prince or by the consent of all mortals. The *jus poli* is the natural equity[12] that permits the breaking of the order in an exceptional case such as the appropriation of the necessities of life. The "natural equity" is the only remnant of natural law in the strict sense in William's system.[13] But he uses the term *natural law*, nevertheless, to cover the man-made law of the *jus gentium;* and he even goes so far as to extend the term to any human enactment that is not contrary to evident reason.[14] We have, therefore, to distinguish between a natural law of the state of innocence and a natural law of the fallen state. The natural law of the fallen state is for the larger part man-made law; within the man-made law there is a distinction between a prepolitical customary *jus gentium*, including the property order, characterized as a natural, higher law, and the enacted civil law. And, finally, the fallen state is governed by the principle of natural equity, by the reason of fallen man as against the pure reason of the state of innocence.

§7. The Order of the World and the Order of Poverty

The intricate legal theory loses its appearance of confused termi-nology as soon as we go beyond the mere classification of types of

---

11. *Opus Nonaginta Dierum,* chap. 65, p. 1110, lines 27 ff.
12. Ibid., lines 53 ff.
13. Ibid., chap. 92, p. 1150, lines 11 ff. Ockham distinguishes the three *aequitates naturales:* (1) quae fuisset in statu innocentiae; (2) quae debet esse inter homines in omnibus sequentibus rationem; (3) quae est inter homines pronos ad dissentiendum et male agendum (*natural equalities:* [1] which had been in a state of innocence; [2] which ought to be among men in all those who follow reason; [3] which is among men who tend to dissent and misconduct).
14. *Dialogus,* pt. III, tract II, bk. III.6, distinguishes three natural laws: (1) quod est conforme rationi naturali; (2) quod servandum est ab illis, qui sola aequitate naturali absque omni consuetudine vel constitutione humana utuntur; (3) quod ex jure gentium vel aliquo facto humano evidenti ratione colligitur ([1] which is conformed to natural reason; [2] which is to be preserved by those who make use only of natural equality without all custom or human constitution; [3] which is gathered together by evident reason from the law of nations or some human act). See particularly *Dialogus,* p. 933, lines 51 ff.

law and observe their function in the solution of problems. The principal problem for William is the relation between the order of the world and the order of poverty in imitation of Christ. The order of the world is fundamentally the order of unredeemed man based on force; the life of the true Christian will have to imitate the life of Christ, who did not assume a *dominium* over the world—of which the Jews falsely accused him—but lived without property. The life in poverty has become the life without property, and only now, under the influence of juristic categories, emerges a clear distinction between a worldly and a monastic morality.[15] The tearing of this gap between the worldly sphere and the true Christian life unfolds its full consequences only in the Great Reformation. The order of the world is established as an autonomous human sphere outside the Christian order in the strict sense, and the Christian order is brought nearer to a monastic, ascetic conduct of life. The medieval temporal-spiritual double order is broken up into the two orders of a non-Christian politico-economic order and a Christian ascetic discipline. As a result, the order of the world will follow from now on its own principles without regard to the Christian order of life, or an attempt must be made to keep it within bounds through regulation from the monastic position. Both possibilities are realized in the Reformation of the sixteenth century. The world as the sphere of compulsion was gravely neglected in the idea of Luther and practically left to shift for itself, with the exception of the counsel of disobedience in case the secular authority should be used to command anything against the law of God. Calvin, on the other hand, made the attempt to submit the conduct in the world to Christian discipline, without success in the long run, for the world broke loose from his discipline and retained of it only an added tenseness in the pursuit of its own ends. Ockham does not attempt in his work to connect the theory of the two orders systematically with his fundamental nominalistic-fideistic dichotomy, but it is obvious that the political dichotomy reflects the same tendency of thought as the philosophical.[16] An insight into this connection will contribute appreciably to an understanding of the deeper roots of

---

15. See on this point Dempf, *Sacrum imperium,* 515 ff. This whole chapter is greatly indebted to Dempf's brilliant analysis of William's work.

16. This statement should be qualified, however, in light of the fact that precisely in the discussion of Christ's refusal to accept the *dominium* of the world, Occam introduces the theory of the *potestas absoluta* and *potestas ordinata* of God. See *Opus*

the Reformation problems in the sentiments and social categories created in the fourteenth century. Retrospectively the dichotomy of Ockham reveals more clearly the intramundane character of the spiritualism of Saint Francis: the conformance with Christ has evolved over the new *corpus mysticum* of the *Evangelium Aeternum* into a rule of conduct that can be discussed in legal categories. From the First Reform of the spiritual power, understood as one of the orders in Christian mankind, we are moving toward the Second Reform with its intramundane tendency of absorbing the layman into the spiritual order, by punishment of ejecting him into a non-Christian worldly order (which has taken the place of the former Christian temporal order) if he resists such absorption.

§8. The Pope and the Church

William's second great problem is closely connected with the first. The true Christian order renounces worldly dominion. Hence the power of the pope cannot have the character of a *plenitudo potestatis*, comprising the direction of political affairs in addition to that of the spiritual and claiming a *dominium generale* over all property. The papal power is the subject matter of the first treatise of *Dialogus* part III; the principal results are resumed in Ockham's last work, the *De Imperatorum et Pontificum Potestate* of 1346/47.[17] If the pope had the plenitude of power, the *lex Christiana* would be a law of servitude, worse than the Mosaic (*Imperatorum* I.5). The power of the pope does not extend to *saecularia* (II.2); nor to the imposition of supererogatory works (III); nor to the rights and liberties of man that even Christ did not touch (IV); and in politics the pope has no right of translation of rulership, no right of approval with regard to duly elected kings (XX.1). His functions are confined to the preaching of the word of God and to his supreme judgeship over all the faithful in spiritual matters (X, XVI.2), tempered by the counsel of the wise and by divine and natural law.[18] The temporal

---

Nonaginta Dierum, chap. 95, p. 1171, lines 14 ff.; and Dempf, *Sacrum imperium*, 514 ff.

17. *De Imperatorum of William of Ockham*, ed. Brampton.

18. For a more detailed analysis of Ockham's theory of papal power see Philostheus Boehner, O.F.M., "Ockham's Political Ideas," *Review of Politics* 5 (1943): 462–87. A more extensive study is W. Kolmel, *Wilhelm Ockham und seine Kirchenpolitischen Schriften* (Essen: Ludgerus Verlag Wingen, 1962).

power of the pope does not derive from Christ but has been acquired through human concession, voluntary submission, and explicit or tacit consent. Concerning temporal powers, however, no absolute doctrine is possible. Hence Ockham proceeds to his unique analysis in Aristotelian categories, of the best form of government for the church (*Dialogus* III.I.II).

The best form is the rulership of a monarch who governs according to his wisdom, unbound by positive law, but limited by due regard for the common weal and natural law. But, following Aristotle, Ockham finds that such a monarchy does not exist in his day. The second best form would be a monarchy limited by positive law, but it is possible that under certain conditions an aristocracy would be the best form of government. An alternative to a universal monarchy would be an aristocracy of national kings as the world government. This idea is then transferred to the church, and Ockham envisages the possibility of an aristocratic church-government by a group of national popes (III.I.I, chap. 20, p. 807). The suggestion is important from several aspects. First of all, the problem of church organization is understood as a field of human action; Ockham proves, indeed, at length that the law of the papal decretal with regard to organizational matters is human law. The gentle distinction of Saint Francis between a life in conformance with Christ and a life in conformance with the Roman Church has unfolded its full consequence. The only traditional element retained by Ockham is the conviction that Peter had spiritual primacy over the other apostles and that consequently the Roman pontiff has a spiritual supremacy over the other Christian churches. Of equal importance are the political implications. The experience of a universal Christian mankind has become so weak that a universal monarchy and papacy no longer seem as necessary as they were for Dante. The national sentiment is strong enough to conceive of at least Western Christianity as a free association of nations under their temporal and spiritual leaders. And it should be understood, furthermore, that in the given political situation the implied attack is directed against the French hegemonic policy and the papacy of Avignon under French influence. The sentiments of William, on this occasion, no longer run along the line of tension between the empire and France, but express rather the claim of the rising new nations, particularly the English, to a share in the European balance of powers, both spiritual and temporal.

§9. The Empire

The idea of a world government through an aristocracy of national kings and popes is, however, for William not more than a possibility that merits discussion. The emperor still exists strongly, and William lives under his protection. The second treatise of *Dialogus* part III *(De juribus romani imperii)* deals with the law of the Roman empire. Ockham's legal distinctions now show their value in the construction of the intricacies of secular public law. The treatise of the church had reduced the power of the pope by the radical separation of the "world" from the true Christian order. The treatise on the empire reduces imperial power as well as royal power by subordinating the political order proper to the customary *jus gentium* that precedes all rulership in rank and time. The cause of political order is the depraved nature of man, which requires compulsion; the cause of the Roman empire was the necessity of giving order to a world sinking into anarchy *(Dialogus* III.II.I, chap. 1, p. 869, lines 54 ff.). The emperor does not owe his position to papal sanction, but derives his power indirectly from God and directly from the people—or its proper representatives, such as the electors.[19] Neither a papal coronation in the case of the emperor nor an anointment in the case of national kings adds to their power, which derives from consent *(Octo Quaestiones,* Q.V, in Goldast II, pp. 369 ff.). The thaumaturgic faculties of the French and English kings in particular are not due to the efficacy of anointment by the ecclesiastical authority (p. 373). The strong accent on the element of popular consent seems to point to the influence of English institutions on Ockham; in his system, however, it forms part of the general theory of the subordination of rulership to the law originating in mankind at large. The emperor is not *legibus solutus* but has to respect the customary institutions, which are not of his making. The legal order of property and persons cannot be altered by him, with the exception of an emergency where the public interest may justify an interference with private rights; the subjects are not his or any ruler's slaves, and their property is not his. Max A. Shepard[20] attaches special importance to the argument that even

---

19. For a closer analysis of the construction of secular power see Boehner, "Ockham's Political Ideas," 477–80.
20. "William of Occam and the Higher Law II," 31 ff.

the people could not transfer unlimited powers to the ruler because the politically organized people have no power over the single individual and his rights; only a general communal consent can change the customary property order. While a universal monarchy has obvious advantages for the securing of world peace and order, and while the emperor has a de jure supremacy over the national kings, Ockham is careful to respect the factual order that has arisen in the Western world and is part of the *jus gentium*. The ordering power of the emperor cannot abolish the law of occupations, wars, servitudes, and so on, so that, as a consequence, the order growing from the adventures in power politics of the national kings is as safely beyond his reach as the property order of the subjects.

§10. Reduction of the Substance to Relations

We have arranged the argument of William in such a manner as to make visible the chain of distinctions and reductions that is all but lost in his voluminous, discursive work. First the true Christian, propertyless, spiritual order is set off against the world at large; then the spiritual element in papal power is distinguished from the temporal; then the order of the church from the order of secular politics at large; in the order of secular politics the imperial power from the national royal; and, finally, the order of rulership from the prepolitical order of the individual human beings. We thus arrive at a survey of the ultimate forces in the universe of powers at the time of William: the Roman pontiff and the emperor, the national kings (and potentially the national popes), the consent of the people in the organized polity, and the personal and property rights of single individuals. The *sacrum imperium* is disassociated into its component power elements, and the pneumatic substance with its charismatic order is thinned out to the point of disappearance so that only a relational skeleton remains. In spite of the reduction of the substance to a system of relations, however, the terms of the relations are still parts of a Christian mankind. The nominalistic analysis stops short of the miracle of Christian faith. Hence we have to return now to the initial problem of the mutual accusations of heresy between the pope and the Franciscan Spirituals. In the discussion of the questions of who will render a decision on heresy in the emergency case and how is Christian mankind to deal with a heretical pope, the analysis of relations is linked back to its beginnings in the problem of the true Christian order. This set of questions is presented in the *Dialogus,* part I, of 1334.

§11. The Power of Ultimate Decision—The Council

The center of the problem is the infallibility of the pope and of the general council. The discussion of this question is carefully prepared by an analysis of the nature of heresy. In order to maintain the authority of the theologians in matters of heresy against the canon lawyers, the function of the canonists has to be restricted to the interpretation of decretals and canons and to judicial procedure, while the content of Christian doctrine is reserved for the province of the theological experts (*Dialogus* I.I, chaps. 11–15, pp. 407–10). The pope and the general council have, of course, the authority to define doctrine, but they have to arrive at the content of a decision on the basis of the proper sources. These sources are the Scripture, the recognized tradition of the apostolic doctrine, and new revelations that have to be confirmed by miracles (I.II, chap. 5, pp. 415 ff.). The position is fideistic and intellectual; the church authorities have no power of creative interpretation. The question of whether a doctrine is orthodox or heretical has to be debated by the expert theologians who know the sources. With the transposition of the problem of orthodoxy and heresy to the plane of intellectual debate, it becomes impossible that any single authority within the church should be infallible. The promise of infallibility, that Christ will be with his church, applies only to the church as a whole, that is to the full congregation of the faithful. In a detailed analysis (I.V) infallibility is, therefore, denied in succession to the pope (chaps. 1–5), to the college of cardinals (chaps. 6–10), to the Roman Church (chaps. 11–24), to the general council (chaps. 25–28), to the whole of the clergy (chaps. 29–31), to all men and all women, because the promise of Christ might be fulfilled at a time only through children (chaps. 32–35). We can observe in this relentless reduction the same tendency to dissolve the substance of the spirit into the relations of the component parts of the community that we saw in the theory of law and politics.

As a consequence of this dissolution the emergency case becomes visible: who will exert the sovereignty of the whole church against a heretical pope? In the first place the whole congregation of the faithful would be called upon; but as the whole church cannot be assembled, the authority devolves on a general council, in further sequence to the diocese in which the pope resides, and if the clergy fails, it devolves to the laymen (I.VI to chap. 64 inclusive). The intervention of the laymen is, however, considered only as a last resort, based on the principle of equity; the proper authorities on heresy are above all the expert theologians. A general council, thus, will be the principal agency in the condemnation of a heretical pope and, in order to make it as closely expressive of the congregational opinion as possible, Ockham develops a procedure very much resembling what we should call today a popular initiative. The parishes have to send representatives to the bishop's council or a royal parliament; these bodies in their turn elect the representatives for a general council; laymen as well as women may be delegated (I.VI, chap. 85, pp. 603 ff.). The models for this suggestion could be found in the English institutions and in the procedure for the representative assemblies of the mendicant orders. We have come down again to the ultimate component parts of Christian mankind and to a system of representative relations as the source of spiritual authority.

§12. Conclusion

The political theories of William have all too frequently been misunderstood, and his importance as a political thinker has, as a consequence, been underrated. It is quite possible, of course, to find that his classifications of law do not differ appreciably from those current in the Middle Ages in general; it is equally possible to see in his theory of the church and the empire a continuation of the interminable discussion about *sacerdotium* and *imperium*; it is possible, furthermore, to classify him as an interesting forerunner of the Conciliar movement, but no more, and to say that his suggestions concerning a general council do not differ markedly from those of Marsilius of Padua. It is possible; but only if one chooses to overlook the essentials. The key to the understanding of William is his nominalistic-fideistic dualism, stemming from the early Franciscan position and prognosticating the great future cleavage between the church and the laicistic civilization. The traditional legal categories do no more than cover the nominalistic dissolution of the *sacrum imperium* into its component parts. And the conciliar suggestions are not simply an appeal to the general council—for the general council is denied infallibility, just as much as the pope—but have to be taken as the solution of an emergency case, with the hope that the broad popular basis will make the council expressive of the true spirit. Even then the reservation of the ultimate independence of the theologian preserves the conviction "that the multitude, as a rule, errs," and "that very often one solitary man can put all the rest to flight" (*Imperatorum*, p. 4). His faith compels William to discuss politics under the assumption that the traditional spiritual and temporal powers still exist substantially; but his nominalism so thoroughly dissolves this substance into relations that, indeed, only a miracle of God's *potestas absoluta* can prevent this system of relations from breaking into pieces. The reduction of the Christian pneumatic substance to a manifold of individual subjects, political peoples, kings, emperors, heretical popes, fallible councils, presumptuous canonists, and battling theologians is the convincing symptom of the internal dissolution of the *sacrum imperium*, to be followed by the successive phases of external disintegration; and it is the expression of the forces that will dominate the scene of the future: the individuals and their rights, the nations and their kings, the spiritual revolt of the monks and theologians, of the laymen and their congregations against the authority of the church, the future national churches, and the reliance on the Scripture as the source of doctrine in the Reformation. It would be overstretching the nominalistic element in Ockham's work if we should say, without reservations, that he was the first postmedieval, modern philosopher; but one may give him this title with the qualification made necessary by his fideism.

19

The English National Polity

Under the heading of the English national polity we intend to deal with a group of phenomena that cannot very well be classified as ideas and still less as theories, but that are, nevertheless, of the greatest importance in a history of political ideas because they form the substratum that stimulates a new evocation. The high and late Middle Ages witnessed the sentimental and institutional integration of the social bodies that later appeared as the Western national states. Their growth presents a problem of the same type as the growth of the Western empire; namely, a factual situation of sentiments and institutions developing over centuries before the idea of the new political entity could be evoked in a decisive manner. In Chapter 15, "French Kingship," we have dealt with the integrating function of the thaumaturgic royal person, culminating in the acute exuberance of French national consciousness at the beginning of the fourteenth century. In the English case the function of kingship was balanced more evenly than in France by the growth of institutions that incorporated the estates and communes into the apparatus of government. While the national growth of France received its characteristics from the king, the royal administration, and the absolute state, the English growth was characterized by the early formation of the strong national political society that overpowered the royal administration in the great struggle of the seventeenth century. The English institutions became the models that determined our modern ideas of representation and parliamentary and constitutional government. In an analysis of these institutions, as far as they grew from the thirteenth to the fifteenth centuries, it will be most suitable, therefore, to use the English case as the center of orientation and to deal with the parallel phenomena in other countries by comparing and contrasting them with the English pattern.

§1. Insularity—Absence of Disturbing Factors

For the facts of English constitutional history we have to refer the reader to the excellent treatises on the subject. We do not intend to review them in even a cursory fashion but shall rather clarify the interaction of sentiments, institutions, and ideas. In order to arrive at an adequate presentation of the problem we first have to tear away the veil of teleological symbolism that still covers historical reality. Although more recent studies have contributed much to a more realistic interpretation of the processes with which we have to deal, our general picture of English government is still determined disturbingly by a teleological approach to its history. As the starting point for the interpretation, a highly complex modern compound is selected, consisting of a rich cluster of institutional accretions that receive a semblance of unity from late evocative symbols such as "representative government," "parliamentary system," "constitutional government," and so on; the historical analysis then tries to penetrate to the "origins" of the modern compound in order to show the evolutionary process that connects the two terms of the series. The metaphysical premise of this approach is the assumption of germinal institutions, endowed with an entelechy, evolving or growing into the modern differentiated form like an organism. This approach can derive a certain empirical justification from a comparison of the English evolution with the more fitful, revolutionary history of governmental institutions in other countries, but beyond this point of comparison the conception is more apt to obscure the issues than to illuminate them.

No growth toward a perfect end is discernible in the history of the English polity. The general structure of the process in which the polity grows toward its final phase of national consciousness is the same as in the continental instances. The sentiment of social unity becomes slowly accentuated; the strongest integrating factor is kingship, aided by geographical, ethical, linguistic, and general civilizational factors, until the counteracting forces of the diffuse field of feudal relations are overcome and, after the painful operation of the Hundred Years War, the spatial delimitation of the social unit is approximately fixed. Under the pressure of sentiment the institutional elements that are introduced at various points in time then converge toward an integrated system of governmental functions; and, in a last stage, the appropriate formulas are found by which the compounds of institutional elements receive their symbolic fixation. In one respect only does the general structure of the English process differ from that of similar processes in other countries: in the English sequence of sentiment, institutional integration, and symbolic formula there appears a curious time lag between the growth of institutions and their symbolization. The Anglican church development moved ahead of the Gallican, but Gallicanism as an idea developed earlier than Anglicanism; the English constitutional achievements of the seventeenth century gained their full evocative force only in the French doctrines of the eighteenth century; and the constitutional evolution after the Settlement reached its belated formulation only by the middle of the nineteenth century through Bagehot. This peculiarity is usually accounted for by a passing reference to the English national character and its reluctance to indulge in philosophical speculation. The explanation, however, overlooks the fact that the "national character" is a type constructed precisely out of such traits as the time lag of symbolization; this time lag itself requires an explanation unless we choose to fall back on racial character as the biological constant. Resorting to blind constants of this kind is faulty method; we have to exhaust first the possibilities of intelligible causation, and the general factor that offers itself as the most probable cause of the peculiar phenomenon is the English geographical position in its two aspects, first of insularity, and second of peripheral position in relation to the main territory of Western civilization. It is fair to assume that, due to geographical isolation, the internal and external tensions of England were less strong than those of the continental countries, and that consequently stimuli for intellectual activity were less plentiful in England. At the court of Lewis of Bavaria, for instance, the colony of distinguished foreign malcontents like Marsilius of Padua, Jean of Jandun, William of Ockham, Michael of Cesena, and others formed a cosmopolitan group that was not paralleled in England at the time. This view is confirmed by the consideration that, in the period following the Norman conquest with its ethnic mixture and international tribulation, England was leading in Western intellectual life through such men as Anselm of Canterbury and the Anonymous of York.

The assumption that the English evolution is relatively poor in tensions and stimuli can be substantiated by historical facts. The quality of organic growth that has always struck historians as peculiarly English seems, indeed, to be due to the fact that there are fewer complications there than on the Continent. Grandeur of style can be achieved in politics as in art by economy of means. We have referred in an earlier context to the rationalizing effects of the Norman conquest on English institutions. We have to say now with more precision that the situation of the conquest made possible a stronger concentration of royal power and a corresponding weakening of the power of the vassals. As a consequence, a first source of continental difficulties was missing in England: that is, the territorial entrenchment of feudal lords that was overcome finally in France only in the seventeenth century and lingered in Germany into the recent past. Second: the direct grip of the royal administration on the court system achieved early the unification of local customs into the English common law so that in England the continental diversification of the *coutumes* is missing that had to be overcome by the introduction of Roman law and later of the codes as the common law of larger national areas. Its geographical remoteness, third, preserved England from the entanglements through imperial ambitions that absorbed so much of the French efforts in the thirteenth and fourteenth centuries and proved the undoing of a German national kingship; and fourth it preserved her from the problems of control over the papacy that accompanied the French and German imperial efforts. Fifth: the simplification and self-concentration of political existence indicated by these traits enabled England to slide so slowly out of the connection with the Roman Church that the formal separation was comparatively painless. The English polity could, therefore, remain, sixth, on the outskirts of the Reformation struggle that convulsed France and Germany in the sixteenth century, until in the seventeenth the issue had so thoroughly fused with the political that the dogmatic aspects had become secondary; the suppression of the intellectual and spiritual issues was so successful that in the nineteenth century Cardinal Newman's famous *Tract Ninety* could arouse the indignation of the anti-Roman wing of the church by the discovery that the *Thirty-Nine Articles,* drafted with consummate statesmanship in the sixteenth century, did not contradict the teaching of the Roman Church, and that England could be aroused in the 1830s and 1840s by the exciting problem of whether the Established Church was Catholic or Protestant. Seventh: the insular position made it possible, furthermore, for England to dispense with a military establishment on the continental scale, after the country had withdrawn from European expansion since the latter half of the fifteenth century. And, finally, we should mention that the English Civil Service has never developed into continental proportions and influence.

§2. The Integrating Sentiments—The Magna Carta

It is a comparatively simple task to list the traits that are absent from, or underdeveloped in, the English polity. It is much less easy to describe the structure of sentiments that dominate the otherwise unencumbered field. The amount of materials for understanding the critical period is large, but still not large enough to furnish answers to all the questions we should like to ask. Our picture of the process has to be in part hypothetical. There is no doubt that kingship and feudal loyalty are the strongest integrating factors up to the fourteenth century. We have to rank second the religious reenforcement lent to the royal function through papal support beginning with the conquest. We have to rank this support second because it could add to the legitimacy of the royal enterprise when it was given, but could not decisively impair feudal cohesion when it was withdrawn. The murder of Saint Thomas à Becket and the practical ineffectiveness of the excommunication of John Lackland by Innocent III indicate the proportionate strength of feudal and religious sentiments. The national sentiment, finally, ranks third in chronological order but, in perspective, surpasses the other two in importance.

The interplay of the three forces—the feudal, the religious, and the national—can be observed well on the occasion of the struggle that culminated in the granting of the Magna Carta in 1215. The source of the troubles that required a settlement was the enormous weight of royal power, permitting encroachments on the traditional order through abuses of the forest and fishery administration, through the denial and sale of justice, through interference with feudal rights on the occasion of the death of a feudatory, through serious interference with the private lives of the nobility by the demanding of hostages, and so on. The gradual increase of such abuses in the preceding reigns and their rapid increase in the early years of John had the cumulative effect of rousing discontent to the point where under able leadership it could be turned into a force of

resistance against further royal encroachments. The more immediate occasion of resistance, the demand of scutage for the French
war and its refusal by the northern barons, shows, however, that
sentiments other than those of feudal tradition entered into play.
The legal contention that service outside England or the payment
of scutage for a foreign war did not form part of the obligations of
a tenant-in-chivalry was at least dubious considering that prece-
dents for service and scutage of this nature existed. The refusal is
more significant as a symptom of the concentration of sentiment
on English affairs in a territorial sense of the word. The English-
Norman amalgamation had proceeded for more than a century, and
neither the Angevin empire policy nor the crusading adventures of
Richard I could seriously hamper the growth or regional sentiment.
One might be tempted to view the loss of Normandy, after the
unlucky struggle of 1202–1204, as a decisive event in the formation
of English sentiment, and it certainly had its importance in this
respect; but what seems most striking about the loss is the ease
with which the Norman baronage in England adjusted itself to it by
a division of interests between English and Norman branches of the
families affected. And the defeat of Bouvines, ten years later, again
did not give a new direction to sentiments but only accentuated the
existing trend.

Curious, as well as somewhat obscure, is the role of the religious
and ecclesiastical factors in the granting of the charter. In 1213
John had resigned England into the hands of the pope and received
it back in fief. While there is at least one contemporary historian
who reports that the event was felt by many to be ignominious,
the resignation seems to have been due less to papal insistence
than to the wish of the king himself and of at least some of the
barons. The political situation was apparently so critical in 1213
that the prestige of the papal overlordship was indispensable in
the relations with France as well as in order to avoid an internal
revolt; the national interest was on the side of the deal—though
the king's idea of the use to which the new feudal relationship
might be put was in direct opposition to that of the barons. The
opportunity to use it came first for the barons, when early in 1215
a group of malcontents appealed to the pope for support of their
demands for the charter. The barons were well aware that such
support might also be available to the king, and, in order to forestall
papal interference adverse to their interests, they incorporated in

the *forma securitatis* of the *Articles of the Barons* the provision that the king would not try to obtain a revocation of the charter from the pope[1] and that any revocation or diminution should be considered void. Under feudal law the provision could not abrogate the rights of the pope and was, therefore, legally null. The charter was granted June 15, 1215; on August 25 it was quashed by the pope on appeal from John; the subsequent internal troubles found their solution after the death of the king in 1216.

The confused pattern of national sentiments, of internal English feudal loyalties, of the temporal lordship of the pope, and of the impact of his spiritual prestige became still more complicated through the national ecclesiastical leadership of Stephen Langton, the archbishop of Canterbury. He was instrumental in shaping the baronial discontent into the articulate form of the demand for a charter, for he apparently was responsible for the unearthing of the Coronation Oath of Henry I and of the Charter of Liberties given by him in 1100, as well as for the suggestion to use the earlier grants as a precedent for the settlement of the present troubles. In the opinion of the partners to the struggle, the Magna Carta was not a revolutionary constitutional act but rather an attempt to restore the legal order as had become necessary once before after the reign of William II. The charter itself has the form of a concession first to God that the English Church should be free, and the second to all free men of the realm that a series of detailed legal rules would be observed henceforth. The concessions are made for the good of the king's soul, for the exaltation of the church, and for the improvement of the realm, by the advice of a number of counselors of whom the first on the list is Langton. The revolting barons are introduced only at the end of the document as the members of the committee of twenty-five that was to watch over its observation. The charter, by its form, thus preserves the royal initiative, and the archbishop appears as the guardian of the true interests of the realm by his double function as adviser to the barons and to the king. The

---

1. In clause 61 of the charter itself the provision is weakened only verbally "nos nihil impetrabimus *ab aliquo* . . . per quod aliqua istarum concessionum et libertatum revocatur vel minuatur" (we will obtain nothing from anyone through which some one of those concessions and freedoms is revoked or diminished). See James C. Holt, *Magna Carta* (Cambridge: Cambridge University Press, 1965), and his *Magna Carta and Medieval Government* (London and Roncevert, W.Va.: Hambledon Press, 1985).

archiepiscopal influence probably extended not only to the form of the settlement but also to its contents. The older thesis that the Magna Carta marks the beginning of English constitutional governments is by now discarded, but the newer one that it is a feudal document is not quite correct either if asserted rigidly. The charter contains, besides regulations of feudal law, a number of provisions of general importance for the prosperity of the realm: for the reform of the courts, for the distribution of chattels in case a man dies intestate, for a proportioning of penalties to crimes, for standard measures and weights throughout the realm, for a confirmation of the liberties of the cities, for the freedom of travel for merchants within England and across borders, for the freedom to buy and sell without tolls, and for the treatment of foreign merchants in England in time of war, and so on. Such provisions do not reflect the interests of the baronage, and we may doubt that the revolting barons had sufficient statesmanship to conceive them and sufficient legal skill to formulate them. The system of provisions reveals a clear policy to develop in general the economic resources of the realm, and in particular foreign and domestic commerce and the towns in which they center. A national policy of this type may be attributed, if not to the king himself, rather to Langton than to the barons.

The interaction of sentiments and interests that appears on the occasion of the Magna Carta should definitely discourage any attempt at reading an organic growth or a preconceived plan into the evolution of English institutions. The closest we can come to a factor determining a trend is the consciousness of a political order established by the conquest and a desire of the partners to the internal struggle to avoid an ultimate disruption of the establishment. This sentiment is revealed most articulately by the author of the policy embodied in the Magna Carta, that is, probably by Langton. To a lesser degree the same sentiment is expressed by the king, in his resoluteness in taking decisive steps, when such steps served the interest of the realm, as for example the resignation of England to the pope, and by the barons who in spite of their amply justified discontent had enough political acumen not to break off, as a group, the relations with the king and to accept the leadership offered by Langton. But this sentiment did no more than strengthen the direction in which the institutions evolved; it did not determine their structure. To the question of the structure we shall now turn, with the anticipation that the institutions did not evolve according to a plan but accidentally, and that even the persistent institutions will undergo profound changes of meaning.

§3. The Institutions

a. The Strength of Royal Power

The earlier discussed conception of an organic growth of English institutions fails to distinguish between the direction given by sentiment and the institutions themselves. It fails, furthermore, by not recognizing the change of meaning that the institutions undergo. The picture of a straight evolution becomes possible only if one retrojects the modern meanings of the terms of the people, of representation and liberties, into the world of feudal conceptions. The idea of the people as the substance of the political unit is a late product in Western history and was, in the English case, not politically active before the seventeenth century; the same holds true a fortiori for the representation of the people. The liberties of the Norman and Angevin kings were not rooted in the rights of the individual but were granted by the king "through the respect of God and the love I bear toward you."[2] The modern constitutional system did not evolve on the plane of institutions but through the superimposition of ideas on institutions that had grown in an entirely different field of sentiments and ideas. We can state the issue of the relation between medieval and modern institutions in a simplified manner by saying that the institutions that grew in the feudal power field constituted a new fact, and that this new fact contributed to the rise of the sentiments and ideas that determined the further growth and interpretation of institutions in the constitutional direction.

To speak, therefore, of an early evolution of English liberties ahead of those of other nations is at least in part anachronistic; in terms of feudal categories rather the opposite would be true. Due to the strength of royal power after the conquest, the English kings could exact court attendance from their tenants-in-chief to an extent and with a frequency that was inconceivable in France. The liberties granted were not an achievement to which there was no parallel on the Continent; they were rather the sad minimum that

---

2. *Charter of Liberties of Henry I,* of 1100, in William Stubbs, *Select Charters,* 8th ed. (Oxford: Clarendon, 1895), 100.

the English vassals could wrench from a strong kingship, while the French barons enjoyed an independence from royal power of which the English could never dream. The same considerations have to be applied to the English royal power over the knights of the shire and the towns who were summoned to send their representatives to the assembly of the realm in the course of the thirteenth century. The attendance of the representatives of French *villes* at the first Estates General of 1302 actually does not lag very long after the first appearance of burgesses in the Montfort Parliament of 1265 and the Model Parliament of Edward I in 1295, but the legal basis of the attendance was not the same in France as in England. Regional assemblies of French *villes* began to be called in order to grant *auxilium* during the thirteenth century; in attending, the towns fulfilled a feudal obligation because due to their enfranchisement they had status as feudal *arrière-vassaux*. In England the privileges of the towns were never so complete as to constitute free towns with feudal rights; there was no development in England paralleling the rise of the feudal communes in France. London seems to have been the one exception; for section 12 of the Magna Carta, which provides that no *scutagium* or *auxilium* should be imposed *nisi per commune consilium regni nostri*, is extended expressly to the City of London. The assumption that London was the one and only English town with a feudal commune and ranked, therefore, equal with the tenants-in-chief seems to be the correct explanation of this peculiarity. The English summons of the knights of the shire and the burgesses to the assembly of the realm has its roots not in a specific feudal relationship but in the extrafeudal attendance of county and borough representatives in the county court and the transfer of such attendance to the plane of the national assembly. Hence the earlier, more frequent, and, finally, regular attendance of shire and borough representatives in the English Parliament was not due to a precocious growth of constitutional rights but to the lesser strength of English feudatories and the lesser growth of feudal communes.

The liberties, in feudal terms, were modest, and the attendance at the *consilium* was an obligation, not a right. The only suggestions of a sphere of rights of the barons can be found in sections 12 and 14 of the Magna Carta, which provided that a *scutagium* should not be imposed, without consultation, except in three specified instances; and these two sections were dropped in the new issue of the charter of 1216, in the first year of Henry III. The great importance of thirteenth-century development in England does not lie in the grants of liberties. It lies in the imposition of the obligation, on ever wider strata of English society, to participate in the process of government. These impositions produced the experience of affairs, the habit of communal action, and the feeling of individuals that they were members of estates, which, in turn, prepared English society with the astounding ability for political action. For a masterly balanced presentation of this process we refer the reader to C. H. McIlwain's "Medieval Estates";[3] in the present context we shall only outline the principal phases and results.

b. Articulation and Integration of the Body Politic

The first and fundamental step toward the formation of English political society is effected through the transformation of the baronage from a group of individual tenants-in-chief, temporal as well as spiritual, all holding from the same lord, into a commune capable of collective action. The symptoms of communal action began to appear in the early thirteenth century; the *forma securitas* of the Magna Carta shows the barons as a body transacting with the king. The pattern evolved by the baronage was followed by the representatives of the shires and boroughs when they began to participate in the assembly of the realm. The knights of the shire, as well as the burgesses and the proctors of the parochial clergy, when summoned, deliberated as groups in the same manner as the barons. This formation of communes capable of deliberation and decision is considerably more important than the much discussed incidental development of representation; for the communes were society in form for action, while the representation of shires and boroughs by delegates was an inevitable technique that developed as soon as the substance to be represented was experienced as such. The English case is unique among its kind because here we can observe, with a minimum of disturbance from other factors, the

---

3. C. H. McIlwain, "Medieval Estates," *Cambridge Medieval History* [hereafter *CMH*], vol. 8 (1936), chap. 23. In general see Frederick Powicke, *King Henry III and the Lord Edward: The Community of the Realm in Thirteenth Century England*, 2 vols. (Oxford: Clarendon, 1947); Michael Prestwich, *The Three Edwards: War and State in England, 1272–1377* (London: Weidenfeld and Nicholson, 1980); R. G. Davies and J. H. Denton, eds., *The English Parliament in the Middle Ages* (Philadelphia: University of Pennsylvania, 1981).

process by which Western political society became articulate from the prime estates, that is from the nobility and higher clergy, down to the lowest strata that were socially relevant at the time.[4] The reasons for the rapid and thorough articulation in the course of a century were manifold, and the materials are so scanty that we have only an incomplete picture; but on the whole, the pressure for articulation seems to have come from the top of the social pyramid rather than from the bottom. Whether the earl of Leicester wished to have a broader basis for his civil war parliament of 1265 by introducing burgessess, or whether Edward I wanted to be the king of all his subjects directly without mediation by his tenants-in-chief, or whether he needed more money through direct grants from the lower estates, or whether he wished to insure by their participation in grants a more effective system of tax collection, or whether the barons, temporal and spiritual, desired the presence of representatives from those strata of society on whom the extraordinary tax burden would fall most heavily—the initiative seems to have rested in any case with the king and the barons. However, we must not overlook the fact that the initiative could not have had any important results unless the pressure toward articulation had been brought to bear upon a social substance capable of articulation. Of the dynamics of the lower society that must have suggested the initiative from the top as a promising action we know very little. But from various symptoms, such as the commercial provisions of the Magna Carta, we can draw the conclusion that, by the thirteenth century, economic development must have resulted in the rise of a society of knights and merchants of sufficient wealth to make their taxability in comparison with the feudal revenue a major item in the finances of the realm, and of sufficient consciousness of their own importance to make their consultation advisable.

The elements of an articulate political society were assembled by the end of the thirteenth century; but the elements in themselves were no guarantee that they would amalgamate into a national unit of action. The several communes showed centrifugal tendencies. The attendance of the clergy became difficult to enforce when in 1296 the bull *Clericis Laicos* enjoined the clergy not to pay

4. The term *prime estates* is Spengler's. See *The Decline of the West*, vol. 1, chapters on the state.

taxes to the secular authority. The lower clergy held aloof from the general parliament and assembled in a separate convocation; the institution was continued up to the seventeenth century. The attendance of the higher clergy could be enforced as an obligation under feudal law. A similar tendency on the part of the merchants to deal separately with the king concerning grants that fell on them alone was suppressed by the middle of the fourteenth century.

The four communes remaining after the convocation of the clergy had gone its own way might have evolved into separate houses with equal rights of consent to grants and statutes. The avoidance of this calamity through the coalescence of the two upper and the two lower estates into the Lords and Commons seems to have been a lucky accident. The reasons are not quite clear in detail, but a major factor seems to have been the formality that the members of the upper communes were summoned individually while the representatives of towns and knights were not. The perfection of the coalescence took a considerable time; separate sessions of the two lower communes are reported as late as 1523. The assembling of the communes in two houses had decisive consequences for the structure of the English polity. First, it produced the peculiar phenomenon of the English middle class, a stratum of society formed by the amalgamation of the gentry and the *haute bourgeoisie.* England thus was spared the severe continental class distinction between the nobility and the bourgeoisie or the *Buergertum;* a revolution of the third estate like the French one of 1789 was impossible in the English structure because no third estate existed as an articulate commune. The somewhat arbitrary division of the nobility into the peerage and the gentry and their distribution over the two Houses had, second, the effect that the bicameral apparatus did not evolve divergent interests in the two chambers. The social cohesion of the nobility secured for them an influence on the composition of the Commons sufficient to prevent antagonism and to compel a parallel development of politics. This influence on the Commons remained, with a certain weakening in the eighteenth century, fairly intact into the nineteenth. After the Reform of 1832 tensions began to increase, but the momentum of tradition is still strong—to the great chagrin of Labourites who fume at the fact that large sections of the English people who by their social status should vote for Labour candidates prefer Conservatives.

c. Comparison with Continental Development

The survey of the process of political articulation will enable us now to round out the characterization of the English polity in its differences from the continental types. The formation of the middle class implies negatively, as we have seen, the absence of an articulate third estate as an independent revolutionary factor. Positively it means the integration of the bourgeoisie into the style of politics created by the feudal nobility. The all-pervasiveness of the aristocratic style in the structure and the history of the English polity is the principal cause of its physiognomic grandeur and of its practical success; its appeal is strong enough, as we have indicated, to draw even the new political classes into its orbit and to keep, at least for the time being, the class conflict that inevitably arises from the industrialization of society below the level of revolutionary disruption—though we have to remark that this feat was aided materially by the advantages that the English economy derived from its early industrialization and from the wealth of the empire. The articulation into communes and the integration through the nobility alone, however, do not explain entirely the tradition of political experience accumulated in the English Parliament; we have to take into consideration also the functions of the communes that were welded into the Parliament. The English royal administration had preserved a high degree of concentration of affairs as late as the critical thirteenth century, whereas at the same time a division of functions had already taken place in the French administration: the judicial functions had been assumed by the *parliaments*, and the functions of *consilium* by the king's private council. When the French *villes* were summoned, their primary function was the granting of *auxilium*; the English knights and burgesses, on the other hand, acquired their experience of affairs not only through participation in the county courts but also through participation in the judicial and administrative affairs of the less strictly differentiated central court. It was the combination of structure and function on a national scale that enabled the English Parliament to emerge unscathed from the Renaissance absolutism of the fifteenth to seventeenth centuries and to assume after the Civil War, in addition to the functions of national deliberation and legislation, the functions of rulership and national political action. A similar development in France was impossible because in the critical period royal power was not strong enough to enforce the articulation of society; and it was still less possible in Germany with its strong entrenchment of the territorial princes. When the French monarchy reached its phase of absolutism, beginning after the Hundred Years War, no articulate society could counterbalance the newly concentrated royal power and save the feudal liberties through the dangerous period so they might burgeon as the liberties of the nation. When the third estate finally became articulate the process had to take the form of a social revolution. In Germany we do not find even an articulation of the third estate, with the consequence that the German middle and lower classes had to bear the curse of peculiarly nonpolitical habits and beliefs and of a severe inexperience of affairs when finally, in the nineteenth century, they reached social relevance and political effectiveness on the national level.

d. English Constitutionalism

A word is necessary, in conclusion, concerning English "constitutionalism" as far as its characteristics were founded in the history of the high and late Middle Ages. No satisfactory general definition of constitutionalism is possible for the obvious reason that the differences between the historical types of government covered by this symbol are too profound.[5] If we define as constitutional a government that operates within the framework of a written constitution and is limited by a bill of rights, England has no constitutional government, for the absolutism of the Tudors and the first Stuarts was followed by the even more radical absolutism of Parliament. The attempts at limitation through written instruments during the Civil War did not take hold and were not renewed afterward. If we define constitutional government more liberally as a government that observes a rule of law and has the consent of the governed, practically every de facto government that is not too much riddled

---

5. A good exposition of the problem connected with a definition of constitutionalism is to be found in Hugh M. Clokie's *The Origin and Nature of Constitutional Government* (London: Harrap, 1936), chap. 3. See also Harold J. Berman, *Law and Revolution: The Formation of the Western Legal Tradition* (Cambridge: Harvard University Press, 1983); Brian Tierney, *Religion, Law, and the Growth of Constitutional Thought, 1150–1650* (New York: Cambridge University Press, 1982) and *The Idea of Natural Rights* (Atlanta: Scholars Press, 1997); Manlio Bellomo, *The Common Legal Past of Europe,* trans. Lydia G. Cochrane (Washington, D.C., 1995).

by arbitrary and corrupt practices and that governs in such a manner that the cries of suppressed minorities or majorities do not permanently testify to the absence of consent, appreciable sections of society would fall under the concept. The problem has been obscured by overstressing the aspects of constitutional technique—such as representation, elections, written constitutions, and bills of rights. Some of these technical elements may be absent, and we are still inclined to speak of constitutional government as in the English case, while the presence of some of them as in the cases of the National Socialist and Soviet governments will not induce us to make the subsumption. The issue lies back of the question of constitutional techniques—which quite generally are overrated in their importance—in the articulation of society and the integration of the articulate parts into a unit. We may find, for instance, an excellently law-abiding government with a highly articulate *haute bourgeoisie,* equipped with representation, bills of rights, elections, and other paraphernalia, and still not consider it particularly constitutional if the broad masses of the people linger in a state of illiteracy and poverty so that any communal expression of their interests is impossible, although legally permitted, and on election day the masses are driven to the polls and vote as ordered. In the sense, therefore, of a thoroughgoing articulation of the body politic and of articulate consent, the English polity had reached a high degree of constitutionality.

If we formulate the issue in these terms, however, we can also see that English constitutionality through articulation was approaching a critical point. In England full articulation had not extended beyond the gentry and the upper middle class. With the close of the ancien régime in 1832 the broad masses were gradually absorbed into the system through the technical device of the franchise for the Commons. The dubiousness of this device from the point of view of political articulation has always been understood. It was exposed for the first time in Hegel's brilliant analysis of the Reform Bill of 1831 and of its consequences; it was discussed on similar lines by Disraeli in his *Coningsby;* Earl Grey proposed remedial devices in his treatise on parliamentary reform. In the twentieth century, and particularly after the War of 1914–1918, authors connected with the labor movement have dealt amply with the problem of adequate articulation of the lower middle and working classes and suggested various reforms of the polity, such as the Guild Socialist plan of

G. D. H. Cole, the Constitution for the Socialist Commonwealth of Great Britain of the Webbs, or Harold J. Laski's conception of a pluralistic state. The difficulties that obstruct the movement toward a further articulation of English society stem from the very structure that has weathered the centuries; its firmness is sometimes experienced today as a nightmare of a millennium of history weighing on the industrial age. The social relevance of the communes reaching back to the thirteenth century, and further back to the conquest, is still strong, but it has decreased in proportion to the relevance of the new lower classes. The proper articulation of the new social strata would entail by the sheer weight of their numbers perhaps not simply an extension of the process but a thoroughgoing rearticulation of English society at the expense of the nobility, the Established Church, and the middle class. The consciousness that the present articulation is a medieval survival no longer in accord with the present, coupled with the loyalty of sentiment toward a structure of society that has made England great and still shelters it against the inclemency of the time, produces the peculiar English malaise that expressed itself in the new warmth of feeling toward the royal house after the last war and in the idolization of the parliamentary institution.[6] English political craftsmanship may find a solution for the articulation of the newly relevant groups without disrupting the established system. But if the miracle should be achieved it will be rather doubtful—precisely for the reason of its achievement, as Arnold Toynbee has seen correctly—whether England in the future can be a model for governmental institutions to be followed by other nations as it was in the nineteenth century and even after 1918. The forms of political articulation for the industrial society would have to be evolved elsewhere; and the center of institutional creativeness has indeed already shifted to Russia, Germany, and Italy—however questionable and ephemeral these first experiments of a new age will prove to be.

6. On the problem of malaise and idolization see the pertinent remarks of Arnold J. Toynbee in his *Study of History*, vol. 4 (London: Oxford University Press, 1939), section on the "Idolization of an Ephemeral Institution," subsection on "The Mother of Parliaments," 408 ff.; see also his notes on "muddling through" in the appendix on "Idolatry and Pathological Exaggeration," 638 ff. Insofar as certain elements of the English structure have entered into the composition of the American polity, we meet there with a similar problem. On the American malaise and idolization see Ralph H. Gabriel, *The Course of American Democratic Thought* (New York: Ronald Press, 1940), esp. chap. 30, "The New American Symbolism," 396 ff.

§4. Symbols

With the discussion of constitutionalism we have already transcended the field of institutional development proper and entered on questions of symbolism. In the analysis of institutions we have to use such categories as the social relevance of classes, the growth of communal consciousness to the point where articulation for communal action becomes possible, and the integration of articulate communes into a national system. In the process of articulation and integration we can, furthermore, distinguish the phases of articulation on the level of local self-government only, of integration through grants of *auxilium* with deliberation preceding it, of deliberation concerning consent to legislation, or participation in judicial and administrative matters on the national level, of initiative through petitions addressed to a central political authority, of legislative initiative, and, in a final stage, of the ability to produce leadership for action on a national scale as in the modern English cabinet system. The English case is the ideal type of articulation insofar as since the seventeenth century the articulate society was able to absorb almost completely the royal state structure into its functions, leaving only the small but important residue of the prerogative. The term *constitutionalism*, on the other hand, is not a concept but a symbol signifying a system of articulation as a whole while absorbing into its explicit content only incidental features of the system. The introduction of such symbols is of little use in science, but it is of greatest importance in politics because symbols are emotional concentrates protecting the system by their spell against inroads of all kinds. It may be difficult to ward off an attack on any particular part of a system by rational argument, showing the historical forces that have entered into it and the dangers of tampering with them, but it is easy to organize emotional resistance against an attack by claiming that it is directed against constitutional government. Not less important, but not always happy in the consequences, is the appeal exerted by such symbols *ad extra*. When symbols of this type are made explicit the explication shows a tendency, as we have said, to absorb the incidental technical devices for the operation of the institution and to overlook the articulation that made the operation of the devices possible. When we speak of Athenian democracy in the average political discussion we are thinking of the popular assembly, the courts, and so on, and are inclined to forget the tribal articulation of the Hellenic polis that sets the framework for the techniques of government; and when we speak of constitutionalism we think of parliaments, elections, and representation and are inclined to forget that the English Parliament is not simply a device for transacting the political business of a people but an instrument of action that has grown with the articulation of English society. Because in the explication of symbols we focus on the instrumental aspects and neglect the articulation, the fallacy arises that instrumental patterns can be transferred from one society to another. Insofar as the transfer is actually possible within limits, if the society to which a pattern is transferred happens to have an articulation that makes the transfer bearable, a semblance of truth is given to the otherwise erroneous opinion that transfers are always possible. There is no guarantee whatsoever that the introduction of a constitution in a country will produce constitutional government; it may just as well produce a revolutionary shambles. Freedom of speech, for instance, is considered an essential of constitutionality; and it is appropriate, indeed, as an instrument of government when the society is firmly integrated, for in that case it will produce the conditions for understanding governmental policies that we call consent, while its abuse will be unimportant because social resistance against it is strong enough to prevent disrupting effects. If a society is less well integrated, freedom of speech may produce not public opinion, pressure on the government, and consent—which is its purpose as an instrument—but a degeneration of the society into a wilderness of distrust, disloyalties, and revolutionary chaos, as we have seen it do in the period preceding the fall of France and, with still more disastrous effects, in the marvelously constitutional Weimar Republic.

§5. Representation

a. Definition

We had to discuss the question of the symbols connected with constitutionalism with some care and to draw clearly the distinction between the articulation of society and the technical devices employed in its operation because the neglect of the distinction is one of the most regrettable obstacles to the understanding of institutions. The operational devices are means to an end; they are not independent phenomena. Hence they cannot be treated scientifically as if they were ultimate units of political reality. The failure to understand the instrumental character of governmental devices has obscured especially the problem of representation. We have to deal with it in some detail because representation as a device for operating the national state had its origin in the high Middle Ages. Its discussion has been voluminous and intense, but it has been beset by difficulties stemming from confusion of the emotional values of the symbol with the rather unexciting and even humdrum use of representation as a device for communal action. As a first step in untangling the problem it will perhaps be best to clarify the difference between an agent and a representative. By an agent we shall understand a person who is empowered by his principal to transact a specific business under instructions. By a representative we shall understand a person who has power to act for a social group by virtue of his position in the structure of the community, without specific instruction for a specified business, and whose acts will not be effectively repudiated by the group. An agent, therefore, is not a primary representative of a group but can act only by virtue of the power derived from the representative proper. An illustration would be a conference of ambassadors acting as agents, as distinguished from a conference of prime ministers who are the representatives themselves. Empirically it will be sometimes difficult to say whether a person acts as an agent or as a representative. It is for instance rather doubtful whether a member of parliament in a democracy that enforces rigid party discipline can still be called a representative if he casts his vote according to instructions received from the party leadership; it is especially doubtful if, as in Czechoslovakia, the supreme court rules that a member of parliament loses his seat if he votes frequently or consistently against party instructions. While in specific cases it will be difficult to discern clearly the extent to which a person acts as an agent or as a representative, the distinction is clear in principle. In this context we shall deal only with representation proper.

The traditional treatment of representation and its origins starts, however, implicitly, with a somewhat different definition. Representation is understood traditionally as the device representing a local group in a central assembly through delegates, as for instance the representation of towns through burgesses in the assembly of the realm. Representation of the townspeople of a large territorial realm through their delegates is considered representation proper; as such it is distinguished from the direct democracy of the Hellenic polis or from the appearance, in the royal council, of the barons who represent nobody but themselves. As a consequence, the problem of representation is narrowed down to a device for participation in the governmental process of a social group that is too widely dispersed and too numerous to act as a body and in one place. If we limit the problem in this manner, there arises the question as to when and where the device for integrating towns into the system of government was employed for the first time. We have then to say that Spanish cities began to be represented in the Cortes by the second half of the twelfth century, the Sicilian towns under Frederick II in the first half of the thirteenth century, the English towns in the second half, and the French in the Estates General beginning with the fourteenth century. We may, furthermore, ask the question whether the appearance of representation in England is due to diffusion of the device from Spain, or whether in several instances the institution has developed independently through convergence.

Hence the problem of the origin of representation depends on the definition of representation that we choose to employ. If we change the meaning of the term, the problem will perhaps not disappear entirely, but it certainly will look different. The question imposes itself, therefore, as to whether we are obliged to accept the traditional definition and with it the problem created by it. I think we are under no such obligation because this meaning bears visibly the marks of the anachronistic projection of a modern evocative idea into the thirteenth century. To single out the representation of towns as meriting attention above all other contemporary problems is a procedure that can be explained only as the consequence of an undue preoccupation with the fact that the borough representation in the Commons is historically the system that, by a change of meaning and the enlargement of the franchise, has been converted into the representation of the people. The idea of popular representation, however, forms part of the modern evocation of constitutional government; it is not to be found in the incipient national kingdoms of the high Middle Ages. The device of representation can serve more than one purpose; it is not of necessity linked with the people. If we want to know what it means in the thirteenth century, we cannot start with the dogmatic assumption that it signifies the beginning of the "people's" representation but have to consult the writs by which the delegates were summoned.

b. The Writs of Summons

The writ of Edward I for the Parliament of 1295 enjoins the sheriff to have elected without delay two knights from the county, two citizens from each city, and two burgesses from each borough, and to have them sent to Westminster at the appointed time; the men have to be chosen from the more discreet and fit for this kind of work *(de discretioribus et ad laborandum potentioribus)*; the delegates must be equipped with sufficient power to act for themselves and their communities so that no delay of business will ensue from lack of powers. What the term *election* means under these circumstances is somewhat doubtful. The procedure, as far as we can surmise it from the writs, presupposes communities of a sufficient degree of articulation to possess members who are prudent and skilled in affairs, and officers of the central administration with sufficient powers to persuade or coerce the communities into the "election" of suitable delegates who may be considered "representative" by virtue of their personal qualifications, but still have strongly the character of "agents" with specific powers.[7]

We are justified, therefore, in speaking of a representation of the *communitas comitatus* and the *communitas civitatis*, and we may speak even of a representation of communes insofar as the borough representatives deliberated together and their resolutions were binding for them all. But we can hardly speak of an incipient representation of the people or the nation through the town delegates. Not only are the sources silent on such a relation; they are on the contrary explicit in assigning the integral representative function to the king himself. The realm is the king's, the prelates and the

---

7. On the actual function of the sheriff in producing the representatives, the machinery in the boroughs for the selection and, above all, the successful resistance of boroughs to sending any representatives and their surprising ability to escape being noticed as boroughs for protracted periods, and further details, see the marshaling of material in D. Pasquet, *An Essay on the Origins of the House of Commons* (1925; rpt. Hamden, Conn.: Archon, 1965), 158 ff. Further details, qualifying in many respects the results of Pasquet, are to be found in May McKisack, *The Parliamentary Representation of the English Boroughs during the Middle Ages* (Oxford, 1932; rpt. London: Cass, 1962).

magnates are his, and his are the cities. The merchants, on the other hand, are not his but "of the realm" or "of the city," a language that indicates that the people as an ultimate community of individuals were not in view, but that individuals were articulated politically in the communes and in the realm as a whole.[8] As the person representing the realm the king has to watch over its external security and internal peace "for the honor of God and the welfare of the whole realm";[9] the term *populus* can be used synonymously with *regnum* in the formula of the "common welfare of the realm."[10] For single individuals we find the term *inhabitants (incolae)* or *fellow citizens (concives)* of our realm.[11] A fairly clear theory of the English constitution emerges from these formulas; the king is the representative and responsible head of the realm as articulated in the magnates, the prelates, and the various communes; the single individual has status not as a member of the people but as a member of his commune or of the realm.

We have to bear this conception in mind when we approach the famous dictum of Edward I, contained in the writ to the bishops of 1295: "that what touches all, should be approved by all" *(quod omnes tangit ab omnibus approbetur)*. The formula, taken from the *Codex Justinianus*, has been enthusiastically interpreted as the policy of a great king who wished to give the English people their place in the constitution, or, with a more limited purpose, to establish the principle of no taxation without consent. These older interpretations have been discarded by now as anachronistic, and the formula has been discounted as even the unimportant flourish of a clerk.[12] The radical step of discounting the formula altogether, however, is perhaps not necessary if only we do not insist upon attributing to it either the Roman meaning or a meaning taken from modern constitutional ideas, but are satisfied to place it in the universe of meanings of the age. In the current discussion the

---

8. For the designation of the merchants see the *Writ of Summons to a "Colloquium" of Merchants*, of 1303, in Stubbs, *Select Charters*, 500.
9. For this formula see *Summons to the Parliament*, of 1265, in Stubbs, *Select Charters*, 415.
10. *Summons to the Parliament of Lincoln*, of 1301, in Stubbs, *Select Charters*, 99.
11. *Summons of the Archbishop and Clergy to Parliament*, of 1295, in Stubbs, *Select Charters*, 485.
12. See Pasquet, *Origins of the House of Commons*, 174. [For a discussion of the Roman law context, where the phrase refers to the conflicts arising from several guardians looking after the same ward, see P. G. Stein, "Roman law," in *Cambridge History of Medieval Thought*, 47.]

formula is torn out of its context. In the context it does not state an independent principle at all, but is used as a general premise from which a more specific rule for the occasion is derived; hence the meaning of the premise should not be determined independently but rather in light of the conclusion drawn from it. The full text of the passage runs as follows:

> Sicut lex justissima, provida circumspectione sacrorum principum stabilita, hortatur et statuit ut quod omnes tangit ab omnibus approbetur, sic et nimis evidenter ut communibus periculis per remedia provisa communiter obvietur.
>
> (Just as a proper law, established by the provident foresight of the holy princes, urges and decrees that what touches all should be approved by all, so also it quite clearly requires that common dangers be met with remedies that are provided in common.)

The specific rule for the occasion says "that a common danger should be met by means provided in common." The danger is the war preparation of the king of France, destined to destroy the realm of England. In the classical formula of *res vestra maxime agitur* (literally: your business in particular is conducted), the king addresses himself, therefore, to the communes of the realm with the order to assemble in person or through representatives for deliberation and action in the emergency. The motivation of the danger to the realm, for which provision has to be made by all, is contained not only in the writs to the prelates but also in the summonses of the temporal lords and of the shire and town representatives.

Taking the clear meaning of the special rule as the starting point, the range of meanings for the general premise is narrowed down considerably. It cannot be construed to imply national rights of whatever description, but has to imply the duty of participation and aid in common affairs, particularly in affairs of an emergency nature. A key to a meaning that fits the context can be found in the language of the summons to the bishops for a great council earlier in 1295.[13] Here we find the general premise of the later writ elaborated in specific terms. That which "touches" all are the "difficult affairs"; and they touch "us" (the king), "our realm," and "the prelates of the realm" as well as the magnates summoned to the council. The king does not wish to expedite affairs without the

---

13. *Summons of the Archbishop for a Great Council*, of 1294, in Stubbs, *Select Charters*, 485.

presence of those who are "touched" by them. The general premise of the later writ seems to us a brief formula for the more elaborate motivation of the earlier writ. The most adequate translation would perhaps be: "affairs that concern all should be made his own business by everybody"; and he can fulfill this duty by meeting with the king in Parliament "ad tractandum, ordinandum et faciendum . . . qualiter sit hujusmodi periculis et excogitatis malitiis obviandum (to manage, arrange, and act . . . in whatever way dangers and contrived evils are to be met)."[14] The later writ only enlarges the circle of those "touched" to include the "alii incolae regni nostri" (other inhabitants of our realm). While it would be unsafe in the absence of any evidence to attribute the appearance of the general formula directly to the intention of the king, it certainly reflects objectively the policy of Edward I to accelerate the transformation of the feudal realm into a realm of the estates.[15]

c. Representation and Articulation

In the analysis of representation we are thrown back on the problem of articulation. When the process of integrating articulate strata of society into a national assembly reaches the shires and towns, the device of sending delegates is used as the obvious means for the representation of communities that cannot be present as a body at the meetings of a territorial realm. As the English institutions did not develop in a vacuum, it is quite possible that similar practices in the Cortes of Aragon and Castile, or, as Professor Barker has suggested, the constitution of the Dominican Order, had some influence on the English evolution; but we do not possess any proof of such influence beyond the contiguity of the phenomena in time. The internal articulation of the English county had reached a degree that makes it superfluous, as Professor McIlwain rightly maintains, to search for extraneous influences on the development of the device. The whole question can be magnified into a "problem" only under the assumption that the sending of representative delegates to the assembly of the realm is a feat of inventive intelligence of which Englishmen should not be suspected. The problem does not

14. *Summons of the Archbishop and Clergy,* of 1295, in Stubbs, *Select Charters,* 485.
15. On the motives of Edward I see the summary in Pasquet, *Origins of House of Commons,* 171 ff.

lie in the sending of delegates, which seems to be a matter of course once the political substance is formed and articulate, but rather in the formation and articulation of the community substance itself.

Here lies indeed a problem that merits attention. The device of representation through delegates from local communities to a central assembly was not used for the first time in history in the rising national realms. We have the cases of the Roman provincial diets, of the early church councils, and of the convocations of the mendicant orders. The background of the provincial diets in the Roman empire is obscure in the details, but the church assemblies are clear in their presuppositions: when we have articulate local communities like the early Christian churches, forming part of the larger territorially dispersed Christian community, the assembly of delegates acquires significance as an instrument because the condition of a large community with local subcommunities is fulfilled. Still more revealing is the constitutional development of the mendicant orders in the early thirteenth century. Great importance has been attached to the elective elements inserted in the constitution of the Dominicans: the election of the priors in the convents, and the participation of elected representatives side by side with the ex officio representatives in the provincial and general chapters. We have to say in this case, as in the case of the shire and town representatives, that nothing spectacular is to be found in the device of elected representatives as such. What is new, and indeed revolutionary, is the growth of a community that requires for its articulation elected representatives. Representatives as such existed in the new sovereign orders since the reform of Cluny; but under the Cluniac organization the member houses were represented in the chapters by the priors, not by elected delegates. We may say that the secular type corresponding to the Cluniac organization is the baronial parliament, a *consilium* that could be the *commune consilium regni* under a principle of virtual representation as long as the lower social strata were not sufficiently articulate. The innovation of the Dominican Order is not the representative chapter, but the conception of the friar as "the invincible athlete of Christ" pursuing the apostolic vocation of preaching the word of God. The bull of Honorius III of December 23, 1216, states that the brethren are "to be the champions of the faith and true lights of the world." The formula, applied in the liturgy to the apostles and evangelists, introduces into the framework of the medieval feudal church the community of the spiritually mature and active Christians.[16] This new type of community, consisting of spiritually active and mature individuals, had to become articulate by means of elective processes within single convents, as well as in the larger communities of the provinces and of the whole order.

The evolution of town communities in the secular sphere parallels the evolution of new spiritual communities in the religious. Both phenomena are intimately interwoven socially; and we have to deal with this aspect of the problem in a later chapter, "The People of God."[17] The fact that new community substances entered the field of history, accompanied by new forms of representation, does not justify, however, the assumption that representation as such was a new phenomenon. Representation, as defined above, is to be found as soon as any community becomes articulate. The king is the principal representative of the realm, as long as the baronial community is not coherent enough to act through representatives of its own. But by the beginning of the thirteenth century the internal coherence of the baronage was sufficiently strong to produce representative organs. The *forma securitatis* of the Magna Carta provides that the barons elect a committee of twenty-five whose duty it is to watch that the king observes his obligations; and any four of the twenty-five can form an acting subcommittee approaching the king or the justiciar with their complaints. As far as articulation through representation is concerned the baronage has the same community structure as a convent or a town. Representation is a function of articulation insofar as it is an omnipresent political phenomenon; the institutional forms can vary with the types of articulate communities, but they cannot be absent; new forms of representation are, therefore, symptoms of new communities in formation. The shire and town representation of the thirteenth century not only indicates the growth of local communities but, insofar as it results in a central assembly, it also indicates the articulation of the community of the realm.

16. On the Dominican constitution and its problems see John-Baptist Reeves, O.P., *The Dominicans* (New York: Macmillan, 1930).

17. *The Collected Works of Eric Voegelin*, vol. 22, *History of Political Ideas*, vol. IV, *Renaissance and Reformation*, ed. David L. Morse and William M. Thompson (Columbia: University of Missouri Press, 1998), pt. 4, chap. 3, "The People of God."

d. The Realm

This latter phenomenon, the growth of the "realm," which ulti-mately results in the growth of the "people," is somehow taken for granted, though it is precisely the process that should arouse curiosity. The Greco-Roman civilization had an immensely rich town development; nevertheless, the Hellenic civilization did not achieve any large territorial power structure at all, while the Roman empire had a large expanse but neither a realm, nor a people, nor rep-resentative institutions—setting aside the late Roman provincial development. In the world of the Hellenic polis we find, during the classical period, the religious leagues, which have more the char-acter of an armistice than of a realm, and the hegemonic leagues, which organized a number of poleis into a more or less compulsory alliance under the leadership of the strongest; no amalgamation into a "realm" occurred, though even councils consisting of delegates of the member poleis were not absent. The Roman empire was a vast military conquest with the Roman polis as its power center while the conquered territories were administered and exploited as *provinciae*. The terms *imperium* and *orbis terrarum* refer signifi-cantly to elements of the structure: the Roman power and the extent of its domain. But no articulating and integrating force comparable to Western royal power is visible; there is peace in the foundation, at last, but no life. The community substance of the polis was not capable of softening to a point where the highly articulate local units could have become integrated with each other to form larger communes. The historical drama of royal foundation, aristocratic rule, *fronde,* and rise of the third estate had to be enacted with varying results in every polis individually. The outcome was for Hellas, as for Rome, the curious "drying up" of the center and the disintegration of the periphery into succession states. This compar-ison with the ancient world brings into clearer relief the decisive function of Western kingship with its feudal organization of large territories as the integrating forces of the realm and of the peoples that grow in its shelter and under its pressure. Where this force was absent, as in Italy, the political structure shows certain similarities with the ancient through the rise of city-states and city-leagues like the Lombard, the internecine warfare between them, and the reduction of their number through the rise of hegemonic powers like Venice or Genoa.

§6. Fortescue

We cannot conclude this chapter more aptly than by making some observations on Sir John Fortescue's ideas on the political structure of the realm of England. In his work we find, if not a profoundly analytical theory of late medieval government, at least an attempt at descriptive type concepts, couched in the terms and images of the age. His ideas have been used for a Whiggist interpretation of English constitutional history ever since the seventeenth century. But more recent excellent studies have begun to regard his works as a source of great importance for understanding the medieval realm before the Tudor period.[18] Formerly some misgivings might have been voiced against the use of Fortescue's ideas for the interpretation of the *medieval* realm because his work falls in the sixties and seventies of the fifteenth century and thus is later than the Lancastrian constitutional experiment with its modern touches. But the "Lancastrian experiment," for long a mainstay of English constitutional history, begins to disappear under the impact of a more careful study of the sources. Concerning this question, S. B. Chrimes says: "The detection of any notable constitutional experiment under the Lancastrians becomes more and more difficult, and consequently any theory of backsliding on the part of the Yorkists becomes more and more meaningless. The present writer . . . has not, in the course of his reading of the sources, discerned any such traces, in contemporary ideas, of a conscious constitutional experiment as might have been expected if the older views were justified."[19] The continuity of evolution within the framework of the medieval realm was not yet broken by the time of Fortescue.

The fundamental concepts of Fortescue's political theory are the *dominium regale* and the *dominium politicum et regale.* In this context we need not go into the intricate question concerning

---

18. Cf. McIlwain, *Growth of Political Thought,* 354 ff., and the great study by S. B. Chrimes, *English Constitutional Ideas in the Fifteenth Century* (Cambridge, 1936), esp. chap. 4, "The Theory of the State."

19. Chrimes, *English Constitutional Ideas,* xviii ff. May I remark on this occasion that the argument of Chrimes for the fifteenth century holds true also for the thirteenth? During the period in which town representation took form, no contemporary historian seems to have been aware that anything sensational was happening. Most sources do not mention at all the afforcement of Parliament through the shires and towns; the few who do mention it do not consider it a revolutionary event—which seems to prove conclusively that the growth of town representation did not imply a break with accepted political ideas.

the derivation of this terminology from Saint Thomas, Ptolemy of Lucca, and Giles of Rome because the derivation is rather one of terms than of meaning; for the meaning we have to search in the use that Fortescue makes of the terms in his theory. The two concepts have three functions: (1) they are used to designate two forms of government, distinguished by the differences of their origin; (2) they designate two phases in the evolution of government; (3) they designate contemporary types of government, irrespective of origin or evolutionary phase, like France and England. The three sets of meaning are not distinguished systematically; they are used in accordance with the requirements of the context and sometimes are blended in one passage; they all converge, however, in purpose to give an adequate description of the English polity.

The *dominium regale* originates in the establishment of a rule through the superior force of a strong and ambitious man; the model is Nimrod, the mighty hunter. The law by which the community is governed emanates from the will of the ruler; if the law is good, the regal rule may develop into the earthly analogue of the kingdom of God. The rule "quod principi placuit, legis habet vigorem" (what pleases the prince has the force of law) finds its justification through the identification of the royal will with divinely sanctioned natural law.[20] Such a rule will obtain the consent of the people because the ruler is also the defender of his own position, and the acceptance of the rule will at least protect the subjects against the violence of others.[21] The theory of natural law implied in these passages is elaborated at length in *De Natura Legis Naturae*, part I; for our present purpose it is sufficient to characterize it as the traditional theory of relative natural law.[22] The *dominium regale* of the absolute ruler is the more primitive form. The *dominium politicum et regale* appears later when mankind has become more civilized.[23] In this advanced stage either more primitive governments may become political, as for instance Rome,[24] or new foundations may

20. *The Governance of England*, ed. Charles Plummer (Oxford: Clarendon, 1885), chap. II. The most recent edition of Fortescue is *On the Laws and Governance of England*, ed. Shelley Lockwood (New York: Cambridge University Press, 1997).

21. *De Laudibus Legum Angliae*, ed. Amos (1825), chap. XII. Recent edition: edited by S. B. Chrimes (Cambridge: Cambridge University Press, 1942).

22. *Works*, ed. Lord Clermont (London, 1869), vol. 1.

23. *Governance of England*, chap. II; "whan mankynde was more mansuete" (gentle).

24. *De Natura Legis Naturae* I.16, in *Works*, vol. 1.

start immediately as *dominium politicum et regale*, as for instance England.[25]

On the occasion of the *regnum politice regulatum*, Fortescue wrote a great page that carries the theory of the intramundane realm one step further along the line that had been fixed by John of Salisbury and Marsilius of Padua.[26] John had evolved the concept of the commonwealth and used the organic analogy in order to make the internal coherence of the unit intelligible. Marsilius had seen that the organic whole thus imagined was a blunt fact of inexplicable origin and had evolved the ideas of the *universitas* and the *legislator* as the preexisting whole that brings the single parts and their legal relations into being. The theory of Marsilius was a great advance in the construction of the intramundane political unit insofar as it recognized that the articulate parts of the whole could not derive their origin and authority from each other, but that the whole back of the parts represented a problem. It suffered, however, from the difficulty that the whole was conceived in terms of an already articulate constituting *legislator*, leaving open the more radical question of how the legislator himself became articulate. And it suffered from the limitation that in the construction of the *legislator* Marsilius used the institutional pattern of the Italian towns, which could not be transferred to the transalpine national territorial realms.[27] Fortescue overcame both handicaps, for he made his theory fit the problems of the national realm and he went deeper into the obscure processes by which a political substance is formed and becomes articulate.

His main terms for the designation of this process are the *eruption* and the *proruption* of the people. The organic analogy is extended from the comparison of the constituted body politic with an organism to a comparison of the creation of the realm with the growth of the articulate body out of the embryo. The people erupt into a realm *(ex populo erumpit regnum)* as the articulate body surges out of its embryonic state. In the case of a people hitherto entirely inarticulate Fortescue speaks of eruption; in the case of a realm *tantum regale* that experiences the transition to a political

---

25. *De Laudibus*, chap. XIII; *Governance*, chap. II.
26. *De Laudibus*, chap. XIII.
27. On John of Salisbury see vol. II, *The Middle Ages to Aquinas*, chap. 6, pp. 113–25; on Marsilius of Padua see chap. 17, above.

state, he speaks of proruption. The concept of the people used in these passages should be considered carefully. Fortescue finds fault with Saint Augustine's definition of the people as the multitude associated through consent to a right order and a communion of interests. Such a people would be *acephalus,* without a head; they could not be a body but would be only a trunk. The people that wish to erect themselves into a realm have to erect a head *(rex erectus est)* that will rule the body. The term *people* is obviously used in the two meanings of the politically inarticulate and the politically articulate people; for the second the term *realm* is a synonym.[28] No idea of popular sovereignty can be derived from this conception, though the language may sometimes tempt one to do so, as for instance when Fortescue says that the king must not use *hanc potestatem a populo effluxam* (this power flowing from the people) for any purposes but the protection of the law and of the bodies of his subjects. The people in this passage are not the articulate people to which Fortescue refers in other contexts as the commons but the embryonic people before their articulation. If we look for later parallels to the theory of a people that become articulate as a body politic through the erection of a king, we must not search in the direction of Locke's natural law speculation but rather, as Chrimes has suggested rightly, in the direction of Hobbes's *Leviathan.*[29]

Hence the realm is a people in a state of political articulation, the king being as much a part of it as the baronage or the commons. Fortescue has contributed further to the creation of a terminological framework for dealing with the mystery of a political evocation by using the term *mystical body* for the realm. As the natural body has the heart for its life center, so the *corpus mysticum* of the realm has for its center the *intencio populi* from which is transmitted into the head and the members of the body as its nourishing bloodstream the political provision for the well-being of the people. The transfer of the religious category to the secular

28. See *Governance of England,* chap. II, where Fortescue speaks of "grete communaltes" (the inarticulate people) who are "willyinge to be unite and made a body pollitike callid a reawme, hauynge an hed to gouerne it." *Realm, body politic,* and Latin *corpus* are synonymously used to designate the phenomenon that we called the realm, which has proceeded in its articulation to the lower strata of society.

29. [For an account of the revival of Thomistic analysis along these lines in the sixteenth century see Skinner, *Foundations of Modern Political Thought,* vol. 2, *The Age of Reformation,* esp. his remarks about the superiority of the treatment of Suarez to that of Hobbes on how a people comes to act as a *universitas* (p. 165).]

field is symptomatic of the strength the national realm had reached in the sentiment of the time and, correspondingly, of the weakness to which the imperial mystical body of Christianity had sunk. It, furthermore, is one of the many instances in which we can trace definitely the origin of secular political symbolism in the symbols of Christianity. And, last, it testifies to the excellent understanding that Fortescue still had for the fundamental problems of politics. The origin of the realm is to be sought not in nature or in law but in the forces of the soul that Fortescue covers by his category of eruption. The nature of political evocation, and the rise of the realm out of the forces of a charismatic personality, was no longer as clear to him as it had been to the historians of the migration period and to the authors of the Nordic saga literature, but it still was much clearer to him than to the later natural law theorists who sought the origin of the state in a contract. Only with Vico do we reach again a comparable level of realistic penetration of the problems of political evocation. This understanding of the mythical character of the body politic is, however, not entirely due to a detached insight; it is determined strongly by the fact that Fortescue himself was still living actively in the myth of the realm that goes back in continuity to the Migration. We have seen that for the *dominium tantum regale* the Old Testament had to furnish the leading case of Nimrod. The foundation of the political realm of England is due, for Fortescue, to Brutus, who came to the island with a fellowship of Trojans after their escape from the Greeks. The myth of the foundation by wandering Trojans, which the migration tribes took from Rome in order to achieve equality of status with the Mediterranean civilization, just as the Romans adopted it in order to achieve mythical equality with the Greeks, is still the backdrop of history forbidding a closer inquiry into the actual process of foundation.[30]

---

30. For the myth of Brutus, the eponymous hero of the Britons, and his *comitiva Trojenorum*, see *De Laudibus*, chap. XIII, and *Governance*, chap. II. The principal English source of the myth could have been the account in Geoffrey of Monmouth's *Historia Regnum Britanniae*. For a survey of other sources accessible to Fortescue and for the role of the myth in historical and political argument in England see the note by Plummer in his edition of the *Governance*, 185 ff. On the myth of the Trojan foundation in general see *The Collected Works of Eric Voegelin*, vol. 19, *History of Political Ideas*, vol. I, *Hellenism, Rome, and Early Christianity*, ed. Athanasios Moulakis (Columbia: University of Missouri Press, 1997), pt. 1, chap. 7, §5, "The Myth of Troy with the Gauls and Franks," pp. 145–46.

The idea of the political realm is elaborated in detail for the English case in the *Governance of England*. A *regnum politicum* is a realm governed by laws to which the people have given their assent; by assent is meant institutionally that the king will not change the law of the realm, or lay taxes, without the assent of his people (chap. II). The realm of France in which commons are taxed without the assent of the estates is for that reason classified as a *dominium tantum regale* (chap. III). The definitions seem to imply the idea of a constitutional monarchy; but this impression would be erroneous—just as erroneous as the opinion that Edward I's dictum "what touches all should be approved by all" implied the idea of government by popular consent. The terms *approval* or *assent* simply did not have at the time the modern connotations. The assent is not a right in the modern constitutional sense, and it cannot be denied as well as given. The assent or approval has the character of a participation in the agreement between the estates of the realm concerning the efforts that have to be made for its maintenance. The assent of the commons is at this time rather an extension of the feudal relationship to the newly articulate strata in which the commons have to fulfill their duties just as much as the barons, while they, on their part, can insist that the king fulfill his obligations arising out of his position as the protector of the realm and the administrator of the law. Any doubts concerning this question are quickly dispersed by the main body of Fortescue's work. Its topic is the "estate of the king," which is in danger of deteriorating and by its deterioration of impairing the stability of the realm itself. In this critical situation it becomes the duty of the other estates to stabilize the estate of the king in the interest of the whole.

The estate of the king is a highly complex idea combining the property rights of the king with his charismatic healing powers and with a composite of such charismatic qualities as are expressed by the terms of the majesty of the king, his will, his liberty, his grace; at the same time the estate is an office with duties of ministering to defense and justice (chap. VIII). The king's estate is "the highest estate temporell in the erthe." For the proper representation of this exalted estate and for the discharge of the duties connected with it, the king has to be the wealthiest lord in his realm, for if any of his subjects should equal or surpass him with regard to the property part of the estate that subject might become a rival to the crown and find rebellious subjects to aid him. "For the people will goe with him that best mey susteyne and rewarde ham." Fortescue seems to consider rebellion for this cause the normal thing to be expected. On this occasion we gain perhaps the deepest insight into the structure and dynamics of the realm. The sustenance of the king is as much the duty of the people as the defense of the people is the duty of the king. The subjects would favor the rebellion of a wealthy lord because they desire by his advancement to be relieved of at least a part of their burden of sustenance (chap. IX). A man will be "erected" into a king because his superior wealth is the most tangible symptom of the possession of the other charismatic qualities that are necessary for the estate of the king; under him the realm will enjoy prosperity, which again is most drastically tested by security and low taxes for the commons.

Fortescue's concern is, therefore, the proper endowment of the king's estate with the necessary means. Of first importance is the substance of the commons. If the commons are rich they can bring more easily the sacrifices of treasure that are required for maintaining the king's estate and with it the realm. Prosperous commons are, furthermore, desirable because the common man can then equip himself with bows and arrows and with defensive armor. The English archery is the backbone of the defense of the realm of which England is in great need because of her openness to attack by sea (chap. XII).[31] The more direct means for introducing stability into the royal finances would be the increase and prudent administration of the estate itself. To this problem Fortescue devotes the larger part of his work. He suggests various means for the increase and goes into the details of a plan for a council that should administer the estate in such a manner that it would not be frittered away by improper rewards to the numerous petitioners. If this plan had been put into practice, with the result that the royal revenue would

---

31. In the fifteenth century the insular position of England was still considered a military disability. The feeling that it might be an asset and an aid to security began to grow only after the construction of the coastal fortifications in the sixteenth century. Before the Tudor period there seems to have prevailed an anxiety, nourished by the memories of the invasions up to the Norman conquest and by the permanent frontier war against the "outer barbarian" (Toynbee's phrase) in Scotland and Wales, somewhat similar to the German encirclement complex. For the reaction of the continental Germanic tribes to the defeats of the migration, and for the origin of the German myth of the defeat, see vol. II, *The Middle Ages to Aquinas*, chap. 2, pp. 41–51.

have been sufficient to cover the principal expenses for the king's household, for the domestic administration and the defense of the realm, England would have evolved in the direction of a powerful absolute monarchy and the "assent" would probably have died from atrophy.

We may conclude with the clear theoretical formulation of the royal position in chapter VIII. Fortescue quotes Saint Thomas to the effect that "Rex datur propter regnum, et non regnum propter regem" (A king is given for the sake of the realm, and not the realm for the sake of the king). The dictum implies in the interpretation of Fortescue that the royal estate is an office with duties with regard to the realm. The ministerial element of the estate is, however, for Fortescue the premise from which he derives the duty of the people to sustain the king adequately. Because the estate is an office, the king may say of himself and of his realm what the pope says of himself and of the church: that he is *servus servorum Dei*, the servant of the servants of God. The king is the first servant of his realm, the secular *corpus mysticum*, and the Lord says, *dignus est operarius cibo suo*, the servant is worth his living. In this reversion of the role of master and servant we have the perfect formula for the balanced, reciprocal structure of the realm.[32]

32. We may note again the transfer of categories from the religious sphere and their application to the interpretation of the secular realm. And we may note also that the idea of the *servus servorum* reappears when the situation of the "eruption of the realm" is repeated, as in the famous dictum of Frederick the Great: "I am the first servant of my state."

20

From Imperial to Parochial Christianity

In the preceding chapter we have treated the articulation of the realm as a problem of internal evolution. We have now to bring this internal development into relation with the evolution of the West as a whole from its medieval imperial phase to its modern parochial phase. The growth of the people to the level of social relevance and political articulation presents, in the sphere of the feudal realms, the problem of integrating the new forces into the structure of the realm. In the measure in which this problem is solved successfully in the domestic sphere, it becomes exacerbated on the vaster scene of Western Christianity. The deeper the feudal realms sink their roots into the people, the looser become the ties of the supraterritorial relationships, temporal and spiritual, with the imperial structure of the West. The kingship and the prime estates orient themselves increasingly toward the people within the territorial boundaries of the realm, as the foundation of their strength; and the people, as they become articulate, are oriented toward the structure of the realm in which they find their political form. After the disaster of the Hohenstaufen, the emperor had been practically eliminated, in his function as the temporal lord of Christianity; and no substitute institution had evolved to take his place. The papacy approached in the fourteenth and fifteenth centuries the same fate, as the consequence of the Babylonian Captivity and the Great Schism. The success of the integration of the new forces into the realms, and the failure of such integration, either directly or by mediation of the realms, for Western society as a whole, is the fundamental historical decision that determined the parochial structure of the modern world. Again, as in the preceding chapter, we have to refer the reader for the historical detail to the standard treatises on the period. We shall trace only the main lines of evolution and select the typical facts.

§1. The Transformation of
the Church Organization

The residence of the popes in Avignon from 1305 to 1378 was an event of the greatest symbolic importance. It severed, at least temporarily, in a tangible form the connection with the Roman tradition. The physical proximity to France, in itself not very important, accentuated the fact, which otherwise would perhaps not have been so obvious to broad Christian masses, that the papacy was engulfed in an anarchical struggle that was to result in the parochial order of the West. The so-called Babylonian Captivity was the outward symptom, understood by everybody, that the direction of Western politics had slipped from the hands of the Holy See and that the papacy was adrift on an ocean of forces that it could not master.

The residence at Avignon and its significance as a symptom are clear. Much less clear is the complex situation of which it is the symptom. The change of residence was most directly a consequence of internal troubles in Italy that made a residence at Rome impossible because of the physical danger to the pope. Benedict XI, the successor of Boniface VIII, had lived in exile in Perugia, and the Archbishop of Bordeaux, Bertrand de Got, when he was elected as Clement V in 1305, was advised not to face the baronial anarchy in Rome. The first need of the papacy was a territorial foothold from which it could operate in physical safety in a new world of powers that did not shrink from an attack on the body of the pope, as the Day of Anagni had shown. The peculiar problem had arisen out of the policy of the Curia, since the time of Gregory VII, toward the Papal States. Over its de jure possessions, stemming from the donation of the Carolingians and of Matilda, the papacy did not exert a temporal sovereignty, but favored on the contrary the city-state development in Tuscany as well as in the *Ducatus Romanus* itself. The greatest asset of the papal policy with regard to the "border states" of the empire was the fact that it refrained from exerting secular authority even in Rome. The difficult position of a papacy without temporal power in Rome had induced Boniface VIII, toward the end of the thirteenth century, to lay the foundations of a Caetani state in southern Tuscany as a territorial bulwark against the Roman nobility. The choice of Avignon in 1305 as the residence did not indicate a submissiveness to France but was made because the Venaissin, surrounding Avignon, had been ceded to the papacy by France in 1274 and was under papal administration, while the overlords of Avignon were papal vassals. Avignon itself was purchased by Clement VI in 1348 and thus formed with the Venaissin the nucleus of a church-state. The various military attempts of the popes at Avignon to gain a secure territory in Italy were unsuccessful until the appointment in 1353 as papal legate to Italy of Cardinal Albornoz, a Spaniard who had received his cardinalate as a reward for distinguished services against the Moors in Andalusia. His diplomatic and military achievements laid the foundation for the construction of the church-state as one of the despotically governed Italian principalities, lasting until 1870. The conquest of Albornoz made possible the return of the papacy to Rome, but the fateful step was taken of surrendering the Hildebrandine policy. The church had stained its universal spiritual claim by the narrowness of submitting to the principle of territorial power in emulation of the new parochial realms. How deeply the parochialism of power penetrated into Western sentiment is evidenced by the pose of the popes as the Prisoners in the Vatican, when their territorial sovereignty was abolished in 1870, and by its reestablishment through the Lateran Treaty of 1929—"an error of Papal statesmanship," as Toynbee rightly characterizes this step.

The residence at Avignon imposed itself, furthermore, because of the new problems of foreign politics. On the occasion of the *Unam Sanctam* it had become clear that the papacy was the sole heir to the imperial policy of the West with regard to Islam. The great obstacle to the pursuit of a common Western policy *ad extra* was the preoccupation of France and England with the problems of their national consolidation. A reconciliation of the two realms was the military and economic condition for the resumption of the crusades. In spite of the setback experienced by Boniface VIII, the popes continued, from their vantage point at Avignon, their negotiations for the settlement of the French-English struggle as well as for the undertaking of further crusades. As distinguished a scholar as Professor Guillaume Mollat speaks of an "obsession" of the popes of Avignon with the idea of a crusade.[1] The language used indicates a bias that still too frequently distorts the understanding of the disaster that overcame Christian mankind in the fourteenth

---

1. Guillaume Mollat, "The Popes of Avignon and the Great Schism," *CMH*, vol. 7 (1932), chap. 10.

and fifteenth centuries. The papal "obsession" means simply that at least the spiritual power of Christianity had not yet renounced the idea of a Western community in which the interests of the whole should be more important than the domestic differences. The struggle between England and France, on the other hand, which paralyzed common action, marks the parochialization of Western politics through the elevation of internal problems to the rank of foreign affairs, at the expense of the affairs of imperial Christianity. The repeated attempts to reconcile England and France, the preparation of crusades, and their actual conduct prevented several times a planned departure from Avignon.[2]

By the fourteenth century the population and the wealth of Europe had increased considerably, the towns were growing in number and in population through immigration from the overcrowded countryside, and the money economy was advancing rapidly while the feudal economy of services was declining. Extrafeudal revenue from taxation formed an ever larger part of the total revenue of the realms, and the wars that were made possible by the new money power were perhaps as much wars to broaden the source of income by adding to the flock of sheep that could be fleeced. If the papacy wanted to hold its own in this new struggle of money power, it had to reorganize its financial system to perfection. The expenditures of John XXII, with 63.7 percent for war, 12.7 percent for upkeep and entertainment of the court, 7.16 percent for alms, down to expenses for the library with .16 percent, give a clear picture of the problem. Avignon was geographically the ideal center for an organization that had to cover the area of Christian Europe, considerably better situated for the purpose than the peripheral Rome. In order to provide for an adequate revenue, the Avignonese popes relied mainly on two measures: (1) a reorganization of the financial administration in the *camera apostolica* with the chamberlain as the most important papal official at its head, and (2) extreme centralization of church affairs in the Curia, particularly with regard

---

2. The problem of the campaigns against Islam, which could be solved successfully by crusades of the West under papal leadership, ultimately found its solution within the new structure of territorial sovereignties by the evolution of the Habsburg monarchy into the "carapace" (Toynbee's term) of the West against the Turks. With the decline of the Ottoman empire this universal Western raison d'être of the Habsburg foundation vanished; the Turkish decline was, for this reason, one of the important factors in the decline of the Austrian monarchy.

to the collation to benefices. Neither of these measures can be called an innovation in church government; what was new was the bureaucratic rationalization and the efficiency of the system. The church was making use of its enormous landed property (in England it is said to have had one-third of the country) for raising taxes to an unaccustomed amount and with an unaccustomed exaction, and of the equally enormous apparatus of noninheritable offices for collecting appointment fees, *annates*, first fruits, vacancy revenues, and so on. As a result the church became the first absolute Renaissance monarchy with a competent central bureaucracy and a ruthlessly efficient financial system. Similar standards of efficiency were reached in the national realms only toward the end of the fifteenth century, in Tudor England and in the France of Louis XI— though one should beware of interpreting, as it is sometimes done, the *post hoc* as a *propter hoc*.

§2. The English Reaction

The inevitable clash between the financial administration of the papacy and those of the realms can be studied best in the case of the English reaction. The fourteenth century brought the great series of measures by which the legal framework for the nationalization of the Church of England was created. The Statute of Carlisle, of 1307, formulates as the principal complaint that the funds of the monasteries, priories, and religious houses, which were established to provide for the poor and the sick, were diverted from their purpose by papal taxation. The statute prohibits the export of tax money, and it enjoins all "aliens" in whose obedience the English houses lie not to levy any further taxes. The measure was directed against the flow of revenue outside the country into the hands of an organization that ultimately might use it for the support of France. In 1343 Clement VI was petitioned to abolish his reservations and provisions by which aliens were appointed to English offices because the foreigners were not capable of ministering to the needs of the English people, if they appeared at all, and did not confine themselves to drawing revenue while the office was taken care of by a proxy for a pittance. The Statute of Provisors, of 1351, reestablished the "free election of archbishops, bishops, and all other dignities and benefice elective in England." In 1353 the Statute of Praemunire threatened with outlawry and forfeiture all persons who would take into papal courts cases over which the king's courts had cognizance. In 1366 the tribute to the pope was refused; John Lackland's homage for the realm of England to the pope was declared illegal because it had not the assent of the baronage. In 1390 the Second Statute of Provisors renewed the first and added severe sanctions of exile and banishment for its violation.

The measures constituted a body of law that, if fully enforced, would make the Church of England organizationally almost independent of the pope. The Supremacy Act of Henry VIII, in 1534, added only the keystone to the edifice of the fourteenth century. At the time, however, the facade was more imposing than the reality. The Statute of Carlisle and the Statute of Provisors had to be renewed because they were not observed too strictly. Papal provisions continued, frequently with the connivance of the kings, whose financial and general power position made deals desirable. The principal effect of the statutes at the time was that they put the king in a better bargaining position in his negotiations with the Curia. Besides, the issue did not lie between the kings and the popes alone, but had the parliament as well as the patrons and the elective bodies as a third partner to it. In the end, however, the victory lay with the king. The "free election" of 1351 was a formality because the royal letter-missive, granting the election, nominated the person to be elected and hardly met with resistance. In the sixteenth century, when the royal position was strong enough, the procedure of the letter-missive could be formalized by the Ecclesiastical Appointments Act of 1534 and disobedience be sanctioned by the punishments of the Statute of Provisors and the Statute of Praemunire. The Church of England thus was integrated into the administration of the territorial realm as the parochializing countermove to the intensified administration of the Roman Church in the territories of the realms.

§3. Wycliffe—General Character

The organizational resistance of the realms against the centralized church administration, which is known as Anglicanism and Gallicanism, would not have been possible unless a profound restructuring of religious sentiment had taken place in the direction of what we have called parochial Christianity. The outstanding figure of the fourteenth century, representing the new religious type, is John Wycliffe (1320–1384). He was the outstanding figure and has become the great symbol of the pre-Reformation because of the amplitude of his personality, which could embrace the functions of the scholar, politician, and reformer. He was unique in his age by this amplitude, but the amplitude has sometimes been mistaken for profoundness and intenseness, with the consequence that his rank in the history of ideas is not yet judged quite stably and clearly. We can observe a tendency to overrate him as the pride of Protestantism and of the English nation, and more recently, under the impression of a closer study of his work in relation to that of others, a tendency to underrate him, particularly with regard to his political ideas. The oscillations of judgment are due to the fact that his greatness is sought too narrowly in his doctrines instead of in the qualities of sentiment that enabled him to give expression, in the medium of scholastic theology, to the problems of the age.

In order to gain the proper level of interpretation, we have first to state negatively that Wycliffe was neither a great harmonizing thinker like Saint Thomas nor a great critic like Duns Scotus or William of Ockham; he was not a great mystic like Eckhart, nor did he have the eschatological tenseness of the humble author of *Piers Plowman*; and he had neither the elemental, savage faith of Luther, nor the qualities of ecclesiastical statesmanship of Calvin. Disappointment is inevitable if we search in Wycliffe's work for an extraordinary achievement on the absolute level of the spirit or the intellect. He is sometimes praised as the foremost scholastic of his time, and the judgment may be correct. But scholasticism had run the course of its great problems from realism to nominalism, and one could no longer be foremost in the movement of ideas by being foremost in scholasticism; no particular merit can be attached to Wycliffe's realistic position, though it determined his unorthodox stand on transubstantiation. The much vaunted theory of the foundation of *dominium* on grace was preformed in Fitzralph's *De pauperie Salvatoris* (ca. 1347), his predestinarianism in the position of Bradwardine; for Wycliffe it was characteristic that he never could harmonize the two doctrines in his system. The discussion of the royal office in his *De Officio Regis* falls short of the radicalism of the *York Tracts*. His doctrine of the church, even in its radical form that God gives his charismata to every Christian, thus constituting with him the mystical body and not requiring for this purpose the mediation of an official of the Roman Church, is not more radical than the antisacerdotalism of numerous heretical sectarians. And even his great organizational work, the preparation of the English Bible, is so much in the trend of the time that Herbert B. Workman in his monograph is compelled to say that it "was the expression of a movement which would have produced a translation in the latter years of the fourteenth or the opening years of the fifteenth centuries, altogether apart from Wyclif."[3]

The importance of Wycliffe does not lie in any one of his doctrines or actions taken singly, but in the richness of the agglomeration. Trends that had moved hitherto separately or on the level of the lower social strata or of heretical sects were gathered in his person and raised to the level of the distinguished scholar, the Oxford man, and the man of politics associated with the court. In his life and work a new social and religious movement pierced for the first time the surface of institutional respectability and became politically relevant through its convergence with the organizational measures of the realm against the papacy. If we formulate the problem presented by Wycliffe in this manner, we have formulated at the same time his strength and his weakness. Wycliffe could make an imprint on his age because he was responsive more than any other contemporary to the stirring forces, spiritual and political, of the England of his time. But he could not make more than a passing imprint because he was not stronger than the forces that he focused in himself. In an age that was not yet ripe for the event he sensed religiously and understood intellectually the problems that later precipitated the Reform. But he was not deeply rooted enough spiritually and metaphysically to stand on his own as a great mystic or philosopher. Hence Wycliffe should properly be approached not through his systematic work. His peculiar responsiveness to, and permeability for, the forces of his time make it advisable to characterize them briefly, and then only to analyze his response.

---

3. Workman, *John Wyclif: A Study of the English Medieval Church*, 2 vols. (Oxford: Clarendon, 1926), 2:170. More recent studies include David Jeffrey, trans. and ed., *The Law of Love: English Spirituality in the Age of Wyclif* (Grand Rapids: Eerdmans, 1988); Anne Hudson and Michael Wilks, eds., *From Ockham to Wyclif* (Oxford: Blackwell, 1987); Anthony Kenny, ed., *Wyclif in His Times* (Oxford: Oxford University Press, 1986); Louis B. Hall, *The Perilous Vision of John Wyclif* (Chicago: University of Chicago Press, 1983); and John L. Daly, *The Political Theory of John Wyclif* (Chicago: University of Chicago Press, 1962).

§4. The Regional Spiritual Movements

We have followed the internal evolution of Christian spirituality through the waves of monastic reform to the mendicant orders. With the beginning of the thirteenth century this evolution entered a critical phase insofar as the ability of the church to institutionalize the ever new movements of the spirit in the form of orders seemed to weaken. The energies of the Cluniac and Cistercian reforms could not be channeled only in the new form of the sovereign order, but they streamed directly into the reform of the papacy and the church. The energies of the Military Orders on the other hand went into the crusades, while that of the mendicant orders went into the European town mission and, in the fourteenth century, during the papal residence at Avignon, into the missionizing of Asia. The papacy itself was comparatively little touched by these later developments. That an epoch had been reached in the waves of spiritual intensification and expansion is shown by the decision of the Fourth Lateran Council of 1215 that prohibited the foundation of new orders. Even so the last of the orders proved already a source of trouble. The Order of the Templars was dissolved at the beginning of the fourteenth century because it conflicted with the territorial temporal power of France. The Order of the Franciscans reached its crisis at the same time because the spiritual wing conflicted with the ecclesiastical organization. From both of the centers of the disintegrating imperial community, from the spiritual as well as the temporal, the late orders were forced into the position of a third power. The Templars as the instrument of imperial Western policy had become functionless in the new field of foreign politics between the contracting realms. The Spirituals and their ideal of poverty were incompatible with the evolution of papacy into the foremost bureaucratic money power of the age.

The last orders, the mendicant, were only a partial success. The Franciscans could absorb in their ranks, particularly through the Tertiary Order, a proportion of the religiously moved people of the towns. And both orders, the Franciscans and the Dominicans, could, through their missionary work spreading over Europe, control an appreciable part of the people and attach their sentiments through their orders to the church. But a not inconsiderable part of the movement escaped such control and developed into the heretical sects. As far as these sects remained small and localized, they do not concern us in this context. But parallel with the foundation of the mendicant orders a social form of the movement began to appear in outlines that prognosticate the later events of the pre-Reformation and the Reformation. In the case of the Albigensians, a heretical movement spread through the towns of a large region, the Provence, and found favor with the regional nobility. This is the first instance in which a new religious movement, outside the church, penetrated a cultural area and rose above the level of its origin in the towns into the ruling nobility. The Provence had a culture, but it was not a realm; if it had remained undisturbed it might have developed into a realm and a Provençal nation might have grown. At the beginning of the thirteenth century no more than tendencies of an evolution in the direction indicated were noticeable. The Albigensian movement does not have the characteristics of a national struggle that are typical of the later regional movements in England, Bohemia, and Germany, but we have to classify it, nevertheless, as the first in the series of upheavals that resulted in the parochialization of Christianity. The principal characteristics were present in (1) the break with the Roman Church, (2) the impossibility of absorbing spiritually active minorities into elite organizations of the order type, (3) the penetration into the nobility, and (4) the foundation in a regional culture.[4]

The first regional movement was suppressed by the church successfully with the aid of the Capetian kings—so successfully that one of the finest civilizations of the West was destroyed completely in the process. In the second wave of parochial Christianity, in England and Bohemia, a complete suppression was impossible. The movements associated with the names of Wycliffe and Hus are called the pre-Reformation. The term is established, but it is not quite happy. It focuses attention too much on the Reform of the

---

4. For other aspects of the Albigensian movement and for the problem of the heretical movements in general, see vol. IV, *Renaissance and Reformation*, chap. 3, "The People of God." Malcolm Lambert, *Medieval Heresy: Popular Movements from the Gregorian Reform to the Reformation* (Oxford: Blackwell, 1992); Norman Cohn, *The Pursuit of the Millennium* (New York: Harper, 1972); Bernard McGinn, *Visions of the End* (New York: Columbia University Press, 1979); Gordon Leff, *Heresy in the Later Middle Ages: The Relation of Heresy to Dissent c. 1250–1450*, 2 vols. (Manchester: Manchester University Press, 1967); and the studies of Emmanuel Le Roy Ladurie, such as *Montaillou: Cathars and Catholics in a French Village, 1294–1324*, trans. B. Bray (Harmondsworth: Penguin, 1980).

sixteenth century and puts Wycliffe in the position of a "forerunner"; the real problems are obscured by this somewhat simplistically drawn line of history. What distinguishes the period of the Great Reform from the movements of the fourteenth century is the international reaction that a spark, touched off by Luther unwittingly, could find. By the sixteenth century, the parochialization of Christian sentiment had made such progress that a revolt against the Roman Church as the survival of imperial Christianity, once it had started at any point, could spread over vast areas of Europe so rapidly and so uniformly that it developed the characteristics of an international movement. From Geneva, Calvin was able to pursue the policy of an international protestant federation. The Protestant International was the first international movement in the technical sense of a movement with parochial centers but of sufficient uniformity to make a degree of alliance possible and to embark on a policy of intervention when the movement resulted in civil war in any one of the parochial centers. Internationalism in this sense is a secondary form of spiritual unity that takes the place, in the age of parochialization, of the former imperial unity. We can describe the so-called pre-Reformation, therefore, more precisely as an earlier phase of parochialism, overlapping still with a comparatively strong imperial Christianity. The phenomena of internationalism and intervention were still absent. The military enterprises against the Hussites in the fifteenth century had still the imperial form of the crusade, just as the Albigensian wars of the early thirteenth century.

Although the influence of Wycliffe on Hus is a foreboding of the later situation, the factor of internationalism was on the whole still absent. The factor of organized nationalism in alliance with the parochial Christian movement was, on the other hand, strongly present, so strongly that it even outweighed the religious movement. The struggle of the church in suppressing the pre-Reformation was characteristically successful as far as the religious movement proper and its leaders were concerned, but it was unsuccessful with regard to the national resistance.[5] Wycliffe was silenced; the statute *De Haeretico Comburendo*, of 1401, engaged the power of the realm for stamping out Lollardy, and with the execution of Sir

---

5. [See B. M. Bolton, *The Medieval Reformation* (New York: Holmes and Meier, 1983).]

John Oldcastle in 1417 the Wycliffite movement was effectively driven underground. The resistance of the realm against the papacy, on the other hand, did not flag perceptibly; the endeavors of Boniface IX (1389–1404) to obtain the abolition of the legislative measures that began with the Statute of Carlisle were in vain. In the struggle against the Hussites we can observe a similar pattern: Hus and Hieronymus of Prague were executed in 1415 and 1416, respectively, with the result that the Czech national movement gained its great momentum while the religious movement disintegrated into sects that ultimately merged in the Great Reformation. We may say, therefore, that the organization of the realm and nationalism were the factors, still missing in the Albigensian case, that provided the ethical, civilizational, and political foundation for the continuous evolution toward parochial Christianity, although the religious movement was not yet strong enough to accomplish the ecclesiastical schism. More precisely, the weakness of the movement can be defined as the inability of the pre-Reformation leaders to unify the forces of sectarianism and to direct them into the foundation of parochial counterchurches to the church of Rome. Neither the English nor the Bohemian movements could master the centrifugal tendencies of the Christian revolt and bend them under the yoke of a new ecclesiastical institution. And even in the sixteenth century the disruptive element of sectarianism was still so strong that Luther as well as Calvin had to strain all their efforts to prevent the Reformation from being engulfed in an abyss of civilizational destruction. Wycliffe's Poor Priests of the first phase of his activity and the laymen Lollards of the later phase had still rather the character of an order community of the early Franciscan type, and it is hard to see how they ever could have become the nucleus of a reformed church even if circumstances had been more favorable, because a church does not live of the spirit alone but also on a good deal of crafty statesmanship. The Hussites came closer to a church organization because the struggle against the Germans in the Bohemian territory added the pressure of Czech nationalism to the forces compelling coherence of the various social and religious groups. But even under these exceptional circumstances the welter of incoherent sectarian influences disrupted the movement to the point of civil war. There is hardly a major Western sectarian trend that did not make its impact felt in the Bohemian struggle. The English Wycliffism determined most strongly the attitude of Hus

himself and of his immediate followers; but in addition we find
the Waldensianism of groups in southern Bohemia and of Nicholas
of Dresden, the rational Puritanism of Picard refugees after 1418,
radical chiliastic movements, Adamites, Albigensian Catharism,
and, of course, the great expressions of Czech religiousness: of Jan
Milic and Thomas of Stitny in the fourteenth century and of Peter
Chelcicky in the fifteenth.[6] To what extent direct Eastern elements
entered into the mixture is unknown; but the question merits attention considering that the Hussite iron-clad wagons linked by chains,
developed by Ziska as an instrument of defensive and offensive
warfare, were probably an import from the Ottomans.[7]

§5. English Spiritualism—*Piers Plowman*

The Christianization of the West had begun at the top of the social
hierarchy; by the twelfth century it had penetrated deep into the
rising towns; by the fourteenth century it had reached down to
the peasantry. The religious fermentation in the lower classes and
the political articulation go side by side; the two trends are interwoven so closely that sometimes, as in the Hussite movement, it
is difficult, if not impossible, to distinguish between them. A vast
groundswell of unrest was rising all over Europe, accentuated by
profound revolutions in the sphere of material factors. The twelfth
and thirteenth centuries had witnessed a considerable increase of
population, which expressed itself in the overflow from the countryside into the towns, the difficulties of holding peasants within
the orbit of the feudal agricultural system, the increase of wealth
and the advance of the money economy, the substitution of rents
for services, and so on. The Black Death of 1349 had accelerated the
economic evolution through the sudden decrease of population and
the ensuing scarcity of labor. Inept economic legislation, like the
English Statute of Laborers of 1351, had aggravated the situation
by fixing wages and thereby robbing laborers of the income they
would have received in an unregulated market; the depreciation of
the English silver coinage of the same year had further decreased
the real value of wages. The strong population movement from the

---

6. The utility of the Brotherhood founded by Chelcicky achieved in 1467 an
independent organization, its priesthood breaking with the apostolic succession.
For this reason it may be considered the first reformed church.

7. See for this question Toynbee, *Study of History*, 1:352, n. 2.

country to the towns had, furthermore, created a broad popular basis for the spreading of discontent as well as ideas from the one social sector to the other. In the fourteenth century the peasantry entered the political scene for the first time as an important factor, though the immediate political effects were ephemeral because of the lack of leadership. The French Jacquerie of 1358 and the English Peasant Revolt of 1381 are violent symptoms of the social and economic changes.

The formation of a broad lower stratum of society in spiritual fermentation has to be understood as the background for literary expressions of the fourteenth century that otherwise might appear more isolated and lacking in social resonance than they actually were. The English scene was intellectually and spiritually not so diversified as the German or Bohemian, and the movement of the people's Christianity had not yet produced the vast manifold of sectarian groupings found on the Continent, but the fermentation was sufficiently intense to let Wycliffe's work appear as the culmination of an evolution that had gained already some historical momentum. A powerful center for the diffusion of spiritual religiousness were the Franciscans at Oxford. Robert Grosseteste himself (ca. 1175–1253) had translated the writings of Dionysius Areopagita from the Greek and thereby released a stream of mystical theology. Richard Rolle of Hampole (ca. 1300–1349) was the first great representative of the new spiritual age. He was an Oxford man and probably had a period at the Sorbonne. He must have experienced the influences of Franciscan spiritualism, of the continental mystics of his time, perhaps of Joachimism, and certainly of the pseudo-Dionysian writings. He was a mystic by temperament himself, inclined toward the *vita contemplativa* and living as a hermit outside the institutional framework of the church and the orders. His more voluminous and more important mystical writings are in Latin, but he exerted greater influence through his English works. He translated the Psalter into English and added a translation of the *Commentary* of Peter Lombard, and he was a poet who wrote religious lyrics of great strength and beauty. His work was widespread in England and on the Continent in the century and a half before the Reformation, but it is impossible to judge how deeply it penetrated into the people beyond the institutionalized religious public. His writing in vernacular alone is not a proof of broad popular influence, because for Rolle as for the German mystics the reason for writing in the native language was the need of religious women who had not learned Latin. Another, and perhaps even more important, center of mystical religiousness is the anonymous author of the *Cloud of Unknowing*, who, under pseudo-Dionysian influence, gave one of the profoundest analyses of mystical experience. The same author, or a member of his group, gave the first English free translation of the Dionysian *Theologia Mystica* under the title *Dionis Hid Divinite*. And, finally, Walter Hilton has to be mentioned, the author of the *Scale of Perfection*, a classic of devotional literature, comparable to the *Imitatio Christi*.

The fact that it is impossible to trace direct influences from this class of literature to revolutionary groups should not obscure its importance. The upsurge of mysticism as such, the withdrawal from the institutional order of society, and the contraction into solitary spiritual existence are among the most fateful symptoms of the disorder of a civilization.[8] It is a question of temperament, social circumstance, education, and religious gifts whether the withdrawal from the disintegrating order will assume the form of mystical contemplation, eschatological vision, or social revolution. The civilizational destruction perpetrated by a peasant group fighting for the perfect realm does not differ in principle from the annihilation of the world content in the sentence of the author of the *Cloud of Unknowing:* "It is needful for thee to bury in a cloud of forgetting all creatures that ever God made, that thou mayest direct thine intent to God Himself." The forms of individual mysticism and of eschatological speculation are closely related.

We have to be aware of this relationship when we approach the complex of poems that goes under the general title of *Piers Plowman*. It is a heatedly debated question whether the several parts of the complex have William Langland for their author, or whether we

8. On the relation between the decline of a civilization and the rise of individual mystics, see Friedrich Heiler, *Das Gebet*, 4th ed. (1921; rpt. Munich: Reinhardt, 1969), 250 ff. *Prayer: A Study in the History and Psychology of Religion*, trans. Samuel McComb (London: Oxford University Press, 1932). In general see Steven Ozment, *Mysticism and Dissent* (New Haven: Yale University Press, 1973); McGinn, *Visions of the End*; Marjorie Reeves, *The Influence of Prophecy in the Later Middle Ages* (Oxford: Clarendon, 1969); Cohn, *Pursuit of the Millennium*; Gordon Leff, *Dissolution of the Medieval Outlook* (New York: Harper, 1976); and Johan Huizinga, *The Waning of the Middle Ages: A Study of the Forms of Life, Theory, and Art in France and in the Netherlands in the XIVth and XVth Centuries*, trans. Frederik Jan Hopman (London: Arnold, 1927; rpt. Harmondsworth and Baltimore: Penguin, 1976).

have to assume the existence of several authors.[9] Fortunately this controversy of literary history need not concern us here because the question of single or multiple authorship has little bearing on the analysis of the contents of the several poems. We have to be clear, however, about the identification of the parts of the agglomeration and shall distinguish, therefore, between the *Visio de Petro Plowman*, comprising the Prologue and Passus I–VIII of the so-called A-Text; the *Vita de Dowel, Dobet, and Dobest*, comprising certainly Passus IX–XI of the A-Text, and possibly, but not necessarily Passus XII;[10] and third, the reworking of the poems of the A-Text and their absorption into the great poem of *Piers Plowman* that is contained in the so-called B-Text.[11]

The *Visio* is the most accessible and best known of the three poems. It is a critique of the time, comparable in its intention to Dante's *Inferno* and *Purgatorio*, though not on the scale of imperial but within the sphere of parochial English Christianity. The topic of the poem is the orientation of Christian life toward its transcendental purpose in God, the fundamental theological conception being on the whole Thomasic. The greatest of all treasures is Truth and its attainment. The meaning of Truth in the context of *Piers Plowman* receives body through a reference to 1 John 4:8: "God is Love. Who does not love, does not know God" (4:8). The Spirit of Truth (4:6) can be recognized as such because it induces us to love God and each other. The life of the Christian should be oriented toward Truth, but most people live as if the material world were the only reality and let their lives be dominated by worldly cupidity. The

9. For the controversy on the authorship see the collected papers of Manly, Jusserand, Chambera, and Bradley in the edition of the Early English Text Society, nos. 135b and 139b, c, d, and e. See also John A. Alford, *A Companion to Piers Plowman* (Berkeley: University of California Press, 1988); *Piers Plowman: The Three Versions*, ed. George Kane (Berkeley: University of California Press, 1988).

10. For a careful analysis of the two poems of the A-Text see T. P. Dunning, *Piers Plowman: An Interpretation of the A-Text* (London, 1937; rpt. New York: Oxford University Press, 1980).

11. The sources used are: *Langland's Vision of Piers Plowman, the Vernon Text, or Text A*, ed. Walter W. Skeat, Early English Text Society, no. 28 (London, 1867). *Langland's Vision of Piers Plowman, the Crowley Text, or Text B*, ed. Walter W. Skeat, Early English Text Society, no. 38 (London, 1869). *Langland's Vision of Piers Plowman*, ed. Walter W. Skeat, Early English Text Society, no. 67 (London, 1885). *Langland's Vision of Piers Plowman, the Whitaker Text, or Text C*, ed. Walter W. Skeat, Early English Text Society, no. 54 (London 1873). Recent editions: *Piers Plowman: A New Translation of the B Text*, trans. A. V. Schmidt (New York: Oxford University Press, 1992); *Piers Plowman: The C-text*, ed. Derek Pearsall (Exeter: University of Exeter Press, 1994).

description of the religiously disoriented English society of the age fills the main body of the *Visio*. The poem is a storehouse of realistic types of all strata of English society and has become by virtue of this empirical wealth a principal source for understanding English social and economic problems of the fourteenth century.[12] The ideal man who lives the true Christian life is represented by Piers Plowman, the God-fearing, hard-working, and charitable peasant who accepts his station in life. This latter point, the acceptance of station, is important. In the *Visio* there is no tendency noticeable to identify Piers Plowman with the savior figure of a new spiritual realm, as in the poem of the B-Text. The humble laborer of the *Visio* lives in imitation of Christ, but no more. He is the representative of the estate that provides for the *bona temporalia;* the fact that he leads a model life does not impair the legitimacy of the priesthood that provides for the *bona spiritualia* or of the knighthood that defends the two other estates. The social hierarchy is accepted as the proper articulation of the Christian community. Hence the *Visio* is a critique of the age by the standards of the Christian law of love, remarkable for its realism and its sharp and sarcastic characterization of the deviations from the straight line of a life oriented toward Truth, but it is not a revolutionary eschatology. A quiet revolution has occurred, nevertheless, even in the *Visio*. The *rudis homo,* the *idiota* of Siger de Brabant and Saint Thomas, has become the representative Christian figure in Langland's poem. The maturation of the Christian spirit that, in the thirteenth century, had produced the Christian intellectual as its representative type was now expanding below the level of the towns into the unlearned people at large. The political articulation of society in the realm was paralleled by the spiritual articulation reaching down to the lower classes.

The growth of the plain man into full spiritual stature is the topic of the second poem, the *Vita de Dowel, Dobet, and Dobest.* Do-Well as the formula for the Christian life appears already in the latter part of the *Visio*. The *Vita* is devoted to a discussion of the

---

12. For a survey of the empirical materials that can be drawn from *Piers Plowman* see D. Chadwick, *Social Life in the Days of Piers Plowman* (Cambridge: Cambridge University Press, 1922). Recent works: Morton Bloomfield, *Piers Plowman as a Fourteenth Century Apocalypse* (New Brunswick, N.J.: Rutgers University Press, 1962); Britton Harwood, *Piers Plowman and the Problem of Belief* (Toronto: University of Toronto Press, 1992).

phases of perfection from Do-Well through Do-Better to Do-Best. The discussion is connected with the *Visio* insofar as it elaborates a problem touched upon in the earlier poem, but it does not continue the allegorical narrative, and Piers Plowman has no function in it except as the model type of Do-Well. The level of the poem has, furthermore, changed from the general categories of Christian life and worldly life to the mystical process of the soul. The three phases of Dowel, Dobet, and Dobest are obviously conceived under the pseudo-Dionysian influence; they correspond to the three stages of Purification, Illumination, and Union of the *theologia mystica.* The first phase, Dowel, is to fear God; the fear of judgment will induce man to fight against his passions and to live virtuously. The second phase, Dobet, is marked by suffering; the chastised soul will turn from the world and cleave to God by love. In the third phase, self-will is broken and the soul, guided by reason, will live in union with the law of God. The penetration of the soul to its own center of reason—that is, to the point of union with divine reason—has to proceed, in the *Vita,* over the steps of perfection under the guidance of Kind-Wit (*ratio* in the Christian sense). The mature existence of Dobest is possible in every state of life, in the humblest as well as in the highest. This principal thesis of the *Vita* implies, as in the *Visio,* acceptance of the various social forms of the active, the contemplative, and the active-contemplative mixed lives, and at the same time preserves the possibility of full Christian existence in the lower ranks of society.

A specific problem is presented in this connection by the role of Learning in the attainment of perfection. The critique of Study in the *Vita* parallels the critique of Cupidity in the *Visio.* Learning may be useful if a man is in the state of grace, but it may become an obstacle to the Christian life if it is indulged in for its own sake. On this occasion we can measure perhaps most clearly the distance that separates Langland from the climate of Thomas, who speaks of the superiority of the philosophical intellect over the understanding of the *rusticus* (*Contra Gentiles* I.3). Scholastic theology is no longer the supreme expression of Christian reason; the accents have shifted from the aspect of *intellectus* in reason to charity and the natural understanding of Kind-Wit, without learning. The position of Langland is closer to Franciscan spiritualism than to scholastic intellectualism, but the conformance to Christ is not driven to the point of an elitarian life in poverty; mystical perfection can be reached within the plain occupational status in the order of the world. And the Christianity of the individual is, furthermore, not strictly dependent on institutional aid, but can be perfected under the guidance of Kind-Wit, who lodges with Life, the lord of the earth.[13] The adult man, in full possession of his faculties, "is chief sovereign of himself" (*Piers Plowman* X.72): "For worche he wel other wrong, the wit is his owene" (X.74).

The declaration of independence of the Christian "sovereign of himself" is almost protestant in its individualism; it is, further-more, an independence that has its source in the mystical experi-ences of the soul; it reflects, third, the consciousness of the plain man as the basic estate of society, and it is very much aware that the poor have an advantage over the rich in entering the realm of God. We have to be clear about these sentiments dominating even the A-Text in order to understand the surprising development of the figure of Piers Plowman in the B-Text. The *Visio* leaves the problem on the level of an allegory, contrasting the life of self-will and cupidity with the Christian law of love; the *Vita* goes deeper into the mystical process of the soul; the B-Text advances to a symbolistic philosophy of history in the manner of Joachim of Fiore and of Dante with Piers Plowman melting into the figure of Christ, who will defeat Antichrist and bring the realm of the Spirit. We shall confine our analysis to the principal part of the poem, beginning with Passus XV, which corresponds in its contents to the apocalyptic vision of *Purgatorio* 29–33.

The topic is still the same as in the *Vita,* the search of Charity. What is Charity? asks the dreamer (XV.145) and receives the answer that it is a childlike thing; if you cannot become like children you shall not enter the realm; only the childlike soul is "a fre liberal wille" (XV.146). Charity purges the soul of pride; when it has become contrite and humble God will not despise it (XV.188). Charity can be found, however, only with the aid of Piers Plowman. The clergy with its works and words does not know him, but the Plowman looks deeper and divines the quality of the will. Only by the purified will is Charity known, and the will is known only by the Plowman *Petrus, id est, Christus* (XV.206).[14]

---

13. A-Text, Passus XII, v. 43, ff.: "my cosyn kynde wit' knowen is wel wide and his loggyng is with lyf' that lord is of erthe."

14. The importance attached to "free will," the *liberum arbitrium,* by the au-thor of the B-Text shows the influence on him of the voluntarism of Duns Scotus

Following the announcement of Petrus-Christus as the guide, the symbolic history of the search for Charity begins in Passus XVI. In the garden that God has made for himself in the heart of man grows the Tree of Patience, entrusted to the care of Piers Plowman, bearing the fruit of Charity. When the dreamer receives this intelligence, he swoons for joy, and in his dream now unfolds the sacred drama. The first act is the history of the Old Testament. The Tree bears fruit—Adam and Abraham, Samuel and Isaiah, and, finally, John the Baptist. But when the fruits ripen and fall, the devil gathers them, and Piers tries to regain them with the aid of Holy Spirit (XVI.25–89). In a second vision the Spirit becomes incarnate through Mary. Jesus, who will fight the devil and defend the fruit of the Tree, is taught leech-craft by Piers to heal the wounds of sickness and sin inflicted by the enemy (XVI.90 ff.). Passus XVII is an excursus on faith, hope, and charity, the Trinity and grace. The history is resumed in Passus XVIII with the appearance of a figure on an ass, resembling partly the Samaritan and partly Piers Plowman. He is hailed by Faith as the Son of David riding toward Jerusalem to joust with Death. The figure is interpreted (XVIII.22 ff.) as Christ in the armor of Piers, that is in his *humana natura*. With Passus XIX the passion begins. Christ in the human form of Piers reappears, "Painted all bloody" and bearing the cross (XIX.6–7). The life of Jesus is followed through the phases of the Dowel of the minor miracles, the Dobet of the major miracles and the passion, to the Dobest of the Resurrected who gives to Piers the powers to bind and unbind (XIX.183 ff.). The figure of Christ in the *humana natura* of Piers now changes to that of Piers on whom the Spirit descends, Piers the plowman of God and founder of the church (XIX.186–330). But the work of Piers is attacked by Pride; the church becomes corrupt, and the admonitions of Conscience are of no avail (XIX.331–406). The situation of corrupt Christianity is summed up by an "unlearned Vicar" (XIX.407–55), who attacks the popes of Avignon and voices the hope for a last and saving transfiguration of Piers. The special evil of the time singled out is the foreign cardinals who come to England and are a curse to the country with

---

and William of Ockham. This specific relation to the scholasticism of the English Franciscans is suggestive, however, also of deeper relations to the whole complex of Franciscan Spiritualism, which must have existed, considering the general conception of the visions we are about to analyze.

their lechery, pomp, and plunder. The cardinals, the vicar suggests, should not come "among the common people" but be kept in their holiness in Avignon with the Jewish money lenders: "Cum sancto sanctus eris" (XIX.420; With the holy you will become holy). In England, however, he prays, Conscience should be in king's court, and grace the guide of the clergy.

> "And Piers with his new plow and eke with his olde, Emperour of al
> the worlde that alle men were cristene." (XIX.424–25)

In the vision of Passus XX, finally, Antichrist appears and devastates the world; the last force of resistance, Conscience, is attacked by Sloth and Pride in a final assault; Conscience flees and wanders the world as a pilgrim in search of Piers the Savior, who will defeat Antichrist (XX.378–84).

Of necessity the account of the vision has to be brief and dry; it does not do justice to the wealth of elaboration of the principal topics nor to the poem as a work of art. But I hope it brings out with sufficient clearness the plan of the work. The Tree of Patience of the Old Testament is followed by Charity—that is, the Spirit Incarnate—in the church of the New Testament, and it is to be followed by the realm of the Spirit under Piers the emperor in person. Between the first and the second realm appear the corrupter Satan and the healer Jesus; after the second realm appears the corrupter Antichrist with Pride carrying his banner while the savior Piers is yet of the hope that is the substance of faith. The sequence of the realms is held together as a history of the Spirit by the metamorphoses of Piers as the gardener, the logos who teaches Jesus, the *human natura* of Christ, Petrus the vessel of the Spirit and vicar of Christ, and Piers the savior-emperor. The parallel with Dante's symbolic history of the church and the hope for the soteriological *Dux* is too obvious to be insisted upon. We have to stress rather the point where Dante and *Piers Plowman* part ways. Dante envisages the *Dux* as the savior figure of imperial Christianity; his hatred against the political popes of Avignon and the corrupter France does not drive him into a parochial solution of the problem. For the author of the B-Text the popes and cardinals of Avignon are not only the corrupters of the church but also "foreigners" who press on the "commoners" of the realm; the organizational struggle of the realm against the financial exactions and the provisions of the papal administration forms the background for the sentiments of the author of *Piers Plowman*; the sequel to the corrupt church will not be the renovated spiritual church of Western mankind, but a Christian realm of England. The formulas of the B-Text (Emperor of the World; all men are Christians) are certainly universalistic, but the concrete situation to which the author refers is that of the common English people. We must not overlook that the imperial figure of Dante is modeled on the historical emperor of the West, while the emperor of the B-Text embodies the spirit of the common laboring man; the Emperor Piers is of the substance of the people— a problem that hardly has any place in Dante's ideas. We may say, therefore, that the B-Text of *Piers Plowman* is a *Divina Commedia* on the level of parochial Christianity; it is a document of the first importance of the new religiousness of the people within the framework of the realm.

May I add that the B-Text from Passus XV to the end is a masterly constructed work of art and of the intellect. The charges, monotonously to be found in the literature on the poem, of nebulousness and lack of organization, can hardly have another cause but a failure of understanding. The author of the B-Text is no Dante, either in the scope of his work, or in learning, or in poetic and intellectual strength, but his work stands, nevertheless, as a masterpiece of symbolistic art. The reader will, furthermore, have noticed that we have stressed the internal spiritual unfolding of the topic from the *Visio* through the *Vita* to the B-Text. A layman in the field of history of literature cannot venture, of course, a definite opinion on the delicate question of single or multiple authorship. He may observe, though, that it would be very curious, indeed, if the internal evolution in the sequence of the poems should not reflect the internal evolution of a personality but that two or three authors should have followed each other by a historical accident so as to form this series.

§6. Wycliffe—Doctrines

The preceding analysis furnishes us with a frame of reference for ordering the principal doctrines of Wycliffe. As we have indicated earlier, the doctrines themselves are less interesting because of their quality as theories than because of the sentiments and political tendencies expressed by their means. We can classify the sentiments that dominate the doctrinal evolution of Wycliffe under three heads: (1) the religiousness of the free sovereign individual; (2) the anti-ecclesiastical sentiment that tends to break the sacramental order of the church and to reclassify mankind into the memberships of the mystical spiritual church and of the equally mystical *corpus diaboli* of the reprobate or "foreknown" in Wycliffe's terminology; and (3) the enhancement of kingship and the tendency to consider the national realm the ultimate visible organization of the Christians.

The first of these sentiments, the religiousness of the free individual, has found in Wycliffe's work its curious expression in the famous doctrine of dominion by grace. As far as the literary filiation of the theory is concerned, it is still connected with the Franciscan struggle for the ideal of poverty. Clement VI had appointed a commission to investigate the controversy concerning the poverty of Jesus. The archbishop of Armagh, Richard Fitzralph, was dissatisfied with the proceedings of the commission and summarized the problem in a treatise of his own, the *De Pauperie Salvatoris* (ca. 1350). In this treatise Fitzralph formulated the principle that no human being can participate in the dominion over the world, as granted in Genesis, unless he is purged of the sin of Adam and has received grace ("donec a peccato mundetur et gratiam gratificantem reciperet," II.8).[15] He also introduces at length the examples of feudal relationships for the illustration of the meanings of property and dominion. In his *De Dominio Divino* and *De Dominio Civili* (ca. 1375/6) Wycliffe amalgamates these elements into a feudal theory of the dominion by grace that is carried by the sentiment of the free Christian existence. God is the lord of the world because there are creatures to be his servants. Dominion and service are the correlative terms of the relationship that binds man and God. The lordship of God differs, however, from that of other feudal lords insofar as God does not rule by intermediate vassals but immediately himself. Every man holds directly from God, without a mesne lord.[16] By this formula Wycliffe attacks on principle the mediating

---

15. Ricardi Armacharii, *De Pauperie Salvatoris*, in Johannis Wycliffe, *De Dominio Divino*, ed. R. L. Poole (London, 1890), 348. See also K. Walsh, *A Fourteenth Century Scholar and Primate: Richard Fitzralph in Oxford, Avignon, and Armagh* (Oxford: Clarendon, 1981). Recent editions of Wycliffe's works include *On Simony*, trans. Terrence A. McVeigh (New York: Fordham University Press, 1992); *Summa insolubilium*, ed. Paul Spade and Gordon Wilson (Binghamton, N.Y., 1986); *Select English Writings*, ed. Herbert Winn (New York: AMS Press, 1976).

16. Wycliffe, *De Dominio Divino*, ed. Poole, I.5, p. 33.

institution of the church and makes every layman a priest holding from God on equal terms of service with every other man.

In the *Civil Dominion* Wycliffe applies his concepts to the spiritual and temporal institutions. Only a man in the state of grace has a right to the gifts of God; he who is in mortal sin cannot be the rightful owner of anything. Dominion is conferred by God in return for the service due to him; he who incurs mortal sin defrauds his lord-in-chief of the service and forfeits his tenure. Every man in grace is lord of the universe, and as there are a multitude of men the goods of the earth can only be held in common by all men.[17] The natural communistic state of dominion is, however, supplemented by the human institution of civil dominion because after the fall of man the sinful lust of individual dominion made a humanly instituted order of property and its enforcement by civil authority inevitable. The political institution of society has the sanction of God, and it is not permissible to break it by force. These doctrines seem on the surface not more than the conventional theory of relative natural law. But they have unexpected implications in the thought of Wycliffe because the two orders, by nature and by civil law, are not distinguished as a state of innocence and a state of fallen man, separated clearly in time, but penetrate each other in the structure of empirical society. The civil order does not derogate the validity of the natural order in the present age. The world *is,* right here and now, under the dominion of the righteous, for "we know that all things work together for good to them that love God, to them who are called according to His purpose" (Rom. 8:28). The earthly success of the wicked is purely phenomenal while the afflictions of the righteous are instrumental to their salvation.[18] This interpenetration of the phenomenal world of appearance and the noumenal, real world is perhaps the greatest difficulty for an adequate understanding of Wycliffe's ideas. In the realm of formulated doctrine the interpenetration expresses itself in oscillations between the contradictory tendencies of recognizing the civil order as the order of this world and of hollowing it out, at the same time, by applying to it the standards of the natural communistic order by grace. A

17. *De Civili Dominio,* ed. Reginald Lane Poole (London 1885), I.14, pp. 96 ff.
18. See ibid., I.16, pp. 114 ff., on mundane life as a dream: "omnes eterna temporalibus postponentes dormiunt sompno gravissimo" (all who put eternal concerns after temporal are sleeping a very deep sleep).

people, for instance, may approve of a ruler by common consent, but he still is not the legitimate ruler unless he is accepted by God, through his grace, for the office (*De Civilo Domino* I.18, p. 130). Popular election may be the civil rule for electing a magistrate, but under natural law the electing community may be infected in the majority by crime and hence may err in the election (I.29, p. 209). The prudent theologian should, therefore, not rashly decide in favor of any civil institutions but should fall back on his principle that it is better if all things are held in common (I.30, p. 218). Wycliffe is in suspense. He cannot accept the civil order unreservedly under a principle of relative natural law, and he cannot condemn it clearly under a principle of absolute natural law. We can feel the eschatological tension, but the revolutionary hope of a Third Realm cannot crystallize into a doctrine. The eschatological sentiment is capable of manifold variations. In a later context we shall have to speak of Calvin's *respectable* echatology. In the context of the pre-Reformation we may speak of Wycliffe's *suspended* eschatology. Wycliffe's spiritual sensitiveness is strong enough to let historical reality become shadowy in comparison with the spiritual reality of the divine order; but it is not strong enough to find the way either into personal mysticism or into the prophecy of the realm to come. His spiritual order is neither quite the order of the life hereafter nor quite the obligatory order for this life.

The eschatological sentiment remains in suspense and does not annihilate with its intenseness the empirical institutions. Hence Wycliffe can have a theory of the spiritual and temporal powers in the present dispensation. The suspense continues, however, to express itself in the unequal treatment accorded to the two powers. With regard to the civil government a balance between the positivism of the order and its spiritual inadequacy is preserved to the degree, as we have seen, that the ruler while spiritually reprobate is still sanctioned by God and has to be obeyed. With regard to the church Wycliffe is stricter in the application of spiritual standards. Even in the *Civil Dominion* he demands that the church, because of its spiritual character, should not exert dominion in the civil sense over earthly possessions. The temporal exactions of the papacy, such as the lordship over England and the exaction of tribute, are incompatible with the spiritual office and contrary to Scripture; the law of the Gospel alone should be sufficient for the rule of the church; civil or canonical law is not required (I.17). For the church, indeed, Wycliffe expects a new dispensation that will do away with the legal and administrative apparatus of the existing ecclesiastical system. The intervention of the temporal power is in place when the church becomes involved in money transactions; the illegitimately appropriated revenue has to be expropriated for the use of the realm (I.37; II.12). We even find at this earlier stage already formulated the principle that the state of grace under the *caput Christus* is all the Christian needs, as it was sufficient in the primitive church, while the direction by any other head is superfluous (I.44, pp. 394 ff.). A church without a hierarchy, reduced to the level of parish communities within the national realm, is the consequence of these tenets.

The later treatise *De Ecclesia,* finished in the fall of 1376 after the Schism had broken out, elaborates the implications of the earlier work. The Church Militant is now defined as the body of the elect *(universitas electorum).*[19] The historical church has for its members the reprobate as well as the elect; hence it cannot be the necessarily invisible Militant Church. Christ is the head not of the visible sacramental but only of the invisible church (*De Ecclesia* III, p. 58). The "foreknown," on the other hand, form a body with the devil as its head (V, p. 102). The theological materials of these doctrines are Augustinian, mediated through Bradwardine, but the radicalism of the position explodes the structure of the sacramental church; it is more Tyconian than Augustinian in its sectarian implications. The doctrine borders even on Manichaean dualism, as can be seen from Wycliffe's work on the Antichrist, which bears the title *De Contrarietate Duorum Dominorum.*[20] The radicalism is not driven, however, to the extreme of invalidating completely the structure of the sacramental church; we find again the reservations and qualifications that make the doctrine contradictory and create the atmosphere of suspense as in the *Civil Dominion.* The pope is not of certainty head of the church because he may not even be a member of the invisible church at all. The position of the pope does not depend on the charisma of his office but on his personal dignity. Nevertheless, the papal institution is not condemned roundly; Wycliffe stresses that an individual pope may be an anti-Christian

19. *De Ecclesia,* ed. Johann Loserth (London, 1886), chap. IV; also chap. II, p. 37.
20. John Wycliffe's *Polemical Works in Latin,* ed. Rudolf Buddensieg (London, 1883), 1:668 ff.; esp. the formulations of chap. I.

figure, but that not all popes are so of necessity. The criterion of the good pope is his conduct, which has to conform to the life and teaching of Christ (*De Ecclesia* II, p. 34). Thorough knowledge of the Bible as the standard of judgment is, therefore, a duty of the Christian (II, pp. 38 ff.). The pope is not accorded the benefit of the secular ruler, who has to be obeyed even if he is unworthy, because the pope's authority has the sanction of God.

The vacillations in the theory of the church are the consequence of a hopeless struggle with the problem of predestination. It was the decisive weakness of Wycliffe that he could neither stay within the sacramental order of the church nor, if he had to break it, find his way into the militant, collectivist predestinarianism of Calvin or into the faith of Luther. The Augustinian experience of the irresistible grace of God as overcoming the demonically fallen nature of man was inaccessible to him. "For all his dependence on Augustine, Wyclif never grasped his doctrine of grace."[21] And equally inaccessible was the Thomasic experience that a life according to nature is a life according to the will of God. The spiritualism of Wycliffe is permanently on the point of revolt without ever reaching the firm ground of a new foundation; as a consequence, it is permanently in danger of sliding into the isolation of demonic individualism. His timid faith is floundering, therefore, in the dialectics of predestination. He accepts without speculative subtlety the idea of predestination in its most deterministic form of God's immutable decision preceding in time the existence of man, and nevertheless admonishes the Christian to live in the hope of salvation and to believe himself a member of the invisible church. The predestination cannot be influenced by a meritorious or sinful life, and nevertheless the damned will be damned for their guilt, and the elect will be saved by their merits.[22]

Considering Wycliffe's obvious inability to penetrate decisively the speculative problems of a Christian anthropology, we shall not be surprised to find a similarly hesitant attitude in the late treatises dealing with royal and papal powers.[23] The symbolism of these late works is closely related to that of the *York Tracts*.

21. Workman, *John Wyclif,* 2:10.
22. See particularly *Speculum de Antichristo,* in *English Works,* ed. F. D. Matthew, p. 111. (rpt. New York, 1973).
23. *De Officio Regis* (1378); *De Potestate Papae* (1379).

Again the king and the pope appear as the vicar of God and the vicar of Christ respectively, the king representing the divine nature of Christ, the pope his human nature.[24] But Wycliffe does not draw his conclusions from this symbolism with the intellectual radicalism of the Anonymous of York. His treatises dissolve rather into a broad manifold of considerations and suggestions, partly concerned with the duties of a king in his realm, partly with the king's independence of the pope and his supremacy over the clergy of England. Even when in the pamphlets of the last years Wycliffe reaches the position that the papacy should be dispensed with in the interest of Christendom, this last radical formulation is due less to a clear argument than to the pressure of historical circumstance.

In the *De Officio Regis*, chapter 3, Wycliffe gives a Mirror of the king, defining the king's duty to surround himself with wise counselors and to be himself conversant with the divine law. There is a touch of Aristotle in the suggestion that the king should give a few and wise laws and adhere to them himself, suspending them for the single case by his lawgiving power only for good reason (p. 57). And there is a reflection of the ethics of the medieval realm in the remark that the king is more bound to his subjects than they to him (pp. 10, 78 ff.). In his function as the vicar of God the king has to support the clergy. This support has to take the form of disciplining corrupt clergymen, of confining them for their sustenance to tithes and alms, of depriving them of temporal lordships, and of using the forfeited wealth for the support of an improved parochial clergy. The basis for these claims seems to have been Wycliffe's sentiment that the realm of England is a mystical body. For in chapter 6 of *De Officio Regis* he develops the doctrine that the sins of individuals weaken the realm, and that for this reason the king has a supreme power of inquisition into individual sins; this power applies specifically to the clergy up to the episcopal rank. Particular evils to be corrected are the unsatisfactory supervision of the lower clergy on the part of the bishops (pp. 152 ff. and passim), the absentee holding of benefices (pp. 163 ff. and passim), and the state of theological studies (p. 177 and passim).

24. *De Officio Regis*, ed. A. I. Pollard and C. Sayle (London 1887), 13, 19.

Wycliffe's attitude toward the papacy underwent a radicalization in the course of the Schism, after 1378. At first he was inclined to recognize Urban VI as the legitimate pope, but with the unfolding of his career both popes appeared to him in the anti-Christian light. The constant element in the variations of Wycliffe's attitude is the sentiment that we called earlier the suspended eschatology—a recognition of institutions, to be withdrawn at any moment under the temptation of breaking through to a judgment by the standards of the noninstitutional grace of God; all Wycliffe's recognition of institutions is permanently to be qualified by his rule that in matters spiritual the last pauper has to be obeyed rather than a pope or an emperor, if the pauper is the better man (chap. V). The suspense between the recognition of institutions and the revolutionary appeal to the common man in the state of grace expresses itself in the *De Potestate Papae* in the doubling of the spiritual and temporal powers. There are two spiritual and two temporal powers. The first spiritual power is the clerical power to dispense the sacraments; the second, the practice of spiritual deeds of mercy, is shared by all Christians alike. The first political power is the power of the rulers; the second is the general power of the community. All power is from God, and the criterion by which the rightful possession of power is to be known is the righteousness of the incumbent. No institutional procedure conferring authority is beyond the appeal to a standard of righteousness by which will be measured the conduct of the incumbent of the office; who falls into mortal sin, thereby loses his power. Equipped with this conceptual apparatus of the four powers, Wycliffe approaches the question of papal power. He does not doubt the succession to Peter, nor the primacy in Christianity of the successor; the institution of Petrine succession is not discontinued, for Christ has not abandoned his church (*De Potestate Papae*, chap. IV, p. 62). But when it has to be determined who in the particular case is the legitimate successor to Peter, a series of problems has to be clarified. First of all, there is no necessary link between the episcopate of Rome and the succession to Peter; the link between the two is a human institution, due to the imperial power of Rome and the Donation of Constantine (IX, p. 215). Moreover, the election of the pope by the cardinals is scandalous considering that not even all members of the college are priests. Since a procedure has to be used that puts it beyond doubt who at any given time is the incumbent of the office, it would be best to throw the burden of true selection on God and have the pope chosen by lot (IV, pp. 68 ff.).[25] Under no circumstance, however, does the successor of Peter have any jurisdiction over Christendom (pp. 97 ff.). The primacy is purely spiritual, and a true pope is to be recognized by his imitation of the life of Christ: he has to live in poverty; he has to renounce temporal ambitions; he must not strive for juridical rights; and he must preach the Gospel to those who are yet ignorant of it. Both of the schismatic popes betray by their ambitions their anti-Christian character (VII, p. 156).

In the *De Potestate Papae* of 1379, Wycliffe admits still the necessity of a successorship to Peter and even the desirability of a center of Christianity, though not necessarily at Rome, for the discharge of administrative functions, provided that they are discharged in the spirit of Christ. In the following years he goes beyond this conception of a spiritualized papacy[26] and arrives, ultimately under the impression of the schismatic struggle, at the conclusion that Christianity would perhaps fare best under the sole headship of Christ and should give up the summepiscopal construction entirely. The *De Christo et suo Adversario Antichristo* lists the contrasts between Christ and his vicar in such a manner that the pope appears as Antichrist.[27] And Wycliffe finds even some good in the Schism itself because Christ by it has graciously split the head of the Antichrist so that the two parts now fight each other.[28] In these last works the position of the Reformation has been reached with its parochialization of the churches in the realms, held together by the headship of Christ.

25. See also *Responsiones ad argumenta cuiusdam emuli veritatis,* chap. VIII, in *Opera Minora,* ed. John Loserth (London 1913), 282 ff. On papal election see, furthermore, *De Blasphemia,* ed. M. H. Dziewicki (London, 1893), chap. III.

26. For the mystical revelation of the pope see particularly *De Potestate Papae* IX, p. 195: "Sed sicut in brutis dux ostenditur a natura, ut patet ex decreto predicto, sic dux Christiani exercitus debet ostendi revelacione divina, quia nihil falsius, quam quod humana eleccio facit papam, nam solus Deus justificat hominem" (But just as among beasts the leader is revealed by nature, as is clear from the aforesaid decree, so the leader of the Christian army ought to be revealed by divine revelation because there is nothing more false than that election by man makes a pope, for God alone justifies man).

27. *De Christo et suo Adversario Antichristo,* in *Polemical Works,* ed. Buddensieg, vol. 2; the lists mentioned in the text are in chaps. 11 and 12.

28. *De Quatuor Sectia Novellis,* chap. 1 in *Polemical Works,* ed. Buddensieg, 1:243; *Cruciata,* chap. 5 in *Polemical Works,* ed. Buddensieg, 2:604.

21

The Imperial Zone

§1. Subimperial Politics

a. Imperial and Subimperial Politics

The title of this chapter, "The Imperial Zone," epitomizes the difficulties the historian has to face in giving an account of the currents of ideas in the vast area between France and the Slavic East, between the Baltic and Rome. We do not find in this area the growth of a national polity as in England, nor the integrating force of a charismatic kingship as in the France of the thirteenth century. The appearance of a political unit in this area, and of a continuum of political ideas, is created through the fact that, beginning with the tenth century, this region east of France furnished the incumbents of the imperial dignity. The *sacrum imperium*, however, with its double headship of the pope and the emperor, was the comprehensive political institution of Western Christianity, it was not the German kingdom; and while the imperial position, giving control over church lands, certainly was a decisive factor in the military strength of German kingship, the empire was no more than one stratum in the political structure of the German-Italian zone. Underneath there is a level of political problems, in principle of the same nature as those we associate in the West with the rise of the national state. The structure of the problems on this regional level, below the imperial, is not at all unknown, but it is somewhat neglected in the general picture of the Middle Ages, and it is still exposed to misinterpretations.

The sources of the neglect and the misinterpretation are mainly three. The grandeur of the imperial period, the dramatic struggle between the emperor and the papacy in the Investiture Struggle, and the great imperial figures of the Hohenstaufen overshadow the less spectacular regional political processes. The Interregnum of 1254–1273 appears in German history as a deeper incision than it actually was because the postimperial problems of the fourteenth century are seen as succeeding those of the imperial period proper rather than as continuing the subimperial, regional problems of the preceding centuries. Second, the regional political structure did not evolve toward the form of the national state. Historians who are preoccupied with the national idea tend to neglect the unorthodox political forms of the central zone; and in the history of political ideas this tendency is particularly strong because the evocations of the imperial zone did not find their literary expression in systematic political thought. The political principles that give the fourteenth century its signature reveal themselves only in an analysis of the institutions. And third, the German historiography of the nineteenth century has cast a veil of Whiggist interpretation that covered until recently the English institutional history of this period. The movement for national unification and the creation of the empire of 1871 induced an evaluation in retrospect of the medieval period as a time of missed opportunities for building the German national state. The failure to emulate France and England in creating a national realm was attributed to the engrossment of the emperors in the Italian problems, to the dynastic egoism of the Hausmacht builders of the fourteenth century, and for the later period to the Habsburgs as the permanent obstacle to German political unity. We also find, however, the recognition of German particularism as a decisive factor, though this recognition is blurred by the explanation of particularism as a trait in the German "national character."

b. The East Frankish Kingdom and Italy

In approaching the subimperial problems of German politics it will be worthwhile to remember that the term *German empire* was used in a state document for the first time in 1871.[1] The absence of a name designating the German political unit in the same unequivocal manner in which the realms of France and England are identified

---

1. For the following survey of the German problem I have used, wherever possible, Johannes Haller, *Die Epochen der deutschen Geschichte* (Stuttgart and Berlin: Cotta, 1924). See also Horst Fuhrmann, *Germany in the High Middle Ages c. 1050–1200*, trans. Timothy Reuter (New York: Cambridge University Press, 1986), and Geoffrey Barraclough, *The Origins of Modern Germany*, 3d ed. (Oxford: Blackwell, 1988).

by their names is a symptom of the peculiar circumstances that beset German history from its beginning. Germany has no decisive date in its history marking a political epoch, like the Frankish conquest of Gaul, the Carolingian foundation, the Norman conquest of England, or, on a minor scale, the Lombard conquest of Italy. If we assign a beginning to German history, it can only be the year 911, with the election of a duke of Franconia to succeed the last Carolingian as the king of the tribes that had fallen, in the partitions of Charlemagne's successors, into the unit of the east Frankish kingdom. The coexistence of a plurality of *Stammesherzogtumer* is the factor that determined from the beginning the pattern of German so-called particularism, while Frankish and Norman conquests by single tribes introduced a unifying factor into the French and English foundations.

Economically and civilizationally the German duchies were the hinterland of the Frankish empire. Once separated, they were hemmed in between the west Frankish kingdom, the non-Christian Scandinavians and Slavs in the north and east, and the Alps in the south. Since the center of high civilization of the time was the Mediterranean and the Byzantine empire, it became of the first importance for the German backwoods area to keep open the route to the Mediterranean, above all to Venice, in order not to be cut off from world commerce and world affairs. The Italian policy of the German kings has to be seen, therefore, under two aspects. The renewal of the Roman empire through Otto the Great in 962 continued the tradition of the Frankish-Roman empire of Charlemagne, which had ceased to function not even a century back; and the German kings themselves were Frankish kings in the sense that they had succeeded the Carolingian line in the east Frankish kingdom. But Otto was not a romantic dreamer who would have continued a tradition for tradition's sake. His expeditions to Italy served the very realistic purpose of curbing, and ultimately of conquering, the rising Italian kingdom, which threatened to block the roads from Germany to Italy. The expedition of 952 secured the mountain passes through the acquisition of Verona, Friuli, and Istria from Berengar of Ivrea; the expedition of 962 conquered the kingdom completely, and Otto was crowned king of Italy in Pavia. The conquest was followed immediately by a commercial treaty with Venice. The taxes, subsidies, and customs dues from upper Italy must have been a considerable item in the budget of the German kings, who could not extract much cash from the undeveloped money economy of the transalpine region. The control over Rome was of similar importance for strengthening the royal position, principally for two reasons. First, a hostile power in Rome and Tuscany would have been a grave danger to the safe possession of Lombardy; and second, a hostile papacy could have done considerable damage to the German influence in Lombardy because most of the Lombard bishops were suffragans of Rome. In the subimperial stratum of politics, expansion into Italy and control of the papacy were, therefore, a plain geopolitical, financial, and commercial interest of the German kingdom.

c. The Concentration of Royal Power and the Interregna

The evolution of this initial German political structure was determined by events both in Germany and in Italy. North of the Alps the emperors made strong efforts at concentrating royal control over the realm. By the middle of the eleventh century the policy of retaining vacant fiefs in the hands of the royal house had reached a point where only the duchy of Saxony still had a certain degree of independence; the other duchies were held by Henry III (1039–1056). At the same time the hitherto somewhat desultory control over the papacy was more firmly established. At the Synods of Sutri and Rome in 1046, the rival popes were deposed under pressure of the emperor, and the following years brought the series of the four German popes who began the Cluniac reform of the papacy. This highly successful policy of reducing the duchies and of integrating the realm was fatally interrupted, however, by the early death of Henry III. When the emperor died at the age of forty, a regency had to be established for the son, who was only six years of age; this regency proved to be the first of the interregna that destroyed radically the integrating efforts of the strong reigns and ultimately prevented the growth of a German national realm. When Henry IV, on coming of age, could resume the royal policy, the princes, lay and clerical, had split up the royal holdings and distributed the domainal resources and the fiefs lavishly among themselves; the young emperor had to start anew. He reestablished control over church land through openly simoniac practices, and he seems to have attempted to form a nucleus of royal domain in Saxony that would have served as a basis of operation in a manner similar to the Capetian concentration in France. But the times had changed. The Cluniac reform had done its work; the spiritual prestige of the reformed papacy had created a new power; and the simoniac practices that were necessary to control church lands as the principal source of revenue precipitated the conflict with Gregory VII. The struggle, practically a second interregnum, again impaired disastrously the royal position. The renewed attempts of Henry V (1106–1125) and Lothair II (1125–1137) could not mature, and by the time of Frederick I (1152–1190) the damage was irreparable. The new royal house did not have any ascendancy in Germany; other princes, the Welfs and the Babenbergs, were equally strong if not stronger.

As a consequence of the deterioration of the royal position in Germany, the Italian policy of the Hohenstaufen differed radically in its complexion from the earlier, though superficially it continued the Ottonic tradition. In the tenth century the Italian expeditions resulted in a control of Italy from the royal stronghold in Germany; in the twelfth century Italy was needed as a royal stronghold for the control of Germany. The Hohenstaufen could attempt no longer to form a nucleus of royal strength on German soil but had to make the attempt in Italy in order to regain a dominant position in Germany. Frederick's first attempt, the consolidation of Lombardy under imperial rule with a *podestà* government in the cities, was only a partial success; it came to an end with the defeat at Legnano in 1176, and the peace of Constance of 1183 had to recognize the practical independence of the Lombard cities. Still, the resources of Lombardy had been sufficient to wage a successful war against Henry the Lion and to dismember Saxony in 1180, thus reducing the most formidable German opponent. More hopeful than the Lombard policy proved the acquisition of Tuscany, which gave the emperor a strategic position from which he could control the papacy in the south and check the Lombard cities in the north. Most important, however, was the Sicilian marriage arranged for his son; the fruits of this plan, however, were reaped only by Henry VI, who in possession of Sicily could begin the reconquest of Italy and raise the imperial power once more to its former height.

Henry VI died in 1197 at the age of thirty-two; his son, who would become Frederick II, was three years old; the third interregnum began. This third interruption of the royal policy raises a problem concerning the adequate classification of the political phenomena of this period. Traditionally only one interregnum is counted, the great one of 1254–1273, between the end of the Hohenstaufen and the election of Rudolf of Habsburg. The great Interregnum is certainly of specific importance because after its close the political factors that had been in the making during the preceding centuries did determine definitely a new pattern of politics: the medieval imperial tradition was dead and the Renaissance principalities and national states were rising. But if the attention is directed too exclusively toward the great Interregnum, the transitional phases and the slow accumulation of factors that only in the aggregate determined the new power pattern of the fourteenth century are obscured. While the great Interregnum is the epochal incision on the level of imperial politics, we have to consider whether on the level of subimperial politics the whole period from 1197 to 1273 should not be classified as one huge interregnum. The reign of Frederick II resumed the imperial tradition of Frederick I and Henry VI magnificently, and in that sense Frederick is considered quite justly the last great medieval emperor, but under the aspect of the subimperial structure of German politics his reign is characterized by features that appear more clearly only in the time of the great Interregnum and in the fourteenth century. Frederick II was no longer a German prince. That he used Sicily as his basis of operation continued the Lombard and Tuscan policy of Frederick I, but that a "foreigner" should be the German king and try to rule Germany from a principality outside the realm was a new development. A situation had arisen that differed only in degree from the election of William of Holland, Richard of Cornwall, and Alfonse of Castile as German kings. Engrossed in his Italian problems, the emperor furthermore surrendered completely the attempts at creating a royal position in Germany. The Golden Bull of Eger of 1213 surrendered control of the German Church to the papacy, the concessions of the Statute of 1220 made the clerical princes practically independent territorial rulers, and the concessions of the Statute of 1231 established the complete control of the lay princes over their territories. These three acts fixed the structure of German "particularism" and made it impossible for Frederick's successors to revive a strong German kingship by the means that were used by the Saxon and Salic emperors—that is, by control of the church territories and by accumulation of a royal domain. The new Hausmacht policy, beginning with the Habsburgs, had to recognize the particularistic structure of Germany. The kings after the great Interregnum could no longer establish within the territory of the old duchies a royal stronghold that would have given them a power ascendancy over the other German princes. That had already been impossible for the Hohenstaufen. Neither could the Italian territories serve as a basis after the loss of Sicily to the Aragonese and in face of the Lombard resistance. The new solution that offered itself was the creation of a nucleus of power east of the old German territory. This new policy was made possible by the German expansion into the eastern Slavic territories that had occurred in the preceding centuries.

d. The Colonization of the East

The German expansion into the east is the most fateful process of the high Middle Ages because of its permanent effects on the German political structure. In the critical centuries in which the realms of France and England acquired their national characteristics in a fixed territory, in which the Western nations could grow internally into coherent societies, and in which the English nation gained its political articulation, the Germans were on the move and expanded their territory from the old borders on the Elbe and Saale to the east even into the territories that today are Poland and Russia. The German eastern expansion from the twelfth to the fourteenth centuries is the greatest feat of Western colonization before the Anglo-Saxon expansion across the Atlantic. A colonization of this magnitude, in spatial contiguity with the homeland, inevitably had its repercussion on the metropolitan territory. The internal growth of a German national civilization, comparable to the English and French, was broken by this event; and Germany has never completely recovered from this breach. From this time on we have to distinguish in Germany between a western metropolitan and an eastern colonial civilization. The two civilizations began to blend effectively only in the eighteenth century with the preliminaries of the Romantic movement; but the civilizational difference of the two areas can be clearly observed even after this period.[2]

2. See on this question the excellent study by Josef Nadler, *Die Berliner Romantik, 1800–1814* (Berlin: Reiss, 1921). Nadler's monograph gives a clearer presentation of the problem than his vast *Literaturgeschichte der deutschen Stamme und Landschaften*, 3 vols. (Regensburg: Habbel, 1912–1918; 4th ed., Berlin, 1938–1939, under the title *Literaturgeschichte des deutschen Volkes*).

The impairment of the national civilizational coherence is paralleled by the aggravation of the problem of institutional integration. Particularism in the territories of the old duchies was a problem of sufficient magnitude in itself; expansion into the east added new strong principalities to the territorial entrenchment of princes and cities in the west. The growth of national communes of the baronage, the gentry, and the commoners that characterizes England, or the growth of a third estate like the French, was impossible under these conditions. Germany has never produced a style of politics and of a political man because the framework of nationwide institutions within which such types can grow through the accumulation of experience in affairs did not evolve. A good deal of the German political peculiarities that in these days are blandly attributed to a special German "national character" as a constant are simply the behavior patterns that grew in the absence of a stabilizing influence and of the experience of old political institutions as in England and France. A severe blow was, finally, dealt to the self-contained growth of national civilization and of national institutions through the eastern momentum that had been imparted to German politics by the colonization. The expansion carried the Germans far beyond the borders of the present contiguous German settlement into purely Slavic territories. The scattered German settlements in the east and southeast have created the modern minority problems. The German civilizational border in the east is not sharply drawn; it is fading out deep into Poland, Czechoslovakia, Russia, Hungary, and Romania. As a consequence, the political border has remained in the sentiments of the people in a suspense that generates the tendencies to extend the German political influence to the farthest reaches of the medieval German colonizing drive into the Baltic states, into Poland and Bohemia, Hungary and Romania, and perhaps even to the Volga.

The political form of the expansion merits some attention. It was not the result of an imperialistic plan on the part of a central government; and it was above all not directed by the empire. The initiative of the expansion lay with a greater number of subimperial authorities; the process reached into the stratum of empire politics only through the recognition that the imperial chancellery extended to the new holdings. The character of a free movement of local authorities had its consequences for the overall result of the colonization. Because it owed its momentum to the power of the princes and cities, the expansion survived the catastrophe of the empire. Because it was not a planned and directed movement, the expansion occurred haphazardly; important positions had to be surrendered later because they were isolated and surrounded by noncolonized Slav country.

The details of the process are not our concern, but a few dates have to be mentioned in order to characterize its political structure. The movement was under way by the middle of the twelfth century. In 1140 Adolf of Schaumburg penetrated to the east coast of Holstein, and in 1143 he founded Lübeck, creating thereby the first German outpost on the Baltic. In the following year, 1144, Albert the Bear founded the March of Brandenburg. The crusade against the Wends of 1147 extended the German colonial land farther east, brutally exterminating the Slavic population and clearing the land for resettlement with Germans from the west. The drive on the Baltic received a greater momentum when Henry the Lion (1156–1180) began the foundation of a principality east of the Elbe. In 1158 he acquired Lübeck from the count of Holstein and from that time begins the rise of the city to its predominant rank in the Baltic area. The thirteenth century witnessed the conquest of the Baltic coast. In 1201 Riga was founded, and the organization of Livland was completed by 1221 through Adalbert of Bremen. In 1230 the Teutonic Order established itself in Prussia; in alliance with the Livonian Brothers it Christianized the whole southern coast of the Baltic up to Estonia and dotted the country with towns. When in 1346 the order acquired Estonia from Denmark, the German settlement reached from Holstein to Lake Peipus. In this whole series of conquests there is only one instance of an expansion due to imperial intervention: the addition of Silesia through Emperor Frederick I in 1163.

The expansion along the Baltic had overreached itself. East of Pomerania the colonization occupied the seacoast with a comparatively thin strip of hinterland. When the Polish and Lithuanian principalities could unite in politically effective national realms, the hold on the coast would become precarious. This consolidation of Poland and Lithuania occurred in the early fourteenth century. When the two realms were united in 1386 the fate of the upper Baltic settlements was sealed. The order lost the battle of Tannenberg in 1410, and in the peace of 1411 Samogitia had to be surrendered, destroying the land connection between Prussia and Livland. The

Peace of Thorn of 1466, following the long war of the Prussian Revolt, broke the holdings in Prussia. West Prussia with Danzig became Polish; east Prussia, having no longer a land connection with the German main territory, remained German but became a Polish fief; Prussia from then on remained outside the German empire and even the German Bund of 1815 until after 1866.

South of the great colonization, the realm had also experienced a new political articulation since the time of the old duchies. After a passing episode of Christianization from Byzantium, Bohemia was integrated into Western Christianity through German missionary efforts beginning in the late ninth century. In the eleventh and twelfth centuries the German influence increased through imperial interventions in the succession struggles of the Premyslid family. In 1158 Emperor Frederick I made the crown of Bohemia hereditary as a reward for Bohemian aid in the struggle with the Lombard cities. In the thirteenth century, Wenceslas I (1230–1253) organized large-scale immigration of Germans for the clearance of forest country and the foundation of towns in order to offset by this new population element the power of the nobility. A revolt of the nobility in 1247–1250 seems to indicate the importance that the immigration policy had gained in the domestic power balance of the kingdom. By the middle of the thirteenth century Bohemia was a semi-German principality, closely interwoven into the structure of the realm through the electoral dignity of the king as well as through the election of Ottokar II as duke of Austria in 1251. South of Bohemia extended the old duchy of Bavaria. The rearticulation of this considerable territory began at the end of the tenth century with the separation of the duchy of Carinthia; Austria became a separate duchy in 1156 and Styria in 1180.

The German colonization from the Baltic to Bohemia, the growth of a semi-German kingdom of Bohemia, and the rearticulation of the old duchy of Bavaria had created in their aggregate a power field that shifted the German political weight from the old west to the east. Here in the east were the territories from which a political domination and integration of Germany could be attempted with a hope of success. The decisive political area in German history after 1300 is defined by the names of Austria and Bohemia, of Brandenburg and Prussia. The colonization and territorial articulation of the east in the centuries of the high Middle Ages determined the German political structure in the same manner in which the internal articulation of the realm into communes determined the structure of the English polity and the rise of French kingship determined the French centralized, administrative state. The fact that the German development did not result in an integrated national state does not in the least diminish the importance of this process for German politics as well as for Western politics at large. Neither does it diminish its importance for the development of German political ideas in the centuries to come: the turn that German political ideas have taken on the higher systematic level is incomprehensible without a precise knowledge of the institutional articulation just outlined.

e. Summary

Summarizing this survey we should like to distinguish three main phases in the evolution of the German political structure. First, the initial coexistence of the old duchies and the concentration of royal power through control of church lands and the retaining of vacant fiefs in the royal house, which is characteristic of the Saxon and Salic period. Second, the failure of this policy as a consequence of the first two interregna and the new concentration of royal power in the Italian possessions, which characterizes the Hohenstaufen period. Third, the Hausmacht policy with its concentration of power in the new eastern territories, which is characteristic of the period after the great Interregnum. Between the Italian and the eastern policy we have to observe a transitional period of disintegration in which non-German princes assumed the function of kingship and a high degree of independence of the German principalities became part of the German constitution.

§2. The Golden Bull

a. Charles IV

The changes in the German political structure found their recognition and formalization in the Golden Bull of 1356, in the reign of Charles IV (1347–1378). On the negotiations that determined the content of the instrument we have little information. After a period of suggestions and guesses as to who might have been the "author" of the document, the prevalent opinion today seems to be that the emperor himself took the initiative for the legislation,

203

that the document was elaborated by the chancellery on the basis of negotiations between the emperor and the electors, and that it reflects on the whole the emperor's own policy. The personality of the man, however, who determined the German constitutional form for the next four and a half centuries is not yet seen quite clearly. He did not conform to the glamorous imperial style as it had been represented magnificently by Frederick I, nor did he have the warmth and personal appeal that aroused sympathies even for an otherwise minor figure like Lewis the Bavarian. The qualities that made him one of the most successful statesmen on the imperial throne were unpopular qualities—unpopular in his own time, and unpopular also with later historians. He was a devout Christian in the medieval sense, but he entertained no illusions about the political papacy. His ancestry and his education, balancing French, German, and Czech influences, made him a European, not firmly rooted in a national soil. He had his original name, Wenceslas, changed to Charles by Charles IV of France at his confirmation, and the figures of his two patrons, Charlemagne and Saint Wenceslas, were of equal influence in determining his conception of rulership as a Roman emperor and a king of Bohemia. His sensitiveness to history and tradition, however, was not romantic; he was a master of rational politics, averse to violent solutions when diplomacy could achieve results. He was a careful administrator and house-holder, and he was probably the only prince of his time who never lacked money. His financial resources he used circumspectly for political purposes and with a thoroughness that can be explained only by a profound contempt of human nature and by the experience that almost every man has his price. The curious mixture of devotional Christianity and rational statecraft, the assertion of imperial claims—he was the last emperor to be crowned as king of Burgundy—on the one hand and the construction of the empire as an oligarchy of the princes on the other, his position over or between the nations—these complexities are probably why one of the great Western statesmen has remained to this day in a relative historical obscurity.[3]

3. On Charles IV see Fritz Vigener, "Kaiser Karl IV," in *Meister der Politik*, ed. Erich Marcks and Karl Alexander von Müller (Stuttgart: Deutsche Verlags-Anstalt, 1921), vol. 2. For French influence on Charles IV see the interesting dissertation by Wolfgang Klein, "Kaiser Karl IV: Jugendaufenthalt in Frankreich und dessen Einfluss

b. The Form of the Golden Bull

The Golden Bull is a codification of which the first part was promulgated on the Diet of Nuremberg (November 1355–January 1356), the second part on the Diet of Metz (November 1356–January 1357). With regard to its form the bull is a statute, promulgated by Charles "by the fullness of his imperial power," "after the previous mature deliberation," "in solemn court," "in the presence of all the electoral princes, ecclesiastical and secular, and of a numerous multitude of other princes, counts, barons, magnates, nobles and cities."4 With regard to its contents the bull regulates the election of the king, the status of the electoral princes, the status of the kingdom of Bohemia, and a number of other topics that have a relation to the constitution of the empire. As a whole the codification lives in the tradition of Frederick II's *Constitutions of Melfi*, the tradition of a fundamental legislation for the order of the realm.

c. *State*-Imperium *and World*-Imperium

For special treatment in this context, we can select only a few formulations and provisions that have a specific bearing on the German political structure. The reader of the bull is struck, first of all, by the complexities of the terminology that is employed in the designation of the realm and its head. For designating the realm the bull uses the terms *christianum imperium, sacrum imperium, sacrum imperium Romanum,* and *sacro-sanctum imperium Romanum.* Occasionally we find a circumscription like *sacri Romani celsitudo imperii;* and the conception is further elaborated by the interpretation of the realm as an analogue and *fundamentum* of the Divine Trinity, or as a *sacrum edificium* with the seven electors illuminating it like the seven candelabra shining in the sevenfold

auf seine Entwicklung" (Berlin, 1926). For an English monograph on Charles IV see Bede Jarrett, O.P., *The Emperor Charles IV* (New York: Sheed and Ward, 1935). See, furthermore, W. T. Waugh, "Germany: Charles IV," *CMH,* vol. 7 (1932), chap. 5.

4. Arenga of the Golden Bull. On the Golden Bull see Karl Zeumer, *Die Goldene Bulle Kaiser Karls IV. 1. Teil: Entstehung und Bedeutung der Goldenen Bulle; 2. Teil: Text der Goldenen Bulle* (Weimar: Buhlaus Nachfolger, 1908). The literature on the election of German kings and on the Golden Bull is prodigious. One of the important older monographs is Herman Bloch's *Die Staufischen Kaiserwahlen und die Entstehung des Kurfürstentums* (Leipzig and Berlin: Teubner, 1911). A more recent important contribution is the monograph by Heinrich Mitteis, *Die deutsche Königswahl: Ihre Rechtsgrundlage bis zur Goldenen Bulle* (Baden bei Wien, 1938).

unit of the Spirit. The head of the realm, as elected by the seven electors, is designated as *rex Romanorum in imperatorem promovendus*, or as *rex Romanorum futurus imperator;* used synonymously with *imperator* is the term *caesar.* In other contexts, however, the language *imperator vel rex Romanorum* is used, implying that the *rex* has the functions of an *imperator* (particularly chapter V). Further alternative designations are: "the temporal head of the Christian people" *(temporale caput mundi seu populi Christiani)* and "temporal head of the faithful." The predecessors are referred to as *divi Romanorum imperatores et reges.*

The variations of the terms reflect the structure of the empire as it had grown historically. Election to the kingship seems to have implied originally not more than an expectation or hope that the elected king would be promoted by papal coronation to the imperial dignity as the temporal head of the Christian world. A solidification of this expectation into a claim—always recognizing, however, papal approval—seems to have occurred by the twelfth century when the title *rex Romanorum* came into use for the designation of the elected king. This claim is expressed in the Golden Bull in the title of the king as an *in imperatorem promovendus* or as an *imperator futurus.*

Even without the coronation at Rome, however, the election to the kingship had as its immediate consequence the assumption of imperial functions in the sense that the German king had to discharge duties and privileges with regard to the kingdoms that were not part of the German realm—that is, with regard to Italy and Burgundy. The legal complication of imperial functions, discharged by a king who was not crowned emperor, were never rationalized terminologically in a formal act; the several legal strata received only occasional designations. The core of the dignity is the German kingship over the German realm, called *regnum Teutonicum;* this kingship, then, carries with it functions of imperial administration in Burgundy and Italy, called the *imperium.* The distinction of the *regnum Teutonicum* and the *imperium* is to be found for instance in the Concordat of Worms.[5] The imperial implications of the German kingship were recognized even by Innocent III, who spoke on one occasion of the *regnum Teutonicum, et, quantum in eo est,*

5. In the *Calixtinum* of the Concordat of Worms, MGH, *Constitutiones I,* no. 108.

imperium.[6] In this sense, therefore, the *rex electus* was an *impera-tor.* A secular conception of *imperium* as the territories ruled by the emperor de facto parallels the conception of *sacrum imperium,* of the empire of the Christian world. On one occasion an interesting attempt was made to distinguish terminologically the territorially limited and the world conception of the empire, when the electors of Philip of Swabia notified the pope that they had elected their candidate in *imperaturam Romani solii.* The territorial, adminis-trative *imperatura* is clearly set off against the *sacrum imperium.*[7] The emergence of a territorial *imperium* of the German kings is, in the imperial zone, the parallel phenomenon to the rise of the national states in the West. In order to have a definite term for the new phenomenon we shall call it henceforth the *state-imperium* as distinguished from the *world-imperium.*

The tension between the two conceptions became clearest per-haps in the twelfth and thirteenth centuries, when the Hohen-staufen attempted to make the state-imperium coextensive with the world-imperium. Frederick I used the designation of *reguli* for the rulers of neighboring independent kingdoms; Henry VI pur-sued the policy of transforming Christian kingdoms into imperial fiefs (England, Armenia, Cyprus, etc.); until with Frederick II the idea of the *dominus mundi* reached its climax. The expansive Ho-henstaufen policy should not lead, however, to the assumption that the temporal headship of the *sacrum imperium* was devoid of po-litical content without such expansion. The crowned emperor was what the elected emperor was not, the protector of the Christian world; only on the crowned emperor fell the duties of crusades, of missioning among the pagans, and of fighting heretics; and only he had functions in the reform of the church and an influence on papal elections.

In the dignity of the king-emperor we have to distinguish, there-fore, the following strata: (1) the kingship over the *regnum Teuton-icum;* (2) the imperial functions with regard to the state-imperium, including Italy and Burgundy; (3) the claim to the headship of the

---

6. The phrase is to be found in the *Deliberatio Domini Papae Innocentii super facto imperii de tribus electis* (in *Registrum super negotio Romani Imperii,* no. 29, Migne, *Patrologia Latina,* vol. 216, p. 1028 A).

7. MGH, *Constitutiones II,* no. 3, p. 3 f. The printed texts all have *in imperatorem.* The photostatic copy of the original, however, has *in imperaturam.* The point was discovered by Heinrich Mittais; see his *Die deutsche Königswahl,* 99 ff.

world-imperium, contained in the formula *futurus imperator;* and (4) the temporal headship of the *populus Christianus* with the protectorate over the church. These strata can be clearly distinguished, however, only in the analysis; in practice they do not represent separable jurisdictions that could be held by several persons. They have to be understood dynamically in the sense that by the successive procedural steps of election, of papal approval, and of coronation the dignity would be built up from the German kingship to the full imperial dignity. Inevitably a cumulative dignity of this type had to be a source of political conflicts. The election fell into the political sphere of the German princes, while approval and coronation fell into the sphere of the papacy. The election of the princes could and did force upon the popes unacceptable candidates for the imperial dignity; the papal right of approval led to interventions in German affairs through preliminary negotiations with the electors concerning a candidate and through papal influence on the three ecclesiastical electoral votes. The result was the civil wars in Germany and the election of anti-kings, if the first elected king did not find papal approval.

The first important steps to disentangle this situation were taken in the reign of Lewis the Bavarian, under the impression of the disorders during the struggle between the unapproved emperor and the pope. In July 1338 a meeting of the electors at Rense declared that an elected king does not need papal approval in order to assume legally the royal title and to discharge the duties of imperial administration. In August of the same year an election law of the emperor, the *Licet juris,* went even further and stigmatized it as a "pestilential dogma" that the *electus in imperatorem* is not a true emperor unless confirmed, approved, and crowned by the pope. According to Roman and canon law the imperial dignity is directly from God, and the duly elected king is a *verus imperator* without papal approbation.[8] The declaration of the electors still admits papal approval as necessary for completion of the dignity, while asserting the state-imperium of the elected *rex Romanorum.* The *Licet juris* goes to the extreme of having the electors creating

8. *Weistum von Rense* and *Kaiserwahlgesetz Ludwigs des Baiern,* in Mario Krammer, *Quellen zur Geschichte der deutschen Königswahl und des Kurfürstenkollegs* (Leipzig and Berlin: Teubner, 1912), 2:91, 97.

a *verus imperator* having the plenitude of imperial power.[9] The radicalism of these assertions could but aggravate the tension in the imperial-papal relations. When the Golden Bull readdressed the problem in 1356, a different course was chosen. The bull neither declares papal approval irrelevant nor uses the extreme terminology of the *verus imperator.* It simply does not mention papal approval at all, but it regulates the election procedure in such meticulous detail that the newly created *rex Romanorum* is capable of exerting the imperial functions without papal approval. The silence on the approval leaves it open to the pope to give it and to the emperor to accept it, but the procedure does not leave a gap in which approval could be exerted with any legal effect. With masterful diplomacy and legal technique the bull maneuvers the approval out of the procedure that results in the creation of the king-emperor. The feat is facilitated by the (perhaps intentional) variations of titles we discussed earlier. There is no phrase in the bull like the *verus imperator* of the *Licet juris,* but in the election oath (chap. II, sec. 2) the *caput populi Christiani* is identified with the *rex Romanorum in caesarem promovendus,* the first formula anticipating the dignity that is phrased in the future tense in the second.

The improvements in legal technique, particularly in procedural law, that characterize this period, and their deliberate use for the politically nonaggressive solution of a delicate problem, are one of the reasons the regulations of the bull proved successful. The silence on the critical point did no obvious damage to papal prestige and made it unnecessary for the papacy to resort to official protests. But the lawyers of the Curia were, of course, not deceived by a neat trick. That the bull did not cause a new storm was due to other factors in the political situation. First of all, the emperor had chosen the time for publishing the bull most judiciously so that a minimum of papal reaction would ensue: Charles had been crowned emperor in 1355 and with the coronation the pope had lost his chief instrument of pressure. The bull, furthermore, did not indulge in

9. The position of the *Licet juris* is prepared and influenced by the memorandum *Subscripta,* a legal opinion on the election of the king-emperor by an unknown author, probably a Franciscan. See Ficker, "Zur Geschichte des Kurvereins zu Rense," Sitzungsberichte der Bayrischen Akademie der Wissenschaften zu Wien, *Philosophische-historische Klasse* 11 (1853): 673–710. The *Subscripta* is reprinted in Krammer, *Quellen zur Geschichte,* 96 ff.

innovations concerning the structure of the realm, but accepted on the whole the existing custom and, in particular, the policy of the electors as declared at Rense. Only the realistic acceptance of the electors' policy on the part of the emperor was new, including the recognition of the practical sovereignty of the electoral princes, and the transformation of the realm into an oligarchic federation of princes with an elected head. The bull was a compromise between the emperor and the princes, recognizing the particularism of the territorial states that had been growing during the interregnum of the thirteenth century. And, finally, one should not overlook the national sentiment that expresses itself in the new policy. The declaration of Rense had strong overtones of national self-assertion against papal and French influences in German affairs; even more clearly these sentiments can be felt in the drafts for letters of the electors at Rense to the pope.[10] The Golden Bull expresses the rise of German national sentiment in the same manner in which the reaction against Boniface VIII and the beginning of the Hundred Years War with England express the increasing strength of the French national sentiment.

d. The Electoral College—The Majority Problem

While the provisions of the bull codified on the whole the existing custom, they gave it a new precision and put an end to its further evolution. The king had to be elected in Frankfurt by seven electors. When all seven, or a major part of them, had cast their votes for a candidate, the election was to be celebrated as made without dissent (II.4). If three of them voted for a fourth member of the electoral college, the vote of the candidate had to be counted as the fourth, thus completing the majority (II.5). This monopolization of the election in the hands of three ecclesiastical and four secular princes is the last phase of a long history for which we have to refer the reader to the monographs on the subject. Of special interest for the history

10. See the *Entwuerfe*, reprinted in Krammer, *Quellen zur Geschichte*, pp. 92 ff. See particularly the second *Entwurf* where the pope is petitioned to accept Lewis the Bavarian in consideration of the devotion "quam gens Germanica et ejus principes ad sanctam Romanan exclesiam hactenus habuerunt" (which the German nation and its princes have had up to this point toward the holy Roman church). The *hactenus* contains even a faint suggestion that the devotion might be not quite so fervent in the future if the pope should insist on further irritating the *gens Germanica* and its princes.

of ideas are the problems of representation and of majority vote contained in these provisions. The majority of four, of which the bull speaks as sufficient for a valid election, is not quite a majority in the modern sense. The majority of four has rather the character of a quorum: four electoral votes are necessary to elect the king; if the other three should be absent or vote for another candidate, the election would not be a majority election as distinguished from a unanimous election, but it would have to be considered an election "in concord."[11] The quorum of four is the original requirement for a valid election, which is now on the point of being transformed into a majority through the coincidence that the college of electors has come to have seven members. The formula *concorditer* marks the transition from the earlier conception. Here we have one of the rare cases in the history of political ideas where the evolution of the majority vote can be traced clearly to its origins in an earlier phase of representative voting.

The formula of the bull is the last vestige of a development that began with the procedure for the creation of the German king in the tenth and eleventh centuries. In this earlier procedure one cannot discern very well a clear election act at all, but has rather to speak of an "elevation" to the throne, a complicated process sometimes extending over years. The "choice" of an appropriate candidate from several possible ones is a first step in this process: then follow "negotiations" with the chosen candidate; then the "election" proper, the agreement of the electing nobles to the candidate; then his "nomination," to be followed by the "laudation," the singly expressed agreement of the lesser men, and the "acclamation" of the people; then follow "enthronization" and "coronation," still interrupted by acts of laudation and acclamation; the acquisition of the consent of tribes that may have held back; the taking possession of the insignia; and the actual enforcement of functions against possible dissenters.

This complicated and extended process in which the actual consensus of the realm to the king is reached had experienced a considerable reduction by the thirteenth century. The election rules

---

11. "Talis electio perinde haberi et reputari debebit, ac si foret ab ipsis omnibus nemine discrepante concorditer celebrata" (Such an election will have to be held and reflected upon just as if it were engaged in harmoniously by all those people with no one disagreeing; II.4).

of the *Sachsenspiegel* (ca. 1230) are perhaps the best illustration of this transitional phase. The election proper has by now become the legal center of the procedure. The number of leading electors is fixed at six.[12] After the six leading electors have cast their vote, all the princes of the realm, ecclesiastical and secular, join in the election. The six leading electors are enjoined not to vote arbitrarily but for the candidate previously chosen by the princes. Obviously a "choice" precedes the election proper; the voting is a formal act that sanctions a substantial agreement to be reached before the voting begins. The six leading electors have to vote first for the chosen candidate, by virtue of their social prestige and authority; and the others follow suit in the electoral vote.[13]

Further restriction of the actual voting to the electoral princes occurred during the thirteenth century when interest in imperial elections sank so low that in 1273 only considerable papal pressure could persuade the princes to proceed to an election at all. The election by a quorum of four, which can be observed since 1198, is a formal act with the implication that it is representative of the substantial consensus of the realm to the candidate. In the Golden Bull the representation of the consensus is, finally, reduced to the fiction of concord. The earlier production of an actual consensus through the extended process of "elevation," and the leading role of certain votes by virtue of the social prestige and the authority of their bearers, is penetrated by strict procedural forms, approaching the majority vote of a college. The representative character of the act is not reconfirmed on the occasion of every election through the practice of leading votes and following votes; the historically sedimented prestige of the seven electoral votes has become formalized in the institution of the Electoral College.

e. The Oligarchy of the Princes

The election of the king-emperor, free from papal intervention, is the central problem of the bull. Around this center, however, are grouped a number of provisions that in their aggregate can be called a constitution of the realm. The elimination of papal

---

12. Eike von Repgow excludes the king of Bohemia because he is not a German prince (*Sachsenspiegel* III.57); text in Karl Zeumer, *Quellensammlung zur Geschichte der deutschen Reichverfassung,* 2d ed. (Tübingen, 1913), 1:64.
13. The provisions in *Sachsenspiegel* III.57.

approval left the king alone to deal with the electors; hence the status of the electors in the realm and their relation to the king had to be ordered. A common front of king and electors against any attempt of the papacy to resume its former prerogative was secured cleverly by the provision that the *rex Romanorum* had to confirm immediately after his election the privileges of the electors in order to be able to discharge imperial functions with legal effect. Any inclinations of the electors to favor papal claims against the elected king would be checked by the consideration that a doubt cast on the legal status of the king would first of all cast a doubt on the privileges of the electors (II.4). The electoral college was defined and closed through the enumeration of the princes of the Palatine, Bohemia, Saxony, and Brandenburg as the holders of the electoral dignity together with the ecclesiastical princes of Mainz, Cologne, and Trier (VII.1). For the four secular princes enumerated, the bull provides succession by primogeniture so that any partition of territories among several heirs, leading eventually to conflicting claims concerning the electoral dignity, is avoided (VII.1). The electors as a group received precedence on public occasions before all other princes of the realm (VI). The precedence among themselves was regulated meticulously in order to prevent dissensions on this point (III and IV). A vacancy in the empire had hitherto been the occasion for the pope to claim the vicariate until the election of a new king. This possibility was now eliminated by appointing the electors of the Palatine and Saxony as provisors of the realm in case of a vacancy (V). One of the most interesting developments was the provision for annual meetings of the electors as a council to deliberate with the emperor and to advise him on the affairs of the realm. The college of electors became an imperial "cabinet" (XII).[14]

Only the electors are treated by the bull as a *communitas*; the other estates of the realm have single status in relation to the king; no development is visible that would lead to a formation of communes in the English sense. This rule of single status suffers an exception only with regard to the peace-leagues *(Landfriedensbünde)*. Characteristically they are treated in the chapter on "Conspiracies" (XV). The peace-leagues were regional federations between princes

14. This function, however, did not develop in practice.

and cities for the maintenance of public peace in the territory. Such leagues are permitted by the emperor at his discretion. All other associations are stigmatized as "conspiracies" and prohibited; the conspiratorial character is specifically stressed for illicit associations in the cities and for leagues of cities. These provisions are aimed at the rising town-leagues, which impaired the full control of the princes over their territories and subjects. A further chapter prohibits, therefore, in particular the custom of cities to extend their privileges to nonresidents *(pfalburgerii)*, thereby withdrawing them from their subject status under the prince (XVI). The provisions about "conspiracies" tend to preserve the structure of the realm as an aggregate of territorial principalities.

f. Lupold of Babenberg

The problems that were regulated by the Golden Bull were also made the subject of a juristic literature. The theoretical achievement of this literature is none too glorious,[15] but we shall discuss briefly the most important treatise of this class because it conveys something of the new atmosphere in which problems of this type had now to move. The treatise is Lupold of Babenberg's *De juribus regni et imperii Romani.*[16] Lupold was a canonist, later bishop of Bamberg, an ecclesiastic who at the same time was deeply moved by the political sorrows of the nation. His treatise is dedicated to Archbishop Baldwin of Trier, the leading statesman among the German ecclesiastical electors; in the closing chapter he confesses that he was moved to write the treatise out of his "fervent zeal for the German fatherland," the *patria Germania* (chap. XIX). The opening chapters (I–IV) reveal his political attitude: the *sacrum imperium* with the pope and the emperor is not the all-absorbing political reality; instead it is the *regnum* of the Franks, the "free," which existed before there ever was an *imperium*. This *regnum* is centered in the German territory; the Franks who settled Gaul are only an offshoot from the main people. And the Franks are

15. A survey of this literature (Jordan of Osnabruek, Alexander of Roos, Engelbert of Admont, Lupold of Babenberg, Konrad of Megenberg) is to be found in Dempf, *Sacrum imperium,* III.3, "Die Konservativen," 494–503.
16. Lupoldus de Babenberg, *De juribus regni et imperii Romani,* ca. 1340; text in Simon Schardius, ed., *De jurisdictione, autoritate, et praeminentia imperiali, ac potestate ecclesiastica . . .* (Basel, 1566). See also R. Most, "Der Reichsgedanke des Lupolds von Bebenburg," *Deutsche Archiv* 4 (1941): 444–55.

descendants from a fugitive group of Trojans so that in terms of origins and antiquity the German *regnum* is of equal dignity with the Roman. After the *translatio imperii* from the Greeks to the Franks by the will of the Roman people through the agency of the pope, the main political problem is not the relation of the emperor to the pope within the empire, but the relation of the preexisting German *regnum* to the *imperium*. These historical matters settled, Lupold proceeds to the exposition of his juristic theory in five articles.[17]

According to Article I, the king-emperor, if elected unanimously, can assume the title of king and proceed to administer imperial affairs in Italy and the other provinces dependent on the empire. The claim is based on accepted legal principles: Charlemagne held his realm from Aquitania to Bavaria legitimately by succession; the other parts of the realm were acquired by just wars, a legitimate form of acquisition according to *jus gentium*; when the Carolingian line ended, the German princes elected legitimately a successor, for a people without a king have the right, by *jus gentium*, to elect one; and so on. The detail of the argument is less important than its tendency to ground the German political structure on general rules of political foundation and to restrict, as far as possible, the share that the world-imperial dignity of the king has in this structure.

According to Article II the king has the same rights even if the election is not unanimous but only by majority, if it is in *discordia*. The argument is very close to the conception of the Golden Bull. The *discordia* is only apparent, not real, because the electors do not vote singly, but as members of a *collegium* or *universitas*; the majority vote produces *concordia* in the case of a *universitas*. That the electors are a *collegium* and not seven single princes has to be assumed because otherwise all princes would have to participate in the election. The privileged position of the electors makes sense only if they are considered a representative committee of the princes, and ultimately of the people. The conception of the princes as the *repraesentantes populi*, and of the election as an act of the German people through its representatives, strongly colors the argument.

Article III introduces a curious detail. Lupold distinguishes between the administrative function of the king in the empire,

---

17. The five articles are set forth in five chapters, V–IX. Chapters X–XIII present and refute objections to the five articles.

principally extending to acts under feudal law, and a power reserved to the emperor of legitimating illegitimate children, of rehabilitating infamous persons, and so on. These rights, originally reserved to the *imperator*, are now claimed for the *rex Romanorum* before approval and coronation. The rights in question are not exciting, but the argument used in their support is highly illuminating for the national trend in German politics. For Lupold refers to "the general custom of the Western realms" to have these rights enjoyed by their kings, though they are not emperors. The other kings have the position of an *imperator in regno suo*, and the *rex Romanorum* should have, after all, this position, too. Article IV asserts that the elected king is under no obligation to request papal approval or to receive it. And Article V, finally, explains that the oath of the emperor to the pope is not a feudal oath, but an oath faithfully to defend the pope and the church.

Lupold is obviously engaged in disentangling the two spheres we called the state-imperium and the world-imperium. Only in the latter does the papal approval have any significance; for the former, for which Lupold chooses the term *regnum*, the principles of *jus gentium* have to be accepted. We might say that he tries to detach legally the German *regnum* from the empire in the same manner in which France and England were finding their national independence. Still, he does not go to the extreme of the *Licet juris* of declaring papal approval and coronation irrelevant. The world-imperium, implying the protection of the church, is still clearly distinguished, and it can be acquired only through papal acts. The ideas of Lupold are very close to the regulations of the Golden Bull, and it is quite possible that they actually influenced the drafting of the instrument. But such influence would have touched rather the technical side of the bull. The political attitude of Lupold distinctly does not favor an oligarchic construction of the empire; all through his work the idea of the people as the ultimate source of royal-imperial power runs strongly, while the function of the electors is admissible only if understood as a representation of the people.

§3. The City-States

a. The Area of the City-States

The particularization of the empire through the rise of territorial principalities to virtual independence is the first of the processes by which the political structure of the imperial zone came to be distinguished from that of the Western national realms. Of equal importance is the second process, the rise of the city-states. Towns grew in number and size in medieval England and France just as in Germany and Italy, but only in the imperial zone did towns develop into self-contained political units to such a degree that we can speak of the city-states as a political type on the same level of historical importance with the Western national realms and the German territorial principalities. The causes of this development are manifold, and they vary considerably in detail in the single instances of the hundreds of cities. Nevertheless, a few general determinants are suggested by the geographical spread of the city-states. The area, or as Toynbee calls it, the cosmos of the city-states,[18] extends from Tuscany and upper Italy, through Switzerland, southern Germany, and the Rhine valley, to Holland and Flanders; from the Cologne area it branches out through Westphalia to the Baltic, and along the Baltic coast to Estonia. This area covers the great trade routes of the Middle Ages; from the Near East through Italy to the regions north of the Alps, and from Novgorod (on Lake Ilmen) to western Europe. At the intersection of the two routes we find the rich cluster of towns in Holland and Flanders. The position on the trade routes is the economic condition for the rise of settlements that live on commerce and industry instead of agriculture. The area in question can, furthermore, be characterized politically as a no-man's-land between the strong territorial powers. The Italian towns developed in the relative power vacuum between the papacy, Byzantium, the Islamic world, and the transalpine empire; the strip from Switzerland to Holland is the zone between France and the larger German principalities; and the Hansa towns spread in the angle between the northern German principalities and the Scandinavian and Slavic realms. The location in areas between balancing powers is the political condition for the evolution of city-states as minor powers. And, finally, the historical structure of the area has to be taken into account. It is not an accident that the region from upper Italy to Flanders lies between balancing major powers, for this region is identical with the area of the Lotharingian realm as established in 843 by the Treaty of Verdun. The region remained an intermediate

18. See on the cosmos of the city-state Toynbee, *Study of History*, vol. 3 (1934), 341 ff.

zone for a thousand years. Only in the nineteenth century were large parts of it incorporated into the Italian and German national states, while Switzerland, Belgium, and Holland retained their status as minor powers between Italy, France, Germany, and England as balancing major powers, and while Alsace-Lorraine was shifted between France and Germany.[19] The Baltic coast is colonial land that was integrated only gradually into the orbits of the growing powers in the south, the north, and the east. The process of absorption was long drawn out until the last German city-states lost their last vestige of independence with the incorporation of Hamburg, Lübeck, and Bremen into the surrounding territories under the National Socialist regime.

b. The Towns and the Feudal World

The spread of the city-states directly determined the political structure only of the imperial zone; but the magnitude of the phenomenon, that vast, strong arc cutting through Europe from the Mediterranean to the Baltic and splitting the Continent into two halves, raised a serious problem with regard to the future political organization of the Western world at large. Until the rise of the towns, the principal political form of the Middle Ages had been the feudal organization of large territories on the basis of an agricultural economy. With the towns emerged a political organization based on commerce and industry and on the intensified intellectual and spiritual life of densely settled communities. Instead of a scattered agricultural population, integrated politically into larger units through subjection to local lords, who in their turn were bound by feudal relations to a common king, we now find a system of direct relations between the citizens and governmental authorities of the towns. Communes, evoked by *conjurationes* as the founding acts, a community of life between magistrates and people, in a small area, under mutual critical observation, tending toward virtual sovereignty—this is the substance of the new type. The town, understood in this sense, obviously was more than just another form of government; it was rather a new mode of life determining a type of political man who differed radically from

19. On the interpretation of the Napoleonic empire as the organization of the city-state cosmos on the Lotharingian territory see Toynbee, *Study of History*, vol. 5 (1939), 619 ff.

the ruling as well as from the subject types of the feudal order—
that is, from the noble, the ecclesiastic, and the peasant. The town
was, furthermore, not a mere addition to the feudal world, but
rather the representative of a new phase of Western civilization.
Historical dynamics were on the side of the economic services, the
rationality of business and politics, the amenities of luxury, the
superior intellectual aliveness, the advancement of literacy, the arts
and the sciences, and the active religiousness of the towns. It is this
civilizational style of the towns that entered into rivalry with the
style of the primary estates and was ultimately to dominate our
civilization. The character of the towns as models for the future
centuries of Western civilization bestows on the city-states their
importance on the wider European scene. In the towns of the great
arc the political potentialities of the new style of life could develop
in a manner that was impossible for the towns of France and England, which were more closely integrated into the structure of the
realm. Especially in the Italian city-states, forms and techniques of
government were developed in the thirteenth to fifteenth centuries,
and only in the France of Louis XI and the England of Henry VII
were they transferred to the transalpine realms. The city-states
produced on a small scale the problems of democracy, oligarchy,
absolute rulership, proletarian revolts, and party life that recur
with a time lag of some two or three centuries on the scale of the
kingdom.

The historical momentum of the town, its leading role in the
evolution of the postfeudal political forms, was the source of the
great alternative that faced the European political organization in
the centuries under observation. Would the civilizationally leading
town units be able to take the political initiative, conquer the feudal
territories, and submit them to their own rule? Or would the feudal
realms be able to adapt the political forms evolved by the towns to
the organization of the kingdoms, and to integrate the new social
sector into the realm as a third estate? The realms were ultimately
victorious; but in the last centuries of the Middle Ages the alternative had yet to be decided by an intense struggle. The details
of this long struggle in which the issue was settled are a matter of
political history; but the immeasurably variegated and complicated
field of historical details shows at least certain dominant lines of
evolution and produces dominant types of institutions that we have
to list briefly.

c. Trade Routes and Food Supply

First of all, the factors should be considered that compelled the towns to transcend the limits of their settlements and become centers of organization for the surrounding territories. The existence of a town is precarious because an industrial and commercial community is not a self-sufficient political unit. For its economic existence the town depends on markets and raw materials, and for sheer life it depends on the food supply from the surrounding countryside; a stable symbiosis with the countryside and the safety of the trade routes are the conditions of existence. The rational power solutions of these problems would be: (1) political rule over a territory sufficient to feed the city, and (2) the building of strength to the point where the town itself is capable as a military power to insure the safety of its trade routes. In its purest and most successful form this solution was pursued in Italy. The case of Venice is perhaps the most illustrative because it shows the interlocking of the two problems of food supply and trade routes. Since the middle of the thirteenth century, Venice was engaged in intermittent warfare with Genoa over control of the Black Sea and Levantine trade; by the middle of the fourteenth century she suffered the severe defeat of Sapienza (1354), which cost her the fleet, and in the subsequent War of Chioggia (1378–1381) the Genoese were able to blockade Venice; the Venetian counterblockade of Chioggia finally compelled the surrender of the Genoese fleet, a blow that broke the Genoese power decisively. The War of Chioggia had revealed a vulnerability through insufficient control of the mainland food supply, and the first half of the fifteenth century witnessed a determined policy of inland expansion that resulted in the acquisition of Padua, Bassano, Vicenza, Verona, Brescia, Bergamo, and Cremona. The conquest of the mainland was necessary in order to maintain the power position that alone could protect the sea empire. The mainland itself, however, besides securing the food supply, served directly a much needed additional protection of trade routes, for the increase of commerce after the defeat of Genoa made imperative the safe possession of the mountain passes for the transalpine trade. Finally, the Venetian expansion illustrates the process in which the weaker towns were reduced and incorporated into the territories of the few strong city-states. In 1300, Italy north of the Papal States had some seventy to eighty city-states;

by the time of Machiavelli the same area was organized in eight principalities.

d. The Fourth Crusade—Power Distribution in the Eastern Mediterranean

On the Italian mainland the city-states had to expand at the expense of rival towns. In the Mediterranean area, however, they were in competition with the feudal powers. The case is of general importance, for it shows the possibilities as well as the limitations of the growth of city-states. The Mediterranean conquests are the only instance of a submission of feudal territories. Here, in the outposts of the Western crusading conquests, the naval power of the Italian city-states proved stronger than the French feudal dependencies. When the city-states came into conflict with the main powers in Europe itself, the realms proved stronger than the cities. Again the case of Venice illustrates best the trend. The greatest position of Venice in the Mediterranean beyond the Adriatic was established through the Fourth Crusade (1202–1204).[20] This crusade showed for the first time the nonfeudal techniques of political, military, and financial rationalism in full force. The original conception of an attack on Egypt required the aid of the Venetian navy for the transport of troops. The Venetians were ready to invest their navy in the enterprise against the promise of a considerable sum of money and a half share in the booty. In the course of the negotiations the object of the crusade was diverted from Egypt to Constantinople, a decision on which the Venetians probably had some influence. Since the cash prize could not be paid, the crusaders at the request of the Venetians, as a preliminary to the Crusade proper, consented to conquer and destroy the Christian town of Zara. The pope was furious and excommunicated the Venetians but could not prevent the further attack on Constantinople with the conquest of the city in 1204. Upon the conquest followed the partition of the booty. A committee of six Frenchmen and six Venetians elected the count of Flanders as emperor, while the patriarchate went to the Venetian Cardinal Morosini. The emperor received one quarter of the conquest; the other three quarters were divided equally between French

20. See on these questions Charles Diehl, "The Fourth Crusade and the Latin Empire," *CMH*, vol 4 (1923), chap. 14.

and Venetians. The French holdings extended over Thessalonica, Athens, and Achaia; the Venetians took the Aegean islands, Crete, Euboea, and the ports of Coron and Modon in the Morea. By force of its navy and its wealth, the city-state had achieved equality of power with the French princes in the Mediterranean. This equality of power, however, did not last long. In the fourteenth century began the invasion of the city-states into the feudal sphere. The Lusignan had to concede in 1372 the trade monopoly of Famagusta to Genoa. In 1466 the Venetians assumed the protectorate of Cyprus, and in 1489 the island became a Venetian colony, until it fell to the Turks in 1517. On the Greek mainland we can observe the curious rise of the Acciajuoli. Niccolo Acciajuoli, a Florentine merchant, became the business manager of Catherine of Valois, the titular empress of Constantinople, in Naples. In the 1330s he obtained through his negotiations for her and her son the principality of Achaia and was rewarded with considerable estates in the duchy; in 1358 he became hereditary governor of Corinth. In the next generation the Acciajuoli acquired the duchy of Athens through conquest from the Catalan company. Florentine dominion ended only with the advance of the Turks—in Athens in 1456, in Thebes in 1460.

e. The Organization of the Venetian Conquest

The expansion of the city-states reveals their strength; the constitutional order of the conquest reveals their limitations.[21] The town constitutions did not expand with the territory; the newly acquired populations were not integrated into the political life of the town. In the case of Venice, the constitutional order of the sea empire was a mixture of central administration and feudal decentralization; the order of the mainland, a mixture of central administration and local self-government. Crete was parceled out into knights' fiefs for nobles and sergeants' fiefs for burgesses. The island was divided into six districts, corresponding to the *sestieri* of Venice; and settlement of the fiefs in the districts was encouraged by colonists from the *sestieri* in order to transplant the spirit of civic competition to the island. The governor, with the title of a duke, was appointed from Venice and held office for one year; like the doge, he had two

---

21. See for this section William Miller, "Greece and the Aegean under Frank and Venetian Domination (1204–1571)," *CMH*, vol. 4 (1923), chap. 15.

personal councillors; the colonists were represented in a greater and a lesser council; the native population could participate in the order through insurrection, which they readily did in the year of its imposition. The lesser islands were held as fiefs by Venetian noblemen, who did not always preserve their loyalty to Venice. This adventurer acquisition of wealth and power in the Aegean through leading families was an important factor in the *serrata* of 1297, the closure of the Great Council, and the establishment of a hereditary oligarchy. On the mainland the institutions of the conquered towns were left intact on the whole; only the *podestà* or *rettore* was a Venetian magistrate. The three varieties of administration show the means of political order at the disposition of a city-state: (1) extension of the central administration with colonization by fiefs; (2) central administration with local self-government; and (3) feudal administration with repercussion for the oligarchic reconstruction of the metropolitan constitution. None of these forms lends itself to the political articulation of a people in the manner of the national kingdoms.

f. Burgundy

An organizational dynamics opposite to the Venetian can be discerned in the integration of the town cluster of the Low Lands into the realm of Burgundy.[22] In the case of Venice, the city-state is the politically active center that integrated the territory by means of its preexistent constitutional and administrative apparatus. In the case of Burgundy, a feudal lord integrated into a realm a number of fiefs, united in his person but otherwise incoherent, by superimposing on his preexistent personal holdings a central constitution and administration. The concentration of holdings began when Philip II, a son of King John II of France, became duke of Burgundy in 1363 and married the heiress of Flanders and Artois. Through purchases, bequests, and cessions, their grandson Philip the Good acquired Holland, Zeeland, Brabant, Limburg, Luxembourg, Hainault, Namur, Antwerp, and Mechlin. His successor, Charles the Bold (1467–1477), added Guelders and Liege. For the government of his aggregate of personal holdings Philip the Good and Charles

22. On Burgundy see Henri Pirenne, "The Low Countries," *CMH*, vol. 8 (1936), chap. 10.

the Bold created central institutions that transformed them into provinces of a realm. The Great Council of the Duke, under the presidency of the chancellor of Burgundy, composed of representatives of all the provinces, occupied itself with affairs of common interest. A judicial chamber of this Great Council was organizationally separated in 1473 as the Parliament of Malines and became a court of appeals for all dominions of the duke. The financial administration of the realm was organized in three *Chambres des Comptes* in Lille, Brussels, and the Hague. A standing army, recruited from all dominions, was organized in the *Compagnies d'Ordonnance.* In 1463 for the first time the Estates General of the realm was called into session, composed of representatives of the local estates. This federal congress of the local estates served primarily the rationalization of the financial system by consenting to the taxes to be raised in the single provinces. The creation, in 1430, of the Order of the Golden Fleece, finally, shows the attempt of the duke to form a nobility of the realm as distinguished from the nobility of the single dominions. A medieval, feudal area was transformed into a monarchy with a rational central administration, but tempered by recognition of local institutions and by a federal congress of estates. The factor that made it possible for Burgundy to achieve what Venice could not even attempt was the position of the feudal lord, who stood above the various dominions to which he held title. The organization did not proceed from one member of the group of political units but from the common lord who was equidistant to them all. In the Italian city-states we find repeated the difficulties that could be observed in the creation of the empire of Athens as well as, on a major scale, in the construction of the Roman empire. The towns seem to have been unable to enlarge their institutions to a representation of the realm. With the exception of Venice, the end of the difficulties in Italy was brought about by the evolution of the *signoria* in the town, which finally developed into the position of the hereditary absolute prince of larger territories like Tuscany, Ferrara, Milan, and so on.

g. The Hansa

Under the specific conditions of the Baltic area, the Hanseatic League was developed as an organization of towns for the protection of trade.[23] There was no question of conquering and organizing a territory; the association served the mutual protection, the acquisition, and the monopolistic exploitation of trade privileges. The Hansa is of interest to us precisely because *no* attempt was made to organize a territory and a people, but in this case the considerable political power, and on occasion even military strength, of the league served exclusively a well-defined economic interest; no idea of a *societas perfecta* entered the political conception of the Hansa. The fragmentary and one-sided character of Hansa politics, the waste of effort as far as the foundation of a polity is concerned, has to be well understood. Centuries of political initiative of a large and important section of German society went into the building of institutions that meant a good deal for the prosperity of the towns but had little consequence, if any, for the political articulation of the German nation. The flowering of the Hansa was impressive, but when the time for its limited objectives had run it did not even come to an end: it petered out, and the single towns remained to be integrated by the territorial principalities. By the standards of institutional development offered by the Western national realms, we would have to say that German particularism, as fixed in the fourteenth century, was an obstacle to political organization that had to be overcome by severe convulsions, while the Hansa flowering of the same period was a political impasse. Under the conditions of a recently acquired colonial area, the Hansa was an adequate, and perhaps inevitable, form of political protection; under the aspect of postcolonial, national development it is one of the factors that account for the absence, in later centuries, of national institutions with sufficient historical momentum. In spite of the far-flung league, no national patterns of political conduct were created that would have transcended the orbit of the single towns. One cannot stress this point strongly enough in order to counteract the arbitrary and purely imaginative interpretations of the German problem of the nineteenth century and after; the interpretations that operate with the German "national character" are, just as the corresponding operations with an English "national character," shortcuts that ignore the importance of long-range institutional

---

23. On the Hansa see A. Weiner, "The Hansa," *CMH*, vol. 7 (1932), chap. 8.

growth for the determination of political patterns. The more recent German difficulties are determined decisively by the events in the critical thirteenth and fourteenth centuries—that is, by (1) the destruction of the royal integrating work through the interregna, (2) the obstacle to political articulation on a national scale erected by the rise of territorial principalities in the wake of the interregna, (3) the immense expenditure of forces that otherwise might have gone into the building of the internal order of the realm, through the colonization of the East, and (4) the diversion of the political energies of the towns into the ephemeral leagues.

The limited objectives of the Hansa were the cause of its organizational nonchalance. Careful investigation has uncovered some 160 towns that at one time or another were associated with the Hansa, but it is impossible to state for any given time how many members the Hansa actually had and who they were. The Hansa had, furthermore, no definite beginning and end in 1350 and 1450, and its greatest numerical strength was probably reached after 1450, at a time when the decline had already set in. In the evolution of the Hansa two phases can be distinguished. Significantly, the Hansa did not begin as a league of cities at all, but as an association of German merchants in trading places abroad. After the middle of the twelfth century we find German merchants gaining self-administration in Gotland and receiving collective protection in London; before 1200 the factory at Novgorod was organized, with subdivisions in Pskov, Polotsk, Vitebsk, and Smolensk; by the middle of the thirteenth century Wisby, Novgorod, London, Bruges, and Bergen had become the leading associational centers. The very effective political weapon at the disposition of these associations was the trade boycott. When the transition to a league of cities ensued cannot be determined exactly. Usually the year 1241, with its alliance between Hamburg and Lübeck, is given as the formal beginning of the Hanseatic League. But the alliance of 1241 was an agreement between the *mercatores* of the two cities, not between the *civitates* themselves. The *civitates* replaced the *mercatores* in the documents only after the middle of the fourteenth century, for the first time on the occasion of the war with Flanders. The internal subdivisions of the league became visible in the statute of 1347 for the factory at Bruges. The statute recognized three divisions, the so-called Thirds: the Wend and Saxon towns under the leadership of Lübeck; the Westphalian-Prussian group and Cologne; and the Gotland-Livland towns with Wisby. The central organs of the league were insufficiently developed. Since the middle of the fourteenth century general sessions of a Hansa Diet are recorded; the business agenda was to be discussed in advance by regional diets; Lübeck had the chairmanship and served generally as the executive of the league. The climax of the league was reached after the war with Denmark; the Treaty of Stralsund, of 1370, gave the league control of the fisheries and customs of the sound, strongholds in Scania, and the concession that no king of Denmark would be crowned unless accepted by the league and after he had confirmed its privileges. The decline of the league came with the consolidation of the territorial powers surrounding the Baltic: Lithuania and Poland were united in 1386, and the Scandinavian countries entered the Union of Kalmar in 1397. The decline of the international position was followed by internal disintegration because the Hansa had failed to organize the agricultural hinterland. The territorial principalities could compel withdrawals from the league when they began seriously to assert jurisdiction over the cities belonging to their territories. In the second half of the fifteenth century the league was substantially broken through the withdrawal of the towns of Brandenburg and Saxony. Its economically dominant position collapsed, just like the position of Venice, with the shift of the principal trade routes to the Atlantic. This end could have been averted only if the Hansa had gone beyond its economic policy, if it had organized the rural hinterland of lower Germany as a territorial power under its control and gained access to the Atlantic through the incorporation of the Lowlands. That a development of this kind was militarily not out of the question is shown by the respectable display of force in the war with Denmark.

h. Southwest German Leagues

That the Hansa could gain its considerable strength and survive as long as it did in spite of its neglect of territorial organization is due to the colonial character of the Baltic area and the belated growth of territorial powers that first reduced and ultimately dissolved it. In western and southern Germany the town leagues had a brief culmination and then collapsed suddenly in the struggle with the princes. The southwest German leagues were a product of the long Interregnum of the thirteenth century. Beginning with 1247 we find a number of leagues between the cities of the Rhine and Moselle area, and in the fourteenth century began the leagues of Swabian and Bavarian cities for protection of commerce and the highways and for defense against princely encroachments. The crisis came after 1356 with the provision of the Golden Bull that prohibited the expansion of jurisdiction to nonresidents and thereby made any territorial organization from town centers illegal. In the following decades the determination of the towns and the princes began to shape for the settlement of the issue by force. In the 1370s the great Swabian and Rhenish town leagues were formed, and in 1381 the two leagues entered into an alliance. To counter this development in 1383 the League of the Princes was formed. In 1386 the town leagues entered into a further alliance with the Swiss towns of Berne, Zurich, Zug, and Soleure. When the war broke out, the alliance of the towns did not hold. The Swiss, who became the first objects of the attack, had to fight alone at Sempach in 1386 and remained victorious. Without Swiss aid, the Swabian League was defeated in 1386 and the Rhenish in 1388. In 1389 the emperor dissolved the leagues, and the towns went in the following centuries down the road of absorption into the territories.

i. The Swiss Confederation

The Swiss Confederation was the only one of the southwest German leagues to be successful. The cause of the success was the unique political dynamics of the Swiss region. In the Venetian case the city had the political initiative in organizing a territory; in the Burgundian case the feudal lord took the initiative in organizing the town areas into a realm; in the Swiss case neither a city nor a feudal lord but the peasant communes of the rural area had the political initiative. The core of the confederation consisted of the Forest Cantons of Uri, Schwyz, and Unterwalden. Originally the cantons were parts of the duchy of Swabia, but during the Interregnum of the thirteenth century Uri and Schwyz managed to receive declarations of immediacy under the empire from Frederick II. The conflict with the feudal powers began when Rudolph of Habsburg tried, for his house, to restore the full jurisdiction of the duchy of Swabia in the Swiss territories. His imperial preoccupations prevented him, however, from devoting sufficient attention to the submissions of the cantons, and Adolf of Nassau, his successor, renewed to Schwyz and Uri their status as tenants-in-chief under the empire; in 1309 Unterwalden received a similar status from Henry of Luxemburg. This combination of peasant communes with a status of tenant-in-chief was the "territory" that could enter into a confederation with towns. Lucerne joined in 1322, Zurich in 1351. The treaty with Zurich became the model for later accessions to the confederation; and it remained the model of the Swiss conception of federation until 1848, when the new constitution of that year incorporated the American experience in federal government into the Swiss plan. The alliance of 1351 provided for mutual protection, local autonomy, a limited jurisdiction of the confederation, courts of arbitration, and a diet. By 1353 Glarus, Zug, and Berne had joined, thus completing the federation of the eight "old" cantons. The rapid growth of a confederate political sentiment is shown by the Priest's Charter of 1370, which already provided for an oath of allegiance of every resident of the united territory to the confederation itself, thus establishing a direct loyalty relation between the confederation and individuals. The details of the further evolution, which was by no means smooth, is a matter of political history. What is relevant in this study is the solution of the hinterland problem for the cities. The city cantons did not have to conquer a rural territory but could gain the advantages of a food supply and of the military strength of a highly effective peasant infantry through federation. The danger to independence from Habsburg and Burgundy was sufficiently great and lasted long enough to let harmony appear the better part of wisdom in spite of the inevitable and very strong tensions and rivalries between town and country. The military prowess and political initiative of the Forest Cantons did much to offset their feeling of inferiority caused by lesser experience in affairs and the conduct of foreign politics of rural communities in comparison with the town aristocracies. A singular coincidence and interplay of factors favored this one federal solution of the problem of the towns.

j. The Internal Structure of the Towns

The internal structure of the towns is a subject too vast to be treated in this context with any adequacy. The reader will have to consult the monographs on the subject.[24] We shall only refer briefly to one or two problems of the Italian city-states that anticipate on the town scale the political problems of the territorial state. The Italian towns are of greater interest in this respect than the German because they have a richer social stratification that resembles closely that of the realms in the period in which the national constitutions evolved. The nucleus of the town society is the *popolo grasso* and the *popolo minuto:* the upper stratum of merchants, bankers, and industrial entrepreneurs; and the lower stratum of the artisans. Beyond this nucleus, which is typical also for the German cities, the Italian structure is complicated through the presence of the *grandi,* who were missing in the German cities, and of the industrial proletariat, which in the German towns where the small crafts were predominant was not developed to the same degree. The Italian towns show the full scale of strata—nobility, *haute bourgeoisie,* lower middle class, and proletariat—that centuries later is found in the European industrialized national states.

The division of the upper class into nobility and bourgeoisie is the principal cause of the violent factional life of the Italian cities. Two civilizational styles, the feudal and the capitalistic, were in constant friction; and both groups tried to assure their political ascendancy with the aid of the lower classes. The first typical constitutional development under these conditions was the political reduction of the *grandi* through the *popolani.* The Florentine Ordinances of Justice, of 1293, mark this phase. Under the provision of the ordinances no person could participate in the government of the town who was not a member of the guilds, and nobody could be a member of a guild unless he actually pursued his profession. A second typical consequence of the factional strife was the weakening of the communal spirit. The people of the town as a whole were the commune, but every individual belonged to special associations—

24. See the fine survey of problems in M. V. Clarke's *The Medieval City-State: An Essay on Tyranny and Federation in the Later Middle Ages* (London, 1926; rpt. Oxford: Oxford University Press, 1964), with a guide to the immense bibliography up to that date. Later studies, useful as guides to the literature, are, for Italy, Romolo Craggese, "Italy, 1313–1414," *CMH,* vol. 7 (1932), chap. 2, and Cecilia Mary Ady, "Florence and North Italy, 1414–1492," *CMH,* vol. 8 (1936), chap. 6. More recent studies include Henri Pirenne, *Medieval Cities: Their Origins and the Renewal of Trade,* trans. Frank D. Halsey (Princeton: Princeton University Press, 1969); John K. Hyde, *Society and Politics in Medieval Italy: The Evolution of Civil Life, 1000–1350* (New York: St. Martins, 1973); and Skinner, *Foundations of Modern Political Thought,* vol. 1.

the *arti* of the *popolani*, the *consorterie* of the *grandi*—and in the rivalry of the associations to capture the government, the communal magistracies lost their representative value for the people as a whole and became technical power instruments in the hands of the incumbent of the moment. The towns had no integrating institutions comparable to the king as the representative of the realm, and the factional associations proved incapable of producing a representative executive who would have balanced the particular interests of the factions. The rise of the *signoria* over the party strife, which became necessary for the effective conduct of affairs, destroyed the self-government and inaugurated absolute rule. The situation is illustrated perhaps best by the necessity in which Florence found itself in the first half of the fourteenth century of submitting to feudal princes as temporary *signori* for the conduct of military campaigns: to King Robert of Naples for the campaign against Henry VII, to the duke of Calabria against the Tuscan Ghibellines, and to Walter of Brienne, the duke of Athens, for the campaign against Pisa. The third instructive feature of town politics is the failure of the proletariat to gain permanent influence on the government. When the existence of the community depends economically on the international connections and the business knowledge of the ruling merchants and bankers, it seems impossible for the industrial proletariat to dominate the town politically because the passive resistance alone of the business class can maneuver workers rather quickly into an untenable position. The democratic gains of the *ciompi*, in the revolt of 1378 in Florence, were wiped out by 1382.

The survey of these characteristics shows the immeasurable importance that the representative kingship of the national realms has for the evolution of constitutional government. The commune alone, without the integrating services of a king, does not have sufficient coherence to bind the factional interests into a workable political unit once the economic stratification of a commercial and industrial society is fully developed. The rise of the *signoria*, on the other hand, with its stifling effect on civic initiative, shows clearly the consequence of absolute rule for the economic development of the community, a stifling effect that appears also in the transalpine national realms under the absolute monarchy. England is the signal exception from this rule because, as we have set forth in an earlier chapter, the articulation of the people into the communes of the realm proved strong enough to balance and, finally, to overcome the absolutistic effects of the Tudor monarchy. The dissolution of the commune into particularistic associations, none of whom can lend representative authority to governmental institutions, is a problem that only recently has appeared on the scale of the national state—in Germany, France, Italy, and Spain—with the decline of the representative values of the constitutional monarchy. Again England is the exception because the political style of the ruling oligarchy, and of the executive type created by it, has preserved its representative values unbroken by revolutions of the continental type.

k. The Constitution of Venice

Among the Italian city-states, Venice had an exceptional position, comparable to that of the English among the national states. The balance and the stability of the Venetian constitution, for centuries the admiration of Europe,[25] were conditioned by the fortunate absence of the factors that caused instability in the other towns. Due to its peripheral situation in Italy, Venice could keep aloof from the destructive Guelf-Ghibelline struggle that tore the other cities. It had, furthermore, never compelled the nobility from the *contado* to settle in the town and, therefore, did not have the problem of the *grandi*. And the economic structure, finally, was so heavily weighted toward commerce that crafts and industries could not gain the social relevance that would have disturbed the homogeneousness of the commercial oligarchy. The simplicity of the political style was for Venice, as for England, the source of its grandeur. The constitution of Venice began to move away from the original popular assembly after the disaster of 1172, which had been caused by the emotional decision of the people and the hasty reaction of the doge. A body of 480 leading citizens was formed in 1172, elected for one year from the *sestieri*, for the transaction of business; the doge was limited by the presence of six councillors and had to give the *promissione ducale*. In 1297 the constitution began to assume its final form. The Great Council was fixed at some 1,500 hereditary

25. Of the considerable literature on the Venetian constitution, the most important treatise is Gasparo Contarini's *De magistratibus et republica Venetorum.* Contarini lived 1484–1542. English edition: *The Commonwealth and Government of Venice*, trans. Lewes Lewkenor (New York: De Capo Press, 1969); reissued in The English Experience, no. 101 (Amsterdam, 1969); see William J. Bouwsma, *Venice and the Defense of Republican Liberty* (Berkeley: University of California Press, 1968).

members. This body had mainly elective functions. The legislation was put into the hands of a senate, consisting of 120 members of the Great Council and the important officials. A Council of Forty discharged the judicial business. The executive organ was the *Collegio,* consisting of the doge and twenty-six department heads; it had to initiate legislation in the senate and to execute the law. In 1310 the Council of Ten was added, a supreme controlling organ of the oligarchic leaders. This constitution was not the constitution of a people, but rather the self-government of the oligarchy.

§4. Cola di Rienzo

a. State of the Problem

A complicated problem of subimperial politics is presented by the commune of Rome. The internal structure of Rome did not differ substantially from that of other Italian cities, and the revolt of Rienzo in 1347 was on the surface a typical *popolani* revolt against the barons, with Rienzo assuming the functions of a *signore.* Other features of the revolt were more specifically Roman, such as the revival of ancient Roman constitutional forms, or the reforming spiritualism directed against the church. Even these characteristics, however, while not typical of other Italian cities, were not new in Rome: they had been present already two centuries earlier in the commune of Arnold of Brescia. Still there was something extraordinary about Cola's revolt. In the *Florentine Histories* (I.31) Machiavelli speaks of the impression that Cola's reform made on contemporaries, an impression so strong that not only the neighboring towns but all Italy sent their ambassadors to him, and the other European countries raised their heads in surprise "when they saw that Rome had been reborn" *(vedendo come Roma era rinata).* In this passage, the term *renaissance* is used for the first time in connection with a political event. Considering the central function of the *ordo renascendi* in Machiavelli's thought, the use of this term can only mean that Machiavelli recognized in Rienzo a forerunner of his own idea of an Italy who would return to her *principii,* shake off the yoke of foreign tyrants, and resume her leading role among nations.

The interpretation of Machiavelli, who sensed something new in the appearance of Rienzo, is substantially correct, and it should be preferred to the more current view of the tribune as a dreamer, a romantic, and a conservative. In the case of Rienzo we are faced by a problem similar to that of Dante: his world of symbols is medieval, but the sentiments drive toward the future. Since Rienzo, however, is not a figure of the importance of Dante, his person and his work have only recently received the attention they deserve, and the results are still somewhat in suspense. In spite of the magnificent work of Konrad Burdach, the personality of Rienzo has not yet become clear. Attention has been concentrated in the recent literature too much on the wealth of symbols that he uses in his writings; and the symbols have been explored in the context of a history of Renaissance symbolism. The person and the ideas of Rienzo are smothered today under a mountain of detailed knowledge that is badly in need of more thorough and more precise classification. We return, therefore, in our study to the letters of Rienzo themselves, and shall attempt to give a picture of his political conception on the basis of his self-presentation and his retrospective self-interpretation.[26]

b. The Letters to the Italian Cities

Rienzo's coup d'etat took place on Pentecost Day of 1347. Immediately following the successful assumption of power, the tribune circulated letters to the towns of Italy inviting them to equip soldiers, to join in the struggle for the liberation of Italy, to send ambassadors

26. The great standard treatise is Konrad Burdach, *Rienzo und die geistige Wandlung seiner Zeit* (Berlin: Weidmann, 1913–1938). For a critique of Burdach's work see Karl Borinski, "Politische symbolik des mittelalters und werden der renaissance," *Zeitschrift für Deutsche Philologie* 48 (1919): 459–75. See furthermore Konrad Burdach's two studies "Sinn und Ursprung der Worte Renaissance und Reformation" (1910) and "Ueber den Ursprung des Humanismus" (1913), both reprinted in *Reformation, Renaissance, Humanismus* (Berlin and Leipzig: Paetel, 1926); Karl Borinski, "Die Weltwiedergeburtsidee in den neueren Zeiten, I: Der Streit um die Renaissance und die Entstehungsgeschichte der historischen Beziehungsbegriffe Renaissance und Mittelalter," Sitzungsberichte der Bayerischen Akademie der Wissenschaften, philosophische-philologische-historische Klasse (Munich, 1919); Karl Brandi, "Cola die Rienzo und sein Verhaltnis zu Renaissance und Humanismus," in *Bibliothek Warburg, Vorträge, 1925–1926* (Leipzig, 1928); Paul Piur, *Cola di Rienzo: Darstellung seiner Lebens und seines Geistes* (Vienna, 1931); and the chapter "Weltuntergangserwartung und Welterneuerungsglaube als Grundlage der Geistigen Neugeburt Italiens," in Paul Piur, *Petrarcas "Buch ohne Namen" und die Päpstische Kurie: Ein Beitrag zur Geschichte der Frührenaissance* (Halle, 1925). The sources used are *Epistolario di Cola di Rienzo*, a cura di Annibale Gabrielli, Fonti per la Storia d'Italia (Rome, 1890); and *Briefwechsel des Cola di Rienzo*, ed. Konrad Burdach and Paul Piur, *Vom Mittelalter zur Reformation* II.3 (Berlin, 1912). The biography of Cola written by a contemporary is now available as *The Life of Cola di Rienzo*, trans. and intro. John Wright (Toronto: University of Toronto Press, 1975); see also Victor Fleischer, *Rienzo: The Rise and Fall of a Dictator* (London: Aiglon Press, 1948.)

who would participate in his parliament on August 1, and to nominate a lawyer whom he would appoint to his *consistorium* of judges. The first of these letters, of May 24, to the commune of Viterbo, contains already the principal formulations that reveal his political conception (*Epistolario* no. 2, pp. 5 ff.). That the communes may rejoice, he announces to them the gift of the Holy Spirit, which Jesus on this Pentecost Day has chosen to extend "to the people [of Rome], to you and to all our faithful peoples who constitute our members." Rome is conceived as the head of Italy, and the other cities are the members of the *corpus mysticum;* the category of the mystical body is transferred to Rome, not to the papal or the pagan Rome, but to the Rome of a new dispensation, which begins with the descent of the spirit on the city and its people, in the same manner in which the first Christian community was constituted by the Spirit on the first Pentecost. There is a suggestion of a Cesaropapal concentration of powers under the new order, for the tribune styles himself *Nicolaus severus et clemens, severus* indicating the temporal, *clemens* the spiritual power.[27] There is, furthermore, alive the tradition of the *lex regia,* for the descent of the spirit restored "unity and concord" to the Roman people and inspired it to transfer to Rienzo "full and free power and authority to reform and conserve the state of peace in the City and Province of Rome."

The letters of the following weeks elaborate and clarify somewhat these first formulations. Those to the other communes show a text substantially identical with that of the letter to Viterbo. But the letter to Florence announces the intention of striking a new coin (*Epistolario* no. 4, pp. 12 ff.). The second letter to Florence (no. 7, pp. 19 ff.) replaces the *provincia Romana* by the *sacra Italia,* from now on to be used regularly. The letter to Pope Clement VI, of July 8, speaks of the regime that has its "origin and status" from the Holy Spirit, and adds that the people of Rome are not subject to anybody but God, the church, and the pope; it is furthermore the first letter to be dated "in the first year of the liberated republic" (no. 8, pp. 20 ff.). The letter of July 9, to the commune of Mantua, enlarges the function of Rome to the headship, not of Italy only,

27. The spiritual meaning of *clemens* is accentuated through Rienzo's reference to *auctore clementissimo domino nostro Iesu Christo* (by the most merciful author and lord Jesus Christ).

but of "all cities of the *orbis terrarum*," and it announces that the tribune will be promoted to a "knight of the Holy Spirit," on August 1, by the *syndici* of Rome and of the other Italian cities (no. 9, pp. 27 ff.).

c. The Tribunus Augustus

The promotion and coronation of August 1 are surrounded by a number of symbolic acts. For their interpretation and their place in the context of renaissance symbolism, we have to refer the reader to the earlier cited literature, particularly to the treatise by Konrad Burdach. We shall have to mention only Cola's bath in the porphyry fountain in the Baptisterio of San Giovanni in which the Emperor Constantine had received his baptism, because this bath figures prominently in a state document as the source of new authority (summons to the emperor, no. 17, pp. 48 ff.). The bath in the fountain of Constantine repeats analogically the purification and spiritual reformation of the emperor in order to signify the *renovatio* and *reformatio* of a Roman imperial Christianity. Rienzo receives his knighthood of the Holy Spirit in honor of the Holy Mother, the Roman Church, his supreme lord, the pope, and for the prosperity of the holy city of Rome, the *sacra Italia*, and the whole community of the faithful. The date of the ceremony, the first of August, and the acceptance of the title of *tribunus Augustus*, emphasize still further the renovation of a spiritual *imperium* over the whole of Christian mankind.

In this role of the spiritual Augustus, Rienzo issued on the same day his summons to the German emperors and the electors (no. 17, pp. 48 ff.). The summons regulates three subjects: (1) the Roman people are to resume the full power, authority, and jurisdiction over the *orbis terrarum* that they once had; all privileges granted at the expense of Roman authority and jurisdiction are revoked; (2) the city of Rome becomes the head of the *orbis* and the basis of the Christian faith; all Italian cities are declared free; the peoples of the cities and the citizens singly receive Roman citizenship and will enjoy all privileges of Romans; (3) the election of the Roman emperor, and the jurisdiction and monarchy of the *sacrum imperium*, belong to Rome and her people; the emperors (Lewis the Bavarian and Charles IV), the electors, and all other princes are summoned to Rome for the next Pentecost to receive from Rienzo the decision on the new imperial order. A letter of September 19, finally, informs the commune of Florence that the election of the emperor will be from then on in the hands of the Italian people and reveals Rienzo's intention that on the coming Pentecost he will have elected *aliquem Italicum* as emperor.

d. National and Imperial Sentiments

The political conception of Rienzo is not free of contradictions, and it obviously underwent an evolution between May and September 1347; the difficulties of an interpretation are, furthermore, increased by his later explanations, which indicate that not all of his pronunciations were meant seriously, but that some served ulterior purposes. Still, the *reformatio et renovatio* of the state of Rome (letter to Viterbo, May 24) is a clear nucleus of sentiment. The *sacra Italia* is at the center of the idea; her liberation and unification are the main purpose. The symbols around this center, however, are not harmonized. The new dispensation of the Holy Spirit would be on principle both a spiritual and a temporal realm, but Rienzo was most careful in stressing on every occasion his loyalty to the church and the pope. The *sacra Italia* was the new *corpus mysticum*; but, on the other hand, Rome would resume her position as the head of all Christianity. The weight of the summons, furthermore, was rather impaired by Cola's later declaration in the memorandum to the archbishop of Prague that he had never believed, of course, that the German emperors and princes would come to Rome and receive his orders, but he had hoped he could induce the tyrants of Italy to appear at this synod, and when he had them all together he would have had the opportunity to hang the wolves "all equally on one day against the sun."[28] If we consider, furthermore, Rienzo's general confession, in the same memorandum, that he acted the fool and the dignified, the ardent and the hesitant, the simple and the astute as the situation seemed to require, it being his one and only purpose "to abolish the error of division and to reduce the

---

28. *Verus tribuni libellus contra scismata et errores scriptus ad archepiscopum Pragensem,* August 1350, *Epistolario* no. 35, p. 154: "Sperans de eo Deo iustissimo pro liberatione totius sui gregis fideliter complacere, si tot lupos, ad locum universalis iustitie, velut ad retia, concurrentes, suspendissem una die partier contra solem" (hoping thereby faithfully to be pleasing to a most just God for the liberation of his entire flock, if, when so many wolves were running to the place of universal justice as though to a snare, I had hung them all equally on one day against the sun).

people to unity"—his whole apparatus of symbols appears in a somewhat dubious light.[29] Rienzo seems to indulge on occasion in the same kind of intellectual juggling with symbols as did Dante in his political *Letters*. The juggling had only advanced one step—from the context of manifestos to the context of political action. Hence it is necessary all the more to insist on the one sentiment of Rienzo that is not in doubt in this earlier phase of his politics, on the sentiment that expresses itself in the idea of a renovated and unified Italy, of an Italy to be renewed through Rienzo as the chosen instrument of the Spirit.

The confessions of Rienzo show that he was not altogether a dreamer and a romantic but that there was in his character a strain of the actor and political technician to whom symbols are instruments for his plans. Nevertheless, in a measure, the confession invalidates itself. We do not know to what extent this confession itself is a good piece of acting in order to convince the archbishop and the emperor of the sincerity of Cola's new political intentions. We can believe him when he says that the love of the republic rather than the love of the imperium moved him to undertake the reform of justice (*Letter to Charles IV*, July 1350, *Epistolario* no. 30, p. 96), but we need not assume, therefore, that the operation with imperial symbols was mere political tactics. We rather have to acknowledge that in the imperial zone the transfer of the *corpus mysticum* idea to the national bodies did not function quite smoothly. In Italy and Germany the idea of the national mystical body was burdened with the Roman and German imperial traditions. The experiences of spiritual renovation in these countries show frequently a tendency to embrace in the renovation the whole of Europe. Since this tendency is a sediment of the imperial Christian idea, it was present, of course, in the Western nations too. We can recognize it in the French idea of the universal validity of French civilizational values, just as much as in the Anglo-Saxon

---

29. No. 35, p. 155: "Fateor attamen, quod, velut ebrius ex ardore cordis arenti, pro tollendis omnibus parcialitatis erroribus et ad unitatem populis reducendis, nunc fatuum, nunc hystrionem, nunc gravem, nuc simplicem, nunc astutum, nunc fervidum, nunc timidum, simulatorem et dissimulatorem ad hunc caritativum finem, quem dixi, constitui sepius memet ipsum" (I confess, nonetheless, that, like a drunk in the burning ardor of his heart, in order to abolish the error of division and to reduce the people to unity, I have too often set myself up now as foolish, now as dramatic, now serious, now simple, now astute, now eager, now fearful, a pretender and dissembler to this charitable end that I have mentioned).

conviction of the universal validity of political forms evolved under very specific conditions in England and America. But there was a difference of dynamics between the West and the imperial zone. In the West, the imperial sentiment and missionary consciousness were superimposed over a separatist national sentiment that was in principle in opposition to the traditional empire construction, while in Italy and Germany the imperial sentiment lived in direct, affirmative continuity with the medieval imperial idea. As a consequence, political thinkers in the imperial zone frequently were not averse to using the imperial symbolism for the expression of their sentiments; and such usage then easily induced the assumption that the thinker in question was "romantic," "conservative," or "reactionary." We have noted this problem already on the occasion of the contrast between Pierre Dubois's French hegemonic plan for the organization of Europe and Dante's imperial conception. These appearances, however, are misleading. We have to accept as a fact the difference of dynamics between the Western nations and the Italian and German empire peoples. Beginning with the fourteenth century, the imperial symbolism in Italy and Germany can no longer be understood primarily in the medieval sense; its functions become subordinate to the national sentiment. The earlier quoted formula of Rienzo—that the love of the republic moved him more than the love of the imperium—is the perfect expression of this relation.

e. The Emissary of the Fraticelli

We have to bear these reflections in mind when we approach Cola's second political phase, after the breakdown of his *signoria* in Rome. He retired, in 1348, to the Fraticelli in the Abruzzi. Two years later, in 1350, he appeared in Prague, at the court of Charles IV. His long memoranda to the emperor and to Archbishop Ernest of Prague are the sources for the motivations both of his withdrawal and of his return to the political scene. In these memoranda, Rienzo reveals himself as a mystic in the tradition of Joachim of Fiore and the Franciscan Spirituals. The presentation of his experiences and ideas is not systematic, and the several documents show variations that are mutually incompatible; but precisely this manifold of conflicting variations permits an insight into the epochal crisis from which emerged the postmedieval personal attitudes as well as the postimperial community ideas. We do not follow in our presentation the chronological order of the memoranda, which has little bearing on the problems, but arrange them systematically.

(1) First should be considered the new political program concerning Italy and the empire.[30] Rienzo is still the chosen instrument of the Spirit, but his imperial aspirations are broken. He reports the illuminating history of the breaking process. At the time of his promotion to the tribunate he had compared himself to Christ: like Christ, who had ascended to his glory in his thirty-third year, so had he in his thirty-third year ascended to the tribunate. A monk who overheard this remark prophesied dire consequences for such hubris, and the perturbation of his mind through the prophecy had caused him to make the mistake that contributed to his downfall. He then resolved to retire to the Fraticelli and to do penitence for thirty-three months for the blasphemy of the thirty-three years. Then, on September 15, 1350, he would return to political life and fulfill, with the help of Christ, the imperial program. In his retirement, however, he had a revelation that compelled him to renounce this ambitious program, to give himself into the hands of the emperor, and to undertake the liberation and unification of Italy as the emperor's simple tool *(operarius et mercenarius Cesaris)*. Rienzo wants nothing but the permission and order of the emperor to complete the pacification of Italy; when his work is done he will resign *totam Italiam obsequentem Casari et pacificam* to the emperor. This *tota Italia* is to include the whole of the peninsula, including Venice, but not including Sicily, Sardinia, and Corsica. The political program is now definitely reduced to a nationally united Italy under the lordship of the emperor.

(2) Even in this reduced form, Rienzo's program does not envisage simply a military conquest of Italy and a submission by force. The unification is to be the work of the Spirit through his instrument Rienzo. The delicate question of the intervention of the Spirit in history through channels other than those of the sacramental church is now treated with great care (*Memorandum to Charles IV,* August 1350, *Epistolario* no. 32, pp. 131 ff.). Rienzo defends himself against the imputation that the Holy Spirit is making a new appearance in him; he never has maintained that a new Holy Spirit would be

30. *Verus tribuni libellus, Epistolario* no. 35. pp. 158–66.

coming like a new God. The defense reveals that Rienzo was at least suspected of claiming to be the Paraclete; he defends himself strongly against this suspicion, but his own confession concerning the thirty-three years incident shows that some of his utterances lent themselves to the belief. The renewal of the Spirit is now defined as an "amplification" of the first descent that will illuminate and renovate the whole surface of the earth. He refers to the prayer *Veni, creator Spiritus,* and asks what sense it could have if we do not expect the Spirit's advent. This advent is now due: "For we need the renovation of the Spirit, whenever we harden and grow old in sins" (p. 132). About the senescence of the world in sins there can be no doubt, hence the *spiritualis renovatio* is most opportune. The Joachitic philosophy of history is the basis of this conception; the Augustinian *senescens saeculum* will be overcome by a renewal of the Spirit on earth; and not only once but, in principle, every time the renewal is needed.

(3) In spite of the assiduous repression of the personal element,[31] Rienzo cannot avoid an explanation and justification of his own role in the advent of the Spirit. In the first Letter to Charles IV (no. 30) he reveals the prophecy of Fra Angelo, one of the hermits of the Abruzzi. God plans a universal reformation of the church. The end of the present epoch was already revealed in the castigation of the church before Saint Francis. At the instance of Saint Francis and Saint Dominic the downfall of the church was postponed; but now it is again imminent, considering the evils of the residence at Avignon. Great revolutions will happen shortly, resulting in the restoration of the church to its former state of holiness and the inclusion of the Saracens in the community of the faithful. A *vir sanctus* will be the instrument of these revolutions; together with the emperor he will reform the *orbis terrarum.* He, Rienzo, is the "precursor" who will assist the emperor in his work. Through the prophecy of Fra Angelo, Rienzo is relieved of the burden of personal responsibility for his projects; he appears rather as the emissary of the Fraticelli who have revealed to him the plan of God and sent him on his way. The contents of the prophecy are in substance

---

31. In order to avoid all suspicion, he even redefines his former self-designation as the "elect of the Spirit"; by this designation he had not meant that the Spirit had elected him on account of his personal virtues, but—rather weakly—"that the unity of the people is created through the spirit" (*Letter to the Archbishop of Prague,* November 1350, *Epistolario* no. 37, pp. 183 ff.).

Dante's vision of a new dispensation under a Dux and a spiritual leader.

(4) Not quite so modest is the second Letter to Charles IV.[32] The epochal consciousness is the same as in the prophecy of Fra Angelo, but now Rienzo permits the prophecy as the source of his present status and projects that he will recede somewhat into the background; the events of the tribunate, before his withdrawal to the Fraticelli, reappear as the source of authority for his role as the precursor of the coming age. Did God not want to have a man baptized in the chapel of Saint John, in the imperial fountain, accepted and desired by all peoples, in order to have a precursor of the emperor who will wash off the stains of the empire, as the Baptist was the precursor of Christ? The emperor himself had admitted (probably in a conversation with Rienzo) that the empire could not be reformed without a divine miracle. Certainly it looks like a divine miracle when help is coming to the tottering Roman empire through a poor and obscure man *(per virum pauperem et novum)*, as it came to the tottering Roman Church through Saint Francis. The rule of Saint Francis came to the support of the church, the rule of Rienzo will come to the support of the empire—"for I believe that the reform of the empire should not be excluded from the work of the Spirit *[opus spirituale]*" (p. 108). Rienzo will complete the work that was begun by Saint Francis.

The passages reveal excellently the difficulties that beset the transition from imperial to national sentiments in the imperial zone. The general background is formed by the consciousness of epoch. The old unity of Christian mankind had institutionally broken down during the interregna and the residence of the papacy at Avignon. The problem is: what new mystical body will take the place of the disintegrating imperial Christianity? In the imperial zone the question cannot receive the comparatively simple separatist answer of the Western national states because the shadows of the imperial tradition are too strong. The first and most comprehensive solution would be the appearance of a paracletic figure, a Joachitic Dux, as the head of a new European *corpus mysticum.* There are touches of the idea in Rienzo; but the conflict with the

---

32. *Letter to Charles IV*, August 1350, *Epistolario* no. 31; for the analysis following the text see esp. pp. 107 ff.

church hangs over it; the conception of the Third Realm, and of the *Evangelium Aeternum* of the Spirituals, cannot be renewed seriously. Hence the advent of the Spirit has to be an "amplification" of the original descent, a renewal that marks an epoch within the Christian aeon. In the prophecies of Fra Angelo, Rienzo still toys with the idea of a great reformation, only suspended by the intervention of Saint Francis: the princes of the church will be put to flight, the pope will be in personal danger, and a *pastor angelicus* will complete the reform and build the Temple of the Holy Spirit (no. 30, p. 92). A closer approximation to the conditions of historical reality is then achieved in the recognition as successive to the work of Saint Francis and the belief that it has to be supplemented only by the reform of the *imperium.* And he concentrates on the idea of the national reform and unification of Italy. The decisive point is that these sentiments and ideas neither form a chronological sequence nor are harmonized systematically. They coexist; and according to circumstances the one or the other can receive the stronger accents.

f. Spiritual Nationalism and Military Unification

The projects of Rienzo did not materialize. The emperor sent him to Avignon; in 1352 he returned to Italy with Albornoz, and under papal auspices he established again a regime in Rome; in 1354 he was killed by his opponents. The political failure has obscured the importance of Rienzo for the evolution of the Italian national idea. The elements of Rienzo's conception can be found in Joachim, in the Franciscan Spirituals, and in Dante, but the linkage between Franciscan spiritualism and the idea of the *corpus mysticum* of the *sacra Italia* in an actual political attempt to translate the idea into reality is new. It is the problem that still decisively occupies Machiavelli. The later thinker is in despair that spiritual forces alone will renovate the nation, particularly since he recalls the failure of Savonarola in Florence. The prophet who unites his people will have to be a prophet in arms. But Machiavelli leaves no doubt that a nation cannot be created by military action alone; the renewal of the spirit is needed to bind the members into a body; and the "spirit" that will have to provide the internal coherence is still the spirit of Rienzo. In Rienzo, Machiavelli sees the flaring up of the political renaissance in Italy; in Saint Francis he sees, like Rienzo, the opening of the spiritual renaissance.[33] This problem is unknown in the Western national states. In England the nation grew under the pressure of a strong kingship. In the imperial zone the nations gained political unity through the growth of a national spirit and, when the spirit had sufficiently matured, through military action that overcame the particularistic political entrenchments.

33. Machiavelli, *Discorsi* III.1. On this question see Karl Borinski, "Die Welt-wiedergeburtsidee," 69.

22

The Conciliar Movement

§1. The Schism—The General Councils

a. The Schism

The Conciliar movement was a direct outgrowth of the Great Schism of 1378–1417. The idea that a General Council should have the power to decide in matters of faith, particularly against a heretical pope, had been developed earlier by Marsilius of Padua and William of Ockham during the tension between the papacy and Lewis the Bavarian, but at the time the idea had remained academic. The election in 1378 of two rival popes, Urban VI and Clement VII, implied a de facto change of the church constitution, for now the regional churches were compelled to declare which of the two popes they would recognize as the legitimate head of the church. The recognition of the pope through the regional clergy, after his election by the cardinals, inevitably introduced a strong element of constitutionalism into the church structure. This revolutionary character of the situation was further aggravated by the problems of national politics, although the election of a French pope in rivalry with the Italian was not entirely a national question as has been assumed. The French government, on the contrary, seems to have been the only one besides the Spanish that investigated carefully the claims of the rival popes and arrived at a conscientious decision.[1] Nevertheless, the French recognition of Clement VII was bound to have its repercussions in the field of national politics. England automatically recognized the Italian pope; Scotland sided with France; the empire recognized the Italian, the Spanish governments the Avignonese. While the existence of

---

1. See on this point Mollat, "The Popes of Avignon and the Great Schism," 291 ff.

two popes required acts of recognition by the national clergies, the national factor made it necessary to overcome the Schism by a supranational General Council.

b. Conrad of Gelnhausen—Henry of Langenstein

The first reaction against the Schism was a number of treatises, emanating from members of the University of Paris and suggesting the convocation of a General Council in order to deal with the Schism. The University of Paris had a special interest in the problem because it was the leading European institution of learning: its work and enrollment would have been in grave danger if the Germans and Italians, who belonged to the obedience of the Roman pope, were compelled to leave. The most important of these treatises were the *Epistola Concordiae* of Conrad of Gelnhausen of 1380 and the *Consilium Pacis* of Henry of Langenstein of 1381.[2] The authors are sometimes considered the originators of the conciliaristic, constitutional conception of church government. While this judgment is quite justified insofar as they were the first to suggest the conciliaristic solution of the emergency, one should not overlook that the constitutional revolution of the church had already occurred de facto through the Schism. The treatises in question do not provoke a revolution, they rather attempt to restore a normal state through the emergency measure of a council, to be used only in this special situation. They are less interesting for their theoretical achievement than for their common sense and juristic acumen in dealing with the extraordinary problem presented by two rival popes. The intention is clearly formulated by Conrad of Gelnhausen: "Just as

---

2. Conradi de Geilenhusen, *Tractatus de congregando concilio tempore schismatis* (the short title *Epistola Concordiae* is given at the end of the treatise); text in E. Martene and U. Durand, *Thesaurus Novus Anecdotorum* (Paris, 1712), 2:1200–1226. Henry of Langenstein, *Consilium Pacis, de Unione ac Reformatione Ecclesiae*; text in *Joannis Gersonii Opera Omnia* (Antwerp, 1706), 2:809–40. An abridged translation of Langenstein is available in M. Spinka, ed., *Advocates of Reform from Wyclif to Erasmus* (Philadelphia: Westminster, 1953). Among the voluminous literature on the Conciliarist movement the following are representative: Walter Ullman, *Origins of the Great Schism* (New York: Burns and Oats, 1948); Brian Tierney, *Foundations of the Conciliar Theory* (Cambridge: Cambridge University Press, 1955); Anthony Black, *Council and Commune* (London: Burns and Oats, 1979); F. Oakley, *Natural Law, Conciliarism, and Consent in the Late Middle Ages* (London: Variorum Reprints, 1984); C. M. D. Crowder, *Unity, Heresy, and Reform, 1378–1460: The Conciliar Response to the Great Schism* (New York: Edward Arnold, 1977).

a bishops' council is summoned in order to deal with affairs that emerge in a province, in the same manner a general council is to be summoned in order to deal with new and difficult cases that concern the whole world. New and dangerous cases emerging in a province are solved, corrected, and reduced to their proper state by a provincial council. . . . In case of imminent necessity one has to have recourse to a council."[3] The emergency solution is supported by theoretical arguments. The infallibility of the *ecclesia universalis* resides in the congregation of the faithful, or of their representatives in council, while the pope and the cardinals can err. "No weal [salus] can be on earth outside the Catholic Church, but it can be outside the college of the pope and his cardinals."[4] Hence the council is superior to the pope, and it can assemble at the summons of the secular rulers, if the pope should fail to convoke it.[5] It can listen to the statements of rival popes, and it can either decide in favor of one of them or elect a new one.[6] Different methods have been employed for the election of popes in various periods of the church, and the method of conciliar election is, therefore, not a revolution against an unbroken tradition.[7]

c. *The Decree* Frequens

The idea that the emergency measure for settling the Schism could become a permanent part of the church constitution was slow to grow. It actually reached its climax only at the very moment when

---

3. *Epistola Concordiae,* chap. 1, p. 1207. Henry of Langenstein discusses the emergency situation in chap. 14 of his treatise. See, furthermore, Henry's formula in *Consilium Pacis,* chap. 15, p. 832, that in *casu tali necessitatis* the council acts directly under the authority of Christ.

4. Conrad of Gelnhausen, *Epistola Concordiae,* chap. 1, p. 1208; Henry of Langenstein, *Consilium Pacis,* chap. 3.

5. Henry of Langenstein, *Consilium Pacis,* chaps. 5–6. See on this point also *Parisiensis, Oxoniensis, Pragensis et Romane Universitatum Epistola de Auctoritate Imperatoris in Schismate Paparum tollendo, et vera ecclesiae libertate adservanda,* 1380; the latter is addressed to Urban VI and Emperor Wenceslas; text in Goldast, *Monarchia S. Romani Imperii,* 1:229–32. See, furthermore, Conrad of Gelnhausen, *Epistola Concordiae,* ch. 3, p. 1216; Conrad stresses again strongly the emergency character: *in casu necessitatis extremae* can the council meet without papal authorization. The point was still a problem twenty-five years later. See Franciscus de Zabarellis *De Schismatibus authoritate imperatoris tollendis,* 1406 (text is Schardius, *De jurisdictione* [Basel, 1566], 688–711): "Quis habebit congregare Concilium? Respondeo, quod olim Imperator congregabat Concilium" (Who had authority to call a council? I respond that of old the emperor called a council; p. 689).

6. Henry of Langenstein, *Consilium Pacis,* chap. 14, pp. 828 ff.

7. Ibid., pp. 826 ff.

the Schism ended through the election of Martin V in 1417. On October 9, 1417, in the thirty-ninth session of the Council of Constance, the decree *Frequens* was published, which transformed the General Council into a permanent institution. The decree provided that councils should be summoned periodically. The first should convene five years after the end of the Council of Constance; the second seven years after the end of the first; and thereafter the councils should meet every ten years. One month before the end of each council the pope should announce the meeting place for the next one; if he failed to do so, the right to fix the place would devolve on the council. The time and place for the meetings of councils, thus, were permanently regulated. The intention of these provisions was expressly formulated as the guaranty of "a sort of continuity, so that always there would be either a council in session or in due course to be expected."[8] The term for the meeting could be shortened by the pope, but it could not be prolonged. In the case of a new schism, a detailed procedure for the meeting of the council was provided. From the day that two popes functioned the term for the next council was shorted to one year. All persons who had to participate in a council would assemble at the place fixed by the previous council, one year from the date of the schism, without special summons. Further provisions demand that a newly elected pope render the Oath on the Catholic Faith, and they prohibit the transfer of prelates against their will. To the reforms of the decree *Frequens* should be added, finally, the decree *De decimis et aliis oneribus ecclesiasticis* of the newly elected Pope Martin V. This decree restricts the general papal power of taxation to the emergency case while ordinarily the consent of the realms and provinces has to be given to financial impositions.[9]

d. Nominalism and Jurisdictionalism

The provisions of the decree *Frequens* reveal the high degree of conscious constitutionalism that had evolved during the sessions of

8. *Decretum Frequens*, in J. D. Mansi, *Sacrorum Conciliorum Nova, et Amplissima Collectio* (Venice, 1784), 27:1159–63. The quotation in the text runs: "ut sic per quamdam continuationen semper aut Concilium vigeat aut per terminipendentiam expectetur."

9. Forty-third Session of the Council of Constance, in Mansi, *Sacrorum Conciliorum*, 27:1175 ff.

the Council of Constance. Again, as in the beginning of the Schism, a revolution had occurred de facto before it found formal expression. The background for the revolution was formed by the resolution of the fifth session of April 6, 1415, by which the council defined its status and authority. The authority of the council is, according to this decree, derived directly from Christ; everyone, even the pope, must obey it in matters of faith, in matters concerning the extinction of the Schism, and in matters concerning the reform of the church *in capite at membris*.[10] There is nothing revolutionary in the decree as such; as far as the derivation of authority and the extinction of the Schism are concerned, its provisions are the inevitable minimum for establishing conciliar jurisdiction. Nevertheless, the council developed unexpectedly under this authority because of the procedural practices introduced at the same time. For the council organized itself into the so-called "nations"; the first four "nations" organized were the Italian (including Crete and Cyprus), the French, the English (including Scandinavia), and the German (including the Slavic East); when the Spaniards arrived, the Spanish "nation" was organized as the fifth.[11] This organization into "nations" had primarily the purpose of reducing the influence of the Italians, who would have dominated the council by their numbers if the votes had been taken by simple majority; the organization into nations was used in taking the vote in plenary session by nations instead of by majority, as well as for composing the committees by equal numbers of delegates from the nations. As a consequence of this procedural arrangement, the political weight of the council had a tendency to shift into the meetings of the nations who determined through their delegates the procedure of the committees; the traditional hierarchical structure of politics was seriously disturbed because the cardinals were set off as a group for themselves, outside the nations, and could make their influence felt in a formal manner only through the three votes that were allotted to them in the committees of the nations. The situation became serious in the summer of 1415 when general business slackened and the council began to interfere with matters belonging under papal

10. The decree *Haec sancta* of April 6, 1415, in ibid., 27:590 ff.
11. On the voting by nations see the Rev. George C. Powers, *Nationalism at the Council of Constance, 1414–1418* (Washington, D.C.: Catholic University of America Press, 1927), esp. chap. 2. On the Spanish "nation" see Bernhard Fromme, *Die spanische Nation und das Konstanzer Konzil* (Münster, 1896).

jurisdiction. The oligarchic executive was in danger of becoming de-
mocratized, with the evils that inevitably accompany the discharge
of executive matters by revolutionary assemblies.[12] The term *de-
mocratized* just used should not convey, however, the impression
that the atmosphere of the council was particularly democratic in
a populist sense. On the contrary: the men who assumed authority
against the oligarchy of the cardinals were mostly royal appointees;
as a group they represented the forces of the absolute monarchies
and of the bureaucracies of the national realms.[13]

From the evolution just outlined it becomes clear that the reforming zeal of the council was less absorbed by a reform of the spirit
than by a jockeying for jurisdictional positions. The nominalism of
the Ockhamist type had now, indeed, become institutional practice.
The spiritual reality of the *corpus mysticum* was dissolving into
the positions and rights of the factions—that is, of the popes, the
cardinals, the general councils, the "nations" within the council,
and the national councils—and it was dissolving into ordinary jurisdictions and emergency measures. This jurisdictional and factional
disintegration is shown clearly by the history of the councils. The
first of the councils, the Council of Pisa, was called in 1409 by the
cardinals of both obediences in order to abolish the Schism; it resulted in the addition of a third pope, because the two popes in office
refused to resign in favor of the pope elected by the council. Once
the abolition of the Schism was achieved in 1417 at Constance, the
usefulness of the councils became doubtful. Nevertheless, in spite
of the hesitations of the papacy, they were called in accordance
with the decree *Frequens:* after five years the Council of Pisa/Siena
in 1423–1424, and after a further seven years the Council of Basel in
1431. The pope, Eugene IV, however, was able to split the Council
of Basel over the question of the union with the Greek Church and
to call a council of his own at Ferrara/Florence in 1438–1445. The
rump council of Basel continued its sessions and elected a new pope,
Felix V. That an institution that had been summoned originally for
the abolition of the Schism caused a new schism was a severe blow
for the prestige of the Council of Basel as well as for the conciliar

---

12. On the position of the cardinals see Heinrich Finke, *Forschungen und Quellen
zur Geschichte des Konstanzer Konzils* (Paderborn, 1889), chap. 6 on the "Schriften
gegen und fur das Kardinalskolleg." This work of Finke contains in the appendix
Cardinal Fillastre's highly important diary of the council.
13. See on this point Powers, *Nationalism at the Council,* 45 ff.

idea in general. The situation at Basel became hopeless when the pope was able, at the price of moderate reform measures, to come to an agreement with the German princes through the Concordat of Vienna of 1448. In 1449 the Council of Basel was dissolved; in the Jubilee year of 1450 the papacy could celebrate the victory of the monarchical church government over the conciliar movement. The obligation to summon councils every ten years remained a threat hanging over the papacy and was used by opponents on occasion for political pressure, but no council was called for the rest of the century. Only in 1511 Louis XII, of France, called again a council at Pisa in order to check the military expansion of Julius II; the pope was compelled to counter with the Council of the Lateran of 1512. The reforms undertaken by the Lateran Council were, however, of little significance. In 1517 Luther nailed his ninety-five theses to the church door at Wittenberg and the Great Reformation started.

The literature of the period of Constance reflects a generally nominalistic mode of thought. It is interesting for its typical contents only; the individual, theoretical achievements are negligible in spite of the intellectual and moral distinction of some of the authors. It will be sufficient in this context to mention the treatises of Pierre d'Ailly and Jean Gerson.[14] The generation of the Council of Basel presents a different picture. The intellectual situation now was dominated by a group of Christian humanists around the brilliant young Cardinal Giuliano Cesarini, the commander of the crusade against the Hussites and the president of the Council of Basel in its earlier phase. The outstanding members of the group were Enea Silvio Piccolomini, the later Pius II, and Nicholas of

14. Petri de Alliaco, *Tractatus de ecclesiae, concilii generalis, Romani pontificis et cardinalium auctoritate,* 1417; text in Jean Gerson, *Opera Omnia,* 2:925–60. The title indicates the jurisdictional approach of d'Ailly. Jean Gerson, *De unitate ecclesiastica et de origine juris et legum,* 1417 (*Opera Omnia,* 2:225–56). For a brief introduction to the approach of Gerson see his *Propositiones Utiles ad exterminationem praesentis schismatis, per viam Concilii Generalis,* 1408 (*Opera Omnia,* 2:112–13). According to the *Propositiones Utiles,* jurisdictional arguments *debent civiliter intelligi.* The traditional church government is a government for the normal case; in an emergency, a sensible course has to be taken in accordance with the rules of equity, the *epikeia* in the Aristotelian sense. Recent edition of Gerson: *Oeuvres complètes,* ed. P. Glorieux, 9 vols. (Paris, 1961–). See also L. B. Pascoe, *Jean Gerson: Principles of Church Reform* (The Hague: Brill, 1973); A. Black, *Monarchy and Community: Political Ideas in the Later Conciliar Controversy* (Cambridge: Cambridge University Press, 1970); Joachim Stieber, *Pope Eugenius IV, the Council of Basel, and the Secular and Ecclesiastical Authorities in the Empire* (Leiden: Brill, 1978).

Cusa. All of them were at first ardent conciliarists, testifying to the revolutionary momentum of the conciliar movement; but the spectacle of the Council of Basel convinced the most important of them—Cesarini, Enea Silvio, and the Cusanus—of the advantages of a monarchical church government. Dempf speaks of these new monarchists as the *Monarchioptants* in order to relate their importance to that of the *Monarchioptants* of the sixteenth century. Their ecclesiastical monarchism forms the background for the secular monarchism of the next generation, of Philippe de Commynes, Machiavelli, and Thomas More.[15]

§2. Gallicanism—The National Concordats

The conciliar movement was not simply a movement for "democratic" reconstruction of church government. The issue of the General Council, which in itself would be an issue regarding the constitution of the universal church, was complicated by the national question. Side by side with the movement for the General Council ran the movement for independence of the national churches. The most important of these movements, in direct connection with the Great Schism, was the Gallican movement.

a. The French National Council of 1398

In February 1395 the king of France, Charles VI, called the first National Council of the French clergy. The council voted for cession, that is for the joint resignation of both popes and the election of a new one. The popes refused to resign. By 1398 the situation had become serious enough to warrant more radical steps. The third National Council, May–August 1398, discussed the withdrawal of obedience from the pope of Avignon as a measure that would abolish the Schism. The arguments advanced on this occasion are highly revealing as to the degree to which the idea of the *corpus mysticum* had been destroyed and replaced by a political-technical

15. On the literary work of this group see the survey by Dempf, *Sacrum imperium*, 554–56. The most important authors and their works are the *Gubernaculum Conciliorum* of Andreas of Escobar; text in Van der Hardt, *Rerum Omnium Concilii Constantiensis Tomus VI* (Frankfurt and Leipzig, 1700); the *Historia gestorum generalis concilii Basiliensis* of John of Segovia; the *De ortu et auctoritate imperii Romani* of Enea Silvio; the *Concordantia Catholica* of Nicolaus Cusanus—about which at length later in this chapter.

relationism. Simon Cramaut, for instance, pleads in his *Proposi-tions* for withdrawal from the obedience of Avignon as a measure that would rapidly restore union to the church. Cramaut argues that the pope does not have much independent income. Withdrawal is the key to union because papal revenue is chiefly derived from France; the French revenue is the reason the pope clings stubbornly to his office; here is the source of his power. The Church of France should withdraw, therefore, *emolumenta illa, seu obeoedientiam;* obedience is identified with the payment of taxes; once the taxes are withdrawn, the pope will lose interest in his office.[16]

Not quite so crude in form is the argument of Pierre Leroy, the abbot of Saint-Michel, though in substance it does not differ very much from Cramaut's. Leroy suggests an alternative to total with-drawal, to the *subtractio totalis.* If not total, the withdrawal should at least be partial *(subtractio particularis).* Partial withdrawal of obedience would consist in the refusal to pay for the collation of benefices and promotions, or to pay *annates* and other taxes. The confirmation of bishops belonged in the primitive church to the archbishops, the collation of benefices to the bishops and diocesans. This tradition of long standing was abolished by papal usurpation, a usurpation that was *contra bonam et debitam politiam.* The previous state should be restored because the Christian people are too large to be governed by a central authority. The functions of the pope should be reduced to matters of doctrine, the conversion of infidels, and other difficult general affairs of the church.[17] The propositions of Leroy make it clear that the withdrawal of obedience has implications far beyond the abolition of the Schism. The con-ception of a *subtractio particularis* envisages a permanent church constitution with a high degree of independence for the regional churches and a papacy that is deprived of all ordinary functions within the church and restricted, more or less, to emergency cases.

The total withdrawal of France from the obedience of Avignon was decided by a royal ordinance of July 27, 1398. Its most im-portant provision was the restoration of the collation of benefices, acquired by Clement V for the papacy, to the ordinary collators.

---

16. *Acta Tertii Concilii Regis et Ecclesiae Gallicanae;* text in the *Preuves* of Bourgeois de Chastenet, *Nouvelle Histoire du Concile de Constance* (Paris, 1718); the remark of Simon Cramaut is on p. 27.

17. Bourgeois de Chastenet, *Nouvelle Histoire,* 34.

The withdrawal, however, did not work quite as pleasantly as was expected by the French clergy. The immediate effect certainly was overwhelming. Benedict XIII was deserted by his cardinals, and the people of Avignon besieged him in his palace. But the Gallican Church had not obtained much freedom, for the papal exactions were replaced by the royal. The Royal Letters of 1400 organized elaborately the spoils system; the collators had to provide alternatively for the protégés of (a) the king, (b) the queen, (c) the king's brother or his uncles, and (d) the University of Paris. Reluctant bishops were disciplined drastically. When Benedict XIII escaped in 1403 the cardinals and Avignon returned to the obedience of the pope; in May of the same year France returned.[18]

b. The French National Council of 1406

The next crisis came in 1406. The National Council of this year gave Pierre Leroy the occasion to elaborate in detail his conception of the Gallican freedoms. The *estat de l'église,* he argued, is better known locally than centrally; appointments from Rome frequently provide improper persons; such interventions caused schisms, perturbation, and confusion; hence they run counter to the *droit commun* and the will of the founders. In order to remedy these evils, the church, and particularly the Church of France, will have to be restored to its old liberty and custom.[19] The financial exactions of the papacy are so heavy that they destroy the substance of the local churches. Hence the king, in his function as the protector of the oppressed, has to act for the oppressed church. From the papacy no help can be expected in this matter because a change would be against its interest; the General Council is of no use either because dilatory tactics prevent its summoning. Leroy proposes, therefore, that the Gallican Church should withdraw its obedience with regard to benefices; the counterargument that the pope would have to starve is not valid because, as a matter of fact, the *Patrimonium Petri* is quite sufficient for the sustenance of the papacy if properly managed. Concerning financial obligations other than the benefices Leroy

18. The *Subtractio Totalis Oboedientiae* of 1398 in Bourgeois de Chastenet, *Nouvelle Histoire,* 79–84; the *Restitutio Oboedientiae* of May 28, 1403, *Preuves,* 84–86.

19. " . . . que l'Eglise soit ramenée, et especialement l'Eglise de France, à la liberté et manière anciennes" (*Nouvelle Histoire,* 172).

proposes a budget-right of the prelacy. Subsidies should be levied only with the consent of the prelates; the impositions have to be necessary and must not exceed actual needs; no church should pay beyond its ability; particular care should be taken in the case of churches that are in straitened circumstances because of frequent vacancies.[20] The obedience was again withdrawn totally in 1406; and in 1408, through the fifth National Council, the autonomous Gallican Church was organized with provinces and primacies.[21]

The Gallican reaction against the papacy of Avignon is the most interesting instance of the process in which the regional churches gained a relative autonomy and, at the same time, submitted to royal control, because the French movement for independence was accompanied by the theoretical elaboration of the Gallican idea. The movement toward institutional autonomy is to be found in other regions, too. In an earlier chapter we discussed the English legislation of the fourteenth century, which resulted in practice in precisely the *subtractio particularis* that Leroy demanded for the Gallican Church. But we also observed that the English development, while it preceded the French, did not produce a theory of the Anglican Church.

c. The Concordats

This movement for national ecclesiastical autonomy became an important stream in the general conciliar movement. The reforms that ultimately were achieved by the Council of Constance had to be couched in the form of "national concordats"—that is, of agreements between the papacy and the national churches controlled by the princes. The concordats were, indeed, a revolutionary innovation. The idea of the *sacrum imperium*, which contains the spiritual and temporal powers as *ordines* in its mystical body, was now definitely destroyed. The church appears as an autonomous society that can enter into contractual relations with the secular realms. The recognition of this new relationship between the church and the secular powers, we may say, was the most important permanent result of the conciliar period. The new nationalism penetrated the church organization even to the top of the hierarchy, for the first

20. The *Propositions de Pierre Leroy, Nouvelle Histoire,* 172–75.
21. For details of the organization of 1408 see Mollat, "The Popes of Avignon and the Great Schism."

provision of the concordats of Constance was the promise of the pope that he would restrict the College of Cardinals to twenty-four members and that he would recruit the members "indifferently" from all the nations.[22]

The concordats of Constance were concluded for five years only. After their expiration in 1423, the situation became tense again. In 1425 Martin V issued a one-sided constitution for France, which was replaced by the Concordat of Genzano in 1426. In 1438, the Council of the French Church of Orleans/Bourges resulted in the Pragmatic Sanction of Bourges. The title *Pragmatic* is a legal innovation, destined to signify a church constitution issued by the king. Under its provisions the papal rights were in substance restricted to nominations for benefices at the Roman court. A Gallican Church under the leadership of the national monarch had finally been constituted. Only after the death of Charles VII in 1461 was the papacy successful in renewing negotiations. The French Pragmatic Sanction was followed in 1439 by the German *Acceptatio* of the Diet of Mainz. It accepted such parts of the reform decrees of the Council of Basel as suited the princes, with a few additions. This *Acceptatio*, however, developed in practice into nothing more than a manifesto of the princes. The great German settlement came in 1448 with the Concordat of Vienna. Its significance lies in the fact that the "reform" took the shape of a sharing of spoils between the papacy and the territorial princes. The papacy gained by it victory over the conciliar movement, and the princes received an ample share of episcopal taxation and control over the territorial churches. This agreement, which at the time had an advantage for the papacy because the princes withdrew their support of the council, had in the sixteenth century the consequence that the Lutheran reformation could be locally successful with comparative ease when the princes exerted their control of the church in its favor.

§3. *Concordantia Catholica*

a. Nicholas of Cusa

In the *Concordantia Catholica* of Nicholas of Cusa the conciliar movement produced the one work that ranks high above the level

---

22. The concordats of 1418 are to be found in Mansi, *Sacrorum Conciliorum*, vol. 27: the general decree, pp. 1177 ff.; the French concordat, pp. 1184 ff.; the German, pp. 1189 ff.; the English, pp. 1193 ff.

of nominalistic and jurisdictional discussions.[23] The reason for the quality of the work is to be sought in the personality of the Cusanus. He was a humanist and a mystic, with a great metaphysical temperament. As a humanist he had at his disposition the philosophical instrumentarium of the ancients as well as of the patres and of scholasticism; and for the expression of his thought he could draw, therefore, on Plato and Aristotle as well as on Saint Ambrose and Saint Augustine, Dionysius Areopagita and Saint Thomas. As a mystic he had his roots in the *theologia negativa;* the use of the word *concordantia* for his title indicates his will to see the social cosmos as an analogue of the mystical concord of the three persons in the divinity; in his work, there is noticeable a strong influence of Meister Eckhart. It was this mysticism that prevented him from becoming dogmatic and taking sides in the factional struggle. By virtue of his metaphysical temperament, finally, he could attack seriously the problems that are created by the blending of the Hellenic and the Christian images of man. In this respect he was more successful than Saint Thomas, in whose work Artistotelian naturalism and Christian spiritualism exist side by side without entering into a consistent theoretical system. The combination of these three elements—humanism, mysticism, and a metaphysical temperament—marks Cusa as the first great postscholastic philosopher. His work is the first that has a distinct Renaissance atmosphere. The external symptom of this "modernism" is the strong touch of the natural sciences in Cusa's habits of thought; for his similes, as we shall see, he draws at decisive points on mathematics, physiology, and medicine.

b. Spiritual Harmony

In the exposition of the *Concordantia* we shall deal first with the systematically central concepts and then briefly survey the institutional elaboration.

23. Nicholas of Cusa, *De Concordantia Catholica Libri res* (Paris, 1514; facsimile Bonn, 1928, with a preface by Gerhard Kallen). *De Concordantia Catholica,* ed. G. Kallen, in *Nicolai Cusani Opera Omnia* (Berlin: Meiner, 1959), vol. 7. The *Concordantia* was written in 1433. Translation: Cusa, *The Concordance of the Catholic Faith,* ed. and trans. Paul E. Sigmund (Cambridge, 1991); see also Sigmund, *Nicholas of Cusa and Medieval Political Thought* (Cambridge: Harvard University Press, 1963).

Concordantia is "that by reason of which the *ecclesia catholica* is in concord in the one Lord and the many subjects." The *concordantia* is the spiritual harmony that flows, by degrees and steps, from the king of Peace into all the subject and united members "so that there is the one God, all in all." From the beginning *(ab initio)* we are predestined to this harmony by adoption into the childhood of God through Christ *(Concordantia* I.1). In these terms Cusa opens his treatise and defines the spiritual substance of society, the substance that underlies the concord of the members. This fundamental position has to be clearly understood; if we neglect it, we arrive at an interpretation of Cusa—as is sometimes to be found—that isolates his theory of representation and consent and overlooks that the institutionalization of consent presupposes for Cusa the spiritual substance that pervades all members of the community and makes consent possible. Here lies the difference between Cusa and the nominalists. Cusa does not believe that the answer to political evils is to be found in institutional reforms. The idea of representative government is for him not a dogma but a pragmatic instrument for the realization of harmony. When the experience of the Council of Basel convinced him that representative assemblies are not unconditionally the best instrument for the creation of harmony, he could become a monarchist in ecclesiastical government without surrendering his metaphysical and mystical positions. The spiritual substance of the *concordantia* is all-important; the institutions are no more than means for its realization in political practice.

c. Infinita *and* Gradualis Concordantia

The end of human life is for Cusa the eternal union with the spirit and flesh of Christ. In order to make it possible for man to arrive at this *concordantissima unio* through faith, God has ordained the *gradualis concordantia* of the mystical body of the church. The *gradualis concordantia* of society is the earthly analogue of the *summa et infinita concordantia* in the triune divinity (I.1). In this analogical construction, Cusa conceives finite reality under the mathematical symbol of an approximation to the divine infinity. A symbolism makes itself felt that is fully elaborated only in the later work of Cusa. In the *Docta Ignorantia* of 1440, Cusa has performed the unique feat of writing a *theologia negativa* in a mathematical notation—if the musical term is permitted. God is the absolute maximum. The infinite divinity appears as the *coincidentia oppositorum*, the point where the maxima and minima of an infinite series coincide, as the point where the ends of an infinite straight line meet in a circle. Metaphysically speaking, we might say, that the maximum "which is believed to be God by the undoubting faith of all nations"[24] is the *realissimum* in which the finite conflict of differences is transposed into an infinite harmony of differences; it is the absolute in which the unfolding of reality is *aufgehoben* in Hegel's sense of the term. As a consequence, empirical social reality is for Cusa neither an anarchy of conflicts nor a perfect harmony of interests; it is rather, by divine ordinance, an approximate harmony in which no particular position can legitimately be erected into an absolute. Cooperation and consent are the forms in which incessantly this approximate harmony has to be made effective; and this task is not hopeless, for by divine predestination the Spirit pervades society and furnishes the homogeneous substance that inclines the conflicting forces toward unity. "The Father is the fountain of life, Who accepts in the Son the blood vessel, through which the flux of the Spirit goes into all men."[25]

d. Hierarchical Order

The mystical body is hierarchically ordered. The category of hierarchical order is used by Cusa generally as the great principle for the interpretation of the universe; it is the category of Dionysius Areopagita that we met already in a decisive function with Saint Thomas Aquinas. The creation flows from God hierarchically; it descends from the creatures most closely in the image of God to the lower configurations of nature. Every lower grade is, in a Platonic simile, the shadow of the next higher, down to the lowest, which is a shadow casting no light down to a further step of the hierarchy. The series from the splendor of eternal light down to the absolute

---

24. Nicolai de Cusa, *De Docta Ignorantia*, ed. E. Hoffmann and E. Klibanski, in *Opera Omnia*, Jussu et auctoritate Academiae Litterarum Heidelbergensis, vol. 1 (Leipzig, 1932), I.2, p. 7. Translation: Cusa, *Of Learned Ignorance*, trans. Germain Heron (London, 1954).

25. *Concordantia*, I.1. This physiological simile should be compared with the elaborate nature symbolism in *Docta Ignorantia*, II.13. See for the organic analogy esp. p. 111, the conception of the earth as an animal. The source of such similes is Hippocrates; for their influence on Leonardo da Vinci see p. 111 n.

shadow again is expressed by Cusa in the mathematical symbol of a series extending *ab infinito usque ad nihil* (*Concordantia* I.2). This conception of the hierarchy then is used in the interpretation of the mystical body. The body, or the *ecclesia Christi,* consists of the sacraments, the priesthood, and the faithful. The sacraments are the spirit, the priesthood is the soul, the faithful are the body. The three together are bound into the mystical body. The two *ordines* within the body, the priests and the faithful, are ordered hierarchically, from the papal and imperial heads, through the ranks of the ecclesiastical and feudal hierarchies, down to the plain *laici* (III.1).

e. The Augmentation of the Corpus Mysticum

Thus far the general structure of the mystical body corresponds to the idea that had been current since the ninth century: it is the Pauline hierarchy augmented by the ranks of the secular rulers. Cusa, however, takes the revolutionary step of further augmenting the types that have to be included in the *corpus mysticum* so as to make it correspond to the postfeudal structure of his own time. The instruments he uses for this purpose are the Pauline *caritas* and the Platonic-Aristotelian idea of the perfect society.

Cusa interprets the *caritas* of Saint Paul as implying an augmentation of the *corpus mysticum* beyond the specifically enumerated charismata. The *caritas,* the bond of love, which for Saint Paul held together the community and its hierarchical order, becomes for Cusa a general principle that intends to give every faithful his status in the mystical body so that no member is lost to Christ. The body should not comprise only those who are distinguished as saints, but all the faithful and even the superior rational virtues and powers. The whole *natura rationabilis* should adhere to Christ as its head.[26]

---

26. *Concordantia* I.1: "Augmentum enim corporis facit aedificationem sui in charitate: ut assurgat unum templum. . . . In quo non solum sanctorum hominum, sed omnium credentium, omnium etiam superiorum rationabilium virtutum atque potestatum connexionem fidei spiritusque accipiendam arbitror: ut per harmoniam quamdam virtutum ac ministeriorum, corpus unum ex omnibus rationabilis naturae spiritibus adhaereat capiti suo Christo." The uncompressed passage reads: "From him one body of the faithful, united and joined in rational harmony with the Word in every branch of the ministry, helps to increase his body proportionately in charity so as to produce one temple and one spiritual dwelling-place for all. Here I think we are to understand that there is a union in faith and the spirit, not only of the saints but of all the faithful and of all the heavenly hosts and powers so that by a certain concordance of powers and ministries one body made up of all spirits

If the Pauline *caritas* is interpreted in this manner, the *ecclesia* is no longer the community of the saints in a pagan environment; and it is no longer even the *ecclesia* augmented by the emperor and the feudal hierarchy; it has become the *societas perfecta* in the Aristotelian sense, giving room to the unfolding of all the potentialities of human nature, particularly the rational potentialities. It becomes possible now to introduce as new ranks into the *corpus mysticum* the *sapientes et heroes,* that is the Platonic philosophers and guardians, as well as the Aristotelian political hierarchy of the free and the slaves (preface to bk. III).

This introduction of the Platonic and Aristotelian types is more, however, than a reflection of humanistic interests: it serves the very practical purpose of giving status in the mystical body, and a very distinguished status to the *sapientes* as the truly free men. With this creation of status for the *sapientes* a trend reaches its climax that had been noticeable for two centuries. We observed in the thirteenth century, with Siger de Brabant and Saint Thomas, the emergence of the intellectual as a new type in Western society. The philosophers, the trained theologians, the royal and ecclesiastical lawyers, the officeholders of the ecclesiastical and secular governmental bureaucracies represent a mode of life that was not provided for in the feudal pattern of society. In the *Defensor Pacis* of Marsilius of Padua there could be sensed very strongly the self-consciousness and the pathos of the bureaucratic expert who knows that he has to operate the government and to bestow the benefit of his rule on unlearned subjects. In Cusa's augmentation of the *corpus mysticum* by the new rank of the *sapiens* we have to see the assertion of the intellectual in a manner comparable to the assertion of the bourgeois in Calvinism and of the proletarian in Marxism.

The reception of the Aristotelian ranks of the free *sapientes* and the slavish *insipientes* created a formidable problem, for the Hellenic idea of a natural slave is incompatible with the Christian idea of the spiritually free man. Cusa solves the problem by the formula, "Not nature makes a man a slave, but his foolishness

---

of a rational nature adheres to Christ, their head, forming the framework of the church edifice in such a way that the links between the individual adherents are not perceived by the senses." It is a quotation from a letter of Saint Ambrose; *The Catholic Concordance,* 6.

[insipientia]; nor does manumissio make a man free, but discipline" (preface to bk. III). Foolishness and wisdom are characterological types. The foolish man is a slave to cupidity, to avarice, to malice, and to anger. The wise man will not be broken by fear nor changed by power nor carried away by prosperity, nor will he be submerged by sorrow. The wise man is of a stable mind; he will neither be depressed nor elated by the change of things, and he will not, like the little man, be driven around by every wind of doctrine. The free man will live by the law, by a law that is not engraved on tables but impressed in his mind. The wise man can govern himself; the foolish man will be governed by his volitions (preface to bk. III). That a man belongs to the wise or the foolish type may affect his place in the social hierarchy, but it does not affect his membership in the mystical body. The differentiation of free man and slaves does not, as in Hellenic theory, draw a dividing line between membership in the community of the citizen and the apolitical status of the slave.

f. Nature and Grace

The distinction of characterological types and the mere assertion that insipientia does not affect membership in the mystical body would not be sufficient to overcome the Aristotelian naturalism. The principal obstacle to an integration of Hellenic political theory into the Christian is formed by the Hellenic idea of nature: Hellenic nature is nature without grace. The differentiation of types is a brute fact. In the Politeia, Plato had to introduce the metal myth in order to make the lower ranks believe that they have to submit to the rule of the wise; and while in the Nomoi he softens the harshness of the differences somewhat, he still can do nothing better than pray to the gods that they might avert the worst when the lower men participate in government. In a Christian system, nature itself has to be penetrated spiritually in order to make natural differences psychologically bearable and systematically compatible with the fundamental idea of spiritual freedom. It is impossible for the conscientious systematic thinker to have the status of man determined on the one hand by childhood under the divine Father and on the other by a blind fact of nature. Cusa finds the construction that the omnipotent God has given to the foolish a character trait by virtue of which they readily trust the sapientes so that the foolish can be governed with their own assistance *(ipsorum adjutorio)*. "Thus, by a kind of natural instinct, the presidency of the *sapientes* and the subjection of the *insipientes* is brought into concord, and can exist under common laws, of which primarily the *sapientes* are the authors, guardians and executors" (preface to bk. III).

This "kind of natural instinct," the *naturalis quidam instinctus,* is neither the blind Hellenic nature nor the psychological nature that appears later in the natural law speculation of the seventeenth century, as for instance in Hugo Grotius. It is a nature illuminated by divine ordination and oriented toward reason. For the instinct of Cusa is not an instinct of obedience or submission to any ruler who happens to hold power, nor is it a gregarious instinct that compels men to join in community; it is rather a variant of reason. The *sapiens* can govern himself by reason; the *insipiens* has the "trust" that induces him to accept in the rule of the *sapiens* the discipline of reason that he cannot exert himself. Without the rule of the *sapiens,* the *insipiens* is the slave of his volitions; under the government of the wise and through it he achieves freedom. The "trust" that induces obedience assures to the *insipiens* in a social form the government by reason of which he is incapable in the personal form. The "trust" is the condition that makes possible a government of reason by consent. Without it representative government would be no more than a question of jurisdiction and power, and government by consent would degenerate into the tyranny of a majority that gives reign to its emotions and volitions. Trust and the rule of law, as formulated by Cusa, are the principles by virtue of which the idea of democratic government by leadership and consent makes sense.

g. Institutional Elaboration

The conception of Cusa presupposes the faith that God is, indeed, with his people: that the rulers have the law impressed in their minds and that the ruled are induced by their trust to consent to the leadership of reason. Cusa held very strongly this religious faith in the *concordantia* of society. This profoundness of conviction inspired him to elaborate in detail the institutional forms for government by consent; his treatise is practically a handbook of parliamentary procedure. In this respect it is without a parallel in his time, and it could have been written only by the one man to whom government by deliberation and consent was a matter of substantive faith.[27]

In order to be valid, positive laws have to be made in accordance with natural law. In order to secure this accordance, the *sapientiores et praestantiores* have to be elected as legislators. Those who are *ratione vigentes* are the natural rulers of the others. They are rulers by reason, not by coercive law or by decisions inflicted on the unwilling. For "by nature all men are free" *(natura omnes sunt liberi)*; the ruling position can be justified only by adherence to the rule of law. Governmental authority is derived from the *concordantia* and the consent of the subject. "For, since by nature men are equally strong and equally free, the true and ordered power of one, who is by nature not stronger than the others, can be constituted only by election and consent" (II.14). For the validity of a particular piece of positive legislation, furthermore, *usus et acceptatio* are required; a law that does not penetrate into society through observation and enforcement is invalid. For the full validity of a statute three things are required: (1) legitimate power in the lawgiver, (2) approval of the statute through usage, and (3) publication (II.11). Decisions in individual cases can be given in a church province by the metropolitan; general rules, however, have to be approved by the provincial synod. "For in such concord the Most-Highest has His joy . . . God is the presiding officer *[primas]* where there is reached a pure concord without corruption" (II.10).

In the case of a general council all the heads of the universal church have to be present in order to make its decisions valid; a rump council is not representative (II.2–3). In the sessions, full freedom of speech has to be guaranteed: a council is not impressive so much by its numbers as by the degree of freedom and unanimity achieved. No secret negotiations should go on, but public audience has to be given to everybody. If on a question agreement is reached through a concordant sentence, the decision has to be supposed to be inspired by the Spirit and by Christ, who presides over the

27. Dempf suggests *(Sacrum imperium,* 558) that the convictions of Cusa were rooted in the experience of the peasant democracy and the elective ecclesiastical government in his native Moselle region. The native pride plays, indeed, a certain role in the work of Cusa. In the *praefatio* to book 3, he cannot refrain from reporting the myth of Treverus, who was expelled from Babylon and on his wanderings found the city that for him was named Treves, "the oldest city of Europe," "in campe quodam amoenissimo interluente eum Mosella" (in a most pleasant field with the Moselle flowing through it).

congregation held in his name (II.3). When a decision proceeds from *concordantia*, then it proceeds from the Spirit who is the source of *concordantia*. It is not human, but divine, when a multitude of men in assembly, with full freedom of speech, arrive at a decision in *concordantia* (II.4).

h. *The* Concordantia *of Mankind*

In summary we have to say that the *Concordantia* is a magnificent attempt to formulate the principles on which government by consent has to rest in a Christian society. Book II of the *Concordantia*, as we have said, has the distinction of being the first handbook of parliamentary procedure, while book III contains a critique of the feudal survivals in the constitution of the empire (III.25–31) and suggestions for constitutional reform (III.32–41) of which it has been said that the German people would have been spared a lot of political misery if they had been adopted. The conceptual apparatus used in this task is Hellenic, patristic, and scholastic, while the momentum of the elaboration is distinctly that of the Conciliar movement. The energy of a renewed, revolutionary institution, the self-confidence of the *sapiens,* and a certain optimism with regard to the nature of man determine the atmosphere.

There is, however, something more in the *Concordantia* than the temper of the age: for the temper of the age was preponderantly nominalistic, while the work of Cusa is unique in its time by virtue of its metaphysical realism. Is this realism perhaps a reversion to the prenominalistic thirteenth century? Should the *Concordantia* be considered a work of reaction? The answer has to be negative. The realism of Cusa has its roots in his mysticism, and his mysticism is that of the great movement beginning with Eckhart. The faith of Cusa is not fideistic like that of Ockham, and his ecclesiasticism is not jurisdictional and relational. A new source of substantive faith has been opened for the spiritual regeneration of Christianity through the mystical movements of the fourteenth century.

If the mystical experience of the *concordantia infinita* in the triune divinity, and its intellectual interpretation, is elaborated metaphysically into a formula for the interpretation of society, the community of mankind is evoked as the body, mystically in concord by virtue of the Spirit that pervades it, growing in faith and charity toward the infinite without reaching it while traveling on this earth (*Docta Ignorantia*, III.12, p. 159). Cusa's perspective of Christian history is neither the *saeculum senescens* of Saint Augustine nor a new dispensation like the Third Realms of Joachim of Fiore and of Dante, but the open horizon of a mankind ever growing in faith and intellectual penetration of the faith. Intellect and faith determine each other. "For faith implies in itself all that is intelligible, and the intellect is the explication of the faith. Hence the intellect is directed by faith, and faith is extended by the intellect. Where there is no sound faith, there is no true intellect" (III.11, p. 152). The life of the intellectual mystic draws its substance from the Vision of God,[28] and therefore it can be lived historically in a concordant mankind, moving gradually toward the *unio concordantissima*. "By our intellect we desire to live intellectually, that is to enter ever more and ever deeper into the Life and the Joy. And since Life is infinite, the blessed are carried into it continuously by their desire. Those who drink from the fountain of Life are thirsting while their thirst is stilled; and since this drink does not glide into the past—for it is a drink in eternity—the blessed will always drink and always find their thirst stilled, and never will they have drunk and be saturated."[29] Precisely at the moment when the medieval *sacrum imperium* was disassociated into the *societates perfectae* of the church and the nations, precisely at the time when the category of the mystical body was transferred from universal Christianity to the particular national bodies, the new *concordantia* of mankind was evoked by the Cusanus out of the forces of the new intellectual mysticism. The nations emerging from the *sacrum imperium* did not become a plurality of brute power facts without grace: the mystical faith in the *concordantia* of mankind was still extended over them as the eternal arc, far outreaching the discord of the times.

28. See Cusa's *The Vision of God*, trans. E. G. Salter, intro. Evelyn Underhill (New York: Ungar, 1960).

29. *Docta Ignorantia* III.12, p. 160: "Desiderium autem nostrum intellectuale est intellectualiter vivere, hoc est continue plus in vitam et gaudium intrare. Et quoniam illa infinita est, continue in ipsam beati cum desiderio feruntur. Satiantur itaque quasi sitientes de fonte vitae potantes; et quia ista potatio non transit in praeteritum, cum sit in aeternitate, semper sunt beati potantes et semper satiantur, et nunquam biberunt aut saturati fuerunt" ("But the desire of our mind is to live by mind, which is continually to enter more and more into life and joy. But life and joy are infinite; and the blessed are borne into life and joy by ardent desire. They who drink of the fountain of life are satisfied in such fashion as still to thirst; and as this drink never becomes a past thing, for it is eternal, ever are they blessed both drinking and in thirst, and never shall that thirst and its satisfaction pass"; *Of Learned Ignorance*, 168).

Index

260–61n, 266; corruption of, 182–84; historical literalism of, 110; and love, 178–79, 181–83; Marsilius of Padua on, 97–101, 98n, 105; and order, 12–13; "parochial Christianity," 15, 168–75, 192; and *Piers Plowman*, 178–84; and pre-Reformation, 172–75; and Reformation, 9, 15, 69, 119–20, 126, 130, 172, 174, 192, 251, 256; regional spiritual movements, 171–75; and representation, 152–53; of William of Ockham, 108–9; and Wycliffe, 13, 168–70, 172–75, 184–92. *See also* Christ; Church; God; Popes; Trinity

Christianum imperium, 205

Church: and Babylonian Captivity, 163, 164; Christ as head of invisible church, 188; clash between nations and, 40–42; and *Clericis Laicos*, 43, 44; and Conciliar movement, 12, 24, 41–42, 113, 125, 245–66; and *corpus mysticum*, 11, 24, 25, 41, 46, 110, 113, 120, 158–59, 162, 259–62, 260–61n, 266; corruption of, 182–84; Curia in, 166–67, 168, 209; and Donation of Constantine, 57; and ecclesiastical totalitarianism, 52–53; in England, 129, 130, 138–39, 143, 167–70, 255; in France, 253–55, 256; in Germany, 198, 256; Giles of Rome on papal power, 51–52; and Golden Bull, 198, 203–16, 228; and Great Schism, 41, 163, 188, 191, 192, 245–53; Greek Church, 250; Hildebrandine assertion of papacy's universal political authority, 11, 165; and Hussite question, 41–42; and *Index Prohibitorum Librorum*, 112; infallibility of, 111, 124–25, 247; and Investiture Struggle, 15, 40, 66, 79, 92, 103, 116, 193; and Jubilee of 1450, 42; Marsilius of Padua on, 97–101, 98n, 105; monarchical government for, 252, 258; and nationalism, 40–42, 255–56; Nicholas of Cusa on government of, 263–66; papacy at Avignon, 11, 41, 61, 79, 121, 164–67, 182–83, 242, 253–54; papal interference in reign of Louis IV, 83; pope's role in, 11–12, 51–52, 162; as power organization, 41; and pre-Reformation, 172–75; and Reformation, 9, 15, 69, 119–20, 126, 130, 172, 174, 192, 251, 256; regional spiritual movements, 171–75; and representation, 152–53;

and Rienzo, 235, 237, 241, 243; secular civilization and withdrawal of, 109–12; temporal power of, 11–12, 120–21, 187–88, 248, 253; transformation of organization of, 164–67; and *Unam Sanctam*, 43–46, 47; and Universal Inquisition, 112; William of Ockham on, 120–21; and Wycliffe, 13, 168–70, 172–75, 184–92. *See also* Christianity; Popes

Church Militant, 188

Church of England, 167–68

Ciompi, 231

Cistercian Order, 66, 171

City-states: area of, 216–18; Burgundy, 223–24; constitution of Venice, 232–33; feudal world and towns, 218–19; and Fourth Crusade, 221–22; in Germany, 216–19, 224–28; and Hansa, 224–27; internal structure of towns, 229–32; in Italy, 10, 154, 217–18, 220–23, 228, 230–33; organization of Venetian conquest, 222–23; Southwest German leagues, 227–28; Swiss Confederation, 228–29; trade routes and food supply, 220–21

Civil Dominion (Wycliffe), 185, 186–88

Civitas, 86, 87, 93, 95–97

Civitas Dei, 81

Civitates, 226

Civium universitas, 89

Clemens, 235, 235n

Clement IV, Pope, 60

Clement V, Pope, 164, 253

Clement VI, Pope, 165, 167, 185, 235

Clement VII, Pope, 245

Clericis Laicos, 43, 44, 138–39

Cloud of Unknowing, 177

Clovis, 58

Cluniac reforms, 152, 171, 196, 197

Codex Justinianus, 149

Cola di Rienzo. *See* Rienzo, Cola di

Cole, G. D. H., 143

Collegio, 233

Collegium, 215

Colonization, 199–203

Colonna, Cardinal, 38

Commentary (Peter Lombard), 176

Common law, 130

Commune consilium regni, 152

Communes, 136, 218, 230–35

Communism, 72, 110

Communitas, 213

Communitas civitatis, 148

Communitas comitatus, 148

Communitas perfecta, 56, 86, 87